The Anatomy of a Constitutional Law Case

To Bea, who spans the first
and second editions,
and any yet to come

At the first sound of a new argument over the United States Constitution and its interpretation, the hearts of Americans leap with a fearful joy. The blood stirs powerfully in their veins and a new lustre brightens their eyes. Like King Harry's men before Harfleur, they stand like greyhounds in the slips, straining upon the start. Last week, the old buglenote rang out, clear and thrilling, calling Americans to a fresh debate on the Constitution. . . .

The London *Economist*, May 10, 1952,
commenting on the Steel Seizure Case.

Scarcely any political question arises in the United States that is not resolved, sooner or later, into a judicial question. Hence all parties are obliged to borrow, in their daily controversies, the ideas, and even the language, peculiar to judicial proceedings. As most public men are or have been legal practitioners, they introduce the customs and technicalities of their profession into the management of public affairs. The jury extends this habit to all classes. The language of the law thus becomes, in some measure, a [common] tongue; the spirit of the law, which is produced in the schools and courts of justice, gradually penetrates beyond their walls into the bosom of society, where it descends to the lowest classes, so that at last the whole people contract the habits and the tastes of the judicial magistrate.

De Tocqueville, *Democracy in America*, 1835

The Anatomy of a
Constitutional Law Case

YOUNGSTOWN SHEET AND TUBE CO.

v.

SAWYER

THE STEEL SEIZURE DECISION

by Alan F. Westin

COLUMBIA UNIVERSITY PRESS
New York

Quotation from *The Supreme Court: How It Was, How It Is* (pp. 94–97), by William H. Rehnquist (Morrow, 1987), reprinted by permission of the author.

Quotation from *Truman and the Steel Seizure Case* (pp. 228–240 and 245–248) by Maeva Marcus (Columbia University Press, 1977), reprinted by permission of the author.

Columbia University Press Morningside Edition
Columbia University Press
New York   Oxford
© Copyright, Macmillan Publishing Co., Inc., 1958
Morningside Edition:
Copyright © 1990 by Columbia University Press

Library of Congress Cataloging-in-Publication Data

Westin, Alan F.
The anatomy of a constitutional law case :
Youngstown Sheet and Tube Co. v. Sawyer (the steel seizure decision) /
by Alan F. Westin.
—[Morningside ed.]
p. cm.
Includes bibliographical references.
ISBN 0-231-07334-8 (cloth).
ISBN 0-231-07335-6 (paperback)
1. Executive power—United States.
2. Separation of powers—United States.
3. War and emergency powers—United States.
4. Eminent domain—United States.
5. Steel industry and trade—United States.
I. Title.
KF5060.W46   1990
342.73'044.'347.30244—dc20
90-39178
CIP

Morningside Edition 1990

Casebound editions of Columbia University Press books are Smyth-sewn and printed on permanent and durable acid-free paper

∞

Printed in the U.S.A.

c 10 9 8 7 6 5 4 3 2 1
p 10 9 8 7 6 5 4 3 2 1

Preface to the Morningside Edition

Thirty-three years have passed since I prepared the original version of *The Anatomy of a Constitutional Law Case*, and thirty-two years since it was published by Macmillan. My premise in writing the book was that students of the social sciences and law could profit from reading a set of contemporary materials that recreated, as much as possible, the publicly available news presentations and the decision-makers' perspectives surrounding President Harry S. Truman's seizure of the steel mills on April 8, 1952 and the Supreme Court's decision on June 2, 1952 declaring the seizure to be unconstitutional. My goal was to illustrate by this in-depth portrayal of one celebrated decision the structural and dynamic elements of public-law litigation in the United States—the "anatomy" of cause célèbre constitutional law cases.

Confirming the value of that premise, *The Anatomy of a Constitutional Law Case* has been used widely in political science and law courses for three decades and has been referred to often by historians, political scientists, and legal commentators writing about the Steel Seizure. The book is now being reissued in a new edition by the Columbia University Press, hopefully to make it accessible to students and scholars for several more decades.

The reissue raised an interesting problem for me. Should I leave the book just as it was—a carefully selected set of contemporary materials and editor's explanations depicting events as of 1952, with only minor additions that were drawn from the 1952–1957 period? Or should I rework the materials and commentary to insert important accounts and analyses of the motives, perceptions, and actions of the key players in the Steel Seizure case, as these have been revealed over the past four decades?

In teaching this case to my undergraduate and graduate political science classes at Columbia, I always threaded post-1957 materials into the classroom discussion, as these became known. But I did this as a supplement to my students' having read as their primary source the original, 1957-based presentation of the Steel Seizure events.

On reflection, I have chosen to leave the original presentation intact for the new Columbia University Press edition. Following this, in a new section, "The Steel Seizure Case: Four Decades Later," I have presented new material and my own commentaries on the following topics:

- What went on within the Truman Administration
- What went on within the Supreme Court
- How the Steel Seizure ruling has been used as a precedent

This book is a documentary portrait of one constitutional law case, *Youngstown Sheet & Tube Co. v. Sawyer*, from its rise in a bargaining dispute in the steel industry during 1952 to the aftermath of its decision by the United States Supreme Court. The purpose of this detailed canvas is to represent, as no set of opinions by themselves can, the full sweep of the American constitutional process: how political and social issues are shaped into legal controversies in our system, how a case moves through administrative and judicial channels on its way to the Supreme Court, how the tactics of litigating parties affect the formulation of constitutional principles, how the actions of the political branches of the government mould the controversy as it progresses, and by what criteria and techniques Supreme Court Justices resolve issues presented to them.

Preface

This book is a documentary portrait of one constitutional law case, *Youngstown Sheet & Tube Co. v. Sawyer*, from its rise in a bargaining dispute in the steel industry during 1952 to the aftermath of its decision by the United States Supreme Court. The purpose of this detailed canvas is to represent, as no set of opinions by themselves can, the full sweep of the American constitutional process: how political and social issues are shaped into legal controversies in our system, how a case moves through administrative and judicial channels on its way to the Supreme Court, how the tactics of litigating parties affect the formulation of constitutional principles, how the actions of the political branches of the government mould the controversy as it progresses, and by what criteria and techniques Supreme Court Justices resolve issues presented to them.

In keeping with the idea of an explanatory model for college and law school students, the selections from transcripts, briefs, and other official proceedings have been accompanied by notes explaining each phase of the constitutional process as it is reached, by narratives relating tactical and political developments, and by a commentary and question section designed to relate the *Youngstown* case to other types of constitutional cases. I suggest to my own students that they go through it once quickly for "plot," read the questions, and then return to the more important parts of the study for closer examination.

The major part of my work on this project was completed during a year as Senior Fellow at Yale Law School, an opportunity for uninterrupted research and writing for which I am grateful to Dean Eugene Rostow and the Yale Law School Faculty. While in New Haven, I drew encouragement for the concept of such a study from the late Judge Jerome Frank, Professor Harold Lasswell, and Professor Alexander Bickel. For reading the manuscript and saving me from more than my allotment of error, I am indebted to Dean Rostow, Professor Walter Berns of Yale University, Professor-Emeritus Robert E. Cushman of Cornell University, Professor Jack Peltason of the University of Illinois, Professor John P. Roche of Brandeis University, Professor Joseph Tanenhaus of New York University, and Norman Dorsen, Esq. Bruce Bromley, Esq., of Cravath, Swaine and Moore, New York City, was kind enough to lend me his copy of the transcript of proceedings in the Federal Court of Appeals, which was not printed in the Supreme Court record. My students in Government at Cornell University served the role of official tastes in the tradition of royal households; in addition to certifying the dish to be harmless, they had valuable suggestions as to seasoning and serving from which I profited.

Alan F. Westin

Ithaca, New York

Table of Contents

National Mood and the Steel Impasse, 1952

The Politics of Frustration

In an era generally dominated by insecurity, 1952 was a peak of frustration and bitterness on the American scene. The Korean War was entering its third year, 128,000 American casualties had been spent, and the end seemed nowhere in sight. Truce negotiations at Panmunjom were conducted fruitlessly all year, in the midst of ammunition duels and alarming reports of Communist troop build-ups. Riots in the Communist prisoner of war compounds were a constant irritant. As the war continued to unsettle the domestic economy—producing an unpopular draft, uneven wage and price controls, and a mounting inflation—the limited-war effort came under severe attack. Yet extending the war in space or weapons was opposed by our Allies, by most of our military leaders, and by much of the American public as well.

With our foreign policy tied in this Gordian knot, frustrations poured into the domestic debates, particularly on the issue of loyalty and internal security. Set in the context of Senator Joseph McCarthy's charges that government, colleges, and the communications media were "honeycombed with Communists," 1952 saw John Carter Vincent dismissed by the State Department as a loyalty risk, Owen Lattimore indicted for denying to a Senate Subcommittee that he was "pro-Communist," and Julius and Ethel Rosenberg's conviction (for passing atomic secrets to the Russians) upheld on appeal. From hundreds of Republican orators came the charge that Democrats could not be trusted to safeguard the nation from Communist agents, a challenge which added bitters to the already tart cup of political discourse.

On the larger political front, 1952 featured a running battle between the Fair Deal Democratic Administration of President Harry Truman and a Congress firmly controlled by a Republican-Southern Democratic coali-

1

tion. More of Truman's domestic legislative proposals were rejected by Congress in 1952 than in any previous year of his tenure, with Congressional disaffection ranging from Tidelands oil and immigration issues to wage and price policies and re-organization of executive agencies. Throughout the legislative session, the Truman Administration was the subject of steaming investigations into tax frauds, influence peddling and "softness toward Communism," while Republican presidential hopefuls ripped open each Truman proposal to see whether a campaign issue might be hidden inside. Even Truman's announcement in March that he would not be a candidate for re-election failed to sweeten executive-legislative relations. Mr. Truman left no doubt that he considered "his record" to be the issue at the coming presidential contest, thus providing a characterization that Republican Congressmen rushed to second, and Southern Democrats saw as a continued threat to their position within the party. Economic-group lines duplicated this division. Big Labor was happily committed to the party of the "Little Warrior" of 1948, while Big Business was determined to leave no check unsigned in the effort to place a Republican on Pennsylvania Avenue.

One product of these varied tensions was widespread labor unrest. More strikes took place in 1952 than in any year since 1946. Three and one half million workers left their jobs in industries such as coal, construction, petroleum, telegraph, and maritime, with cries from each side that the other would have to bear the stain of Korean casualties on its palms. The most serious labor dispute of 1952 took place in the nation's most important and strategic industry—steel.

Crisis in Steel, The New York Times, April 6, 1952[1]

Last Thursday night [April 3] Philip Murray, president of the United Steelworkers of America, sent this terse note to the presidents of the nation's steel companies:

"You are hereby notified that since a mutually satisfactory agreement has not been reached . . . a strike has been called at the plant of your company . . . effective 12:01 A.M., April 9, 1952."

Thus at the week-end the threat of a crippling steel strike hung over the nation. Yesterday Government representatives were still negotiating with labor and management in an effort to find a formula

[1] From *The New York Times*, April 6, 1952, IV, p. 1, col. 1. Used with permission of *The Times*.

for averting the strike. Late in the afternoon the Government announced it had persuaded union and industry delegates to meet at 10:30 this morning [Sunday] in New York for another try at reaching a settlement.

But whether there is a strike or settlement, there are grave dangers in the situation. A strike would imperil the nation's economy and jeopardize its—and most of the free world's—defense program. A settlement with a boost in steel wages and steel prices would increase the inflationary pressure.

These are the parties involved in the steel dispute:

Union: The United Steelworkers, with 1,100,000 members, 650,000 of them in the basic steel industry. They get an average hourly wage of $1.88.

Management: The 253 companies which produce steel at the rate of 2,100,000 tons a week or 109,000,000 tons a year—enough to make, say, 100,000 cars every day. The industry has 650,000 stockholders who received $320,000,000 in dividends last year. Steel profits were estimated by the Government as $2,600,000,000 before taxes last year; $690,000,000 after taxes.

Government: The President is in over-all command of the mobilization effort and the machinery to check inflation. Under the President is the Office of Defense Mobilization, headed until last week by Mr. [Charles E.] Wilson. Under the O.D.M. is the Economic Stabilization Agency, headed by Roger Putnam, which is directly concerned with inflation controls. And under E.S.A. are the twin wage-price control agencies, the Wage Stabilization Board, headed by Nathan Feinsinger, and the Office of Price Stabilization, headed by Ellis Arnall.

The steel controversy began five months ago when the union asked for raises for its 1952 contract and management said it could not grant wage boosts unless it got higher [price] ceilings. In December, the President referred the dispute to the Wage Board. Four times after that the union scheduled a strike and four times postponed it.

Late last month the W.S.B. announced its proposals: a package settlement of 17½ cents an hour in three stages extending through June, 1953, plus 5.1 cents in fringe benefits. The union accepted the recommendations; management denounced it; the Government split over it. Defense Mobilizer Wilson said it was "a serious threat in our effort to stabilize the economy," and that industry would need substantial price boosts to pay for it. Stabilization officials under Mr. Wilson maintained that the package was fair and that management did not need any price increases.

The showdown in the Government came nine days ago. Mr. Wilson, Economic Stabilizer Putnam and Price Stabilizer Arnall met with the President. The meeting was long and heated. It was plain that Mr. Wilson's implication was: If you approve of the W.S.B. package for labor, you must give industry price relief—or I go.

Wilson went.

Sunday evening he released a letter to the President saying, "I simply do not believe the W.S.B. recommendations and the Government's [price policy] meet the principles of equity . . ."

Mr. Truman replied: "I find that the [W.S.B. recommendations] are by no means unreasonable and do not, in fact, constitute any real breach in our wage-stabilization policies. As far as steel prices are concerned . . . if the eventual settlement of the wage negotiations is such that a price increase is required . . . it will be granted; otherwise it will not."

Throughout last week the O.P.S. and the industry argued over the price increase question. On Thursday industry officials met with union representatives and made an offer which was substantially lower than the Wage Board's recommendations. The union turned it down. Next morning the companies received Mr. Murray's strike notice. Friday afternoon Wage Board Chairman Feinsinger came to New York for the new effort to get a settlement. Meanwhile, the industry was banking its furnaces.

The basic wage-price arguments in the steel dispute now come down to this:

Management: The W.S.B. package has breached the Government's wage control line and will set a pattern for most of the rest of U.S. workers. If the Government insists upon supporting this package, the companies must have a price increase of $12 a ton over the current average of $110—$6 to pay the direct wage costs, the other $6 because the steel wage boost will mean hikes for other unions which, in turn, will send up the prices of the products the steel companies must buy. Steel profits after taxes have been falling—from $803,000,000 in 1950 to $690,000,000 in 1951.

Government: The W.S.B. package does not breach the line; it merely allows steel labor to catch up with labor in other industries. Average hourly earnings in steel are $1.883 compared with $1.987 in autos and $2.242 in coal. The companies can afford to pay for wage boosts out of profits. Under the O.P.S. formula a company is not supposed to raise prices unless its profits before taxes are running 85 per cent of its average for the best three of the years 1946–1949. The steel industry's profits before taxes last year were about 200 per cent of those of the base years.

Barring an unexpected break in the situation, the Government has three courses open to it: (1) it can invoke the Taft-Hartley law's injunction provisions against the union; (2) it can try to seize the steel plants; (3) it can do an about-face and grant the companies a price boost—perhaps $5.50 or $6.50 a ton—which is less than industry demands but is believed to be acceptable.

The first course—invoking the Taft-Hartley law which provides eighty-day injunctions against strikes affecting the "national health or safety"—seems unlikely. The President is reluctant to use the law against his political ally, Mr. Murray, particularly because the union has already postponed its strike for ninety-nine days at the Government's request.

As for the second course, legal authorities are divided about whether the President has the right to seize the steel plants. Under the Selective Service Act, the Government has limited seizure powers. The law says the President can "take immediate possession of any plant, mine or other facility" if the plant fails to make delivery on mandatory orders to the Government. But steel sells very little directly to the Government. Therefore some observers believe the President might rely upon his broad, "inherent powers" to deal with emergencies.

With regard to the third course—granting the companies some kind of price boost—Mr. Truman said last week that if a price increase is required "in the interest of national defense, it will be granted." This statement leaves the President plenty of room to change his mind and make a deal with industry.

President Truman's Dilemma

In December of 1951, according to a story obtained by reporters from members of the Truman Administration, the President had been informed by his "top advisors" that they doubted whether there was any "sound legal basis" for seizing the steel mills.[1] Having campaigned energetically in 1948 for repeal of the "unjust" and "oppressive" Taft-Hartley Act, Truman was unreceptive to the use of the Act against Labor.[2] By April, with a strike set for the ninth of that month, lawyers in the Justice and Defense Departments were set to work studying legal bases for Government intervention. At this announcement, lawyers for the steel industry indicated they were ready to contest Government seizure in court, and lawyers for the steel workers' union declared themselves equally ready to oppose any move to obtain an eighty-day Taft-Hartley injunction. On April 4, Attorney General J. Howard McGrath resigned. Although his successor, James McGranery, was named by the President the same day, the Senate was slow to confirm the nomination, and the steel seizure case went from start to finish without an Attorney General in office. During this period, the Solicitor General, Philip Perlman, served as Acting Attorney General and top legal counselor.

Newspapers on April 8 reported that last minute negotiations had failed and that a seizure order was being drafted at the White House. What the President felt at this moment is reviewed in the following selection from his memoirs.

---

[1] *The New York Times*, April 6, 1952, IV, p. 10E, col. 5.

[2] Senator Robert Taft (Rep.-Ohio) declared that Mr. Truman had used the Taft-Hartley Act "12 or 15 times" since its enactment in 1947, with "complete success", and the Senator demanded that the President employ it now rather than resort to seizure. *The New York Times*, April 3, 1952, p. 38, col. 2.

Harry S. Truman, Memoirs[1]

The demands of the steelworkers did not seem out of line to me. Korea and the needs of the defense program had greatly increased the volume of business being done by the steel mills, and the steel companies' profits were rising. For the three years preceding the Korean emergency the average profit in the steel industry had been $6.59 per ton. For 1951, however, the first full year of Korean war requirements, the profit, after taxes, was $7.07 per ton. Furthermore, in the light of the huge orders the Defense Department had placed with them on the authorization of Congress as requested by the Executive, 1952 promised to be at least as good for the steel manufacturers, if not better.

We had this economic situation on our hands: The industry was making more money, while the workers in the plants found that the increases in the cost of living had cut down the purchasing power of their pay. The cost of food and clothing and similar basic items had gone up.

Wages, however, were only one of the issues which the union wanted to negotiate. There had been a general worsening of relations between the union and some of the companies, especially United States Steel. The difficulty had arisen over company efforts to introduce an incentive-pay wage system. The workers charged rightly or wrongly, that this system would treat them as if they were machines, and they resented it.

. . . In 1951 the steel industry said that it did not wish to discuss the union's demands for increased wages and changes in working conditions, and the union announced that the workers would strike on December 31. I had no way of knowing why the companies refused to negotiate with the union. Perhaps they thought this was an opportune time to get tough. Perhaps they believed that the urgent needs of the defense program would bring the government into the dispute and force continued production at unchanged contract con-

---

[1] Harry S. Truman, *Memoirs*, vol. II pp. 465–471, Doubleday & Co., N. Y. 1956. Used by permission of *Time, Inc.*

ditions. Whatever the reasons, the officials of the Defense Department and of the defense production agencies viewed the impending strike with the gravest alarm. Secretary of Defense Robert A. Lovett had for months been pointing out to me that the national defense program would be endangered if a strike was allowed to halt production. All the members of the Cabinet agreed with Lovett that it would be harmful to the country and injurious to our campaign in Korea if our steel mills were allowed to close down. We were then not only trying to keep our forces in Korea, as well as elsewhere, fully equipped, but we had allies to whom we had promised arms and munitions and whose determination to resist Communism might depend on our ability to supply them the weapons they so badly needed. It was obvious that the best interests of the nation would be seriously affected if a strike in the steel industry took place.

On December 22, I referred the dispute between the United Steelworkers and the steel companies to the Wage Stabilization Board for solution. The unions immediately responded to this action by agreeing to postpone the strike so that production would not be interrupted.

To put off the strike in the hope of negotiating a solution, I had a choice of two alternatives as provided by the Congress. The first was the Taft-Hartley Act, which had a provision for an eighty-day injunction. Contrary to the claims of some uninformed people, this is not a mandatory provision. On the contrary, it provides in cases of strikes endangering national health and safety that the President *may* appoint a board of inquiry to determine the facts and to report to him. Upon receiving that report, the President *may* instruct the Department of Justice to ask for a court order to enjoin the strike for eighty days. During this period the board of inquiry attempts to bring about a settlement. At the end of eighty days, unless a solution is reached, the strike may legally proceed and the President must then report the facts to the Congress along with his recommendations.

There was the other alternative in the Defense Production Act of

1950 which declared that it was "the intent of Congress, in order to provide for effective price and wage stabilization . . . and to maintain uninterrupted production, that there be effective procedures for the settlement of labor disputes affecting national defense." This authorized the President to provide for procedures similar to those that had existed in World War II with the War Labor Board.

Acting under a directive from Congress, I had set up a Wage Stabilization Board and had assigned to it the function of settling labor disputes affecting national defense. In 1951 Congress had received a full report on the record of how this Board operated as an alternative to the procedure laid down in the Taft-Hartley Act. A move had been attempted in the House of Representatives to deprive the W.S.B. of the right to handle labor disputes. This move was defeated, however, and Congress extended the Defense Production Act with full knowledge that it included an alternative method for the handling of labor disputes.

In deciding on a choice, then, between the two alternatives, I first considered the Taft-Hartley Act. But the Taft-Hartley Act had been designed primarily for peacetime labor problems. The Wage Stabilization Board, however, had been established especially for defense labor disputes and had been reaffirmed by the Congress in this function within the year. The kind of situation we were facing caused me to turn to the Wage Stabilization Board.

From January 10 through February 26, 1952, the Wage Stabilization Board held extensive hearings and discussion with the parties, and on March 20, it submitted its report to me. On the wage issue it recommended that the union be given an increase in three stages over an eighteen-month period, for a total increase of 26.4 cents per hour. This was less than the union asked for. On the other points, too, the Board pared down the union's requests. On some it recommended that the union's requests be rejected altogether. Weighing the result against the current and prospective earnings of the industry, the proposal seemed to me to be fair and workable.

Charles E. Wilson, Director of Defense Mobilization, reported to me on March 24 that the companies would flatly reject the recommended settlement. He said that there would be an industry refusal followed by a prolonged strike and that the only thing that would prevent a shut-down of the mills would be to grant the price increase requested by the companies.

. . . I realized, of course, that any wage increase means adding cost to production, but I was *not* willing to commit myself to a flat [price increase] figure to be applied across the board, without proof that it was made necessary by the wage increase.

Steel is of such importance in our highly mechanized economy that any rise in the price of steel is soon reflected in price increases of a large range of goods, from refrigerators and automobiles to tin cans and bobby pins. A disproportionate rise in the cost of steel would have an inflationary effect. Because of this I felt that I would be justified in agreeing to a steel-price increase only if the steel industry would carry more than its normal share of the production cost. In this case, however, the steel industry was actively seeking to get much more than its share of the profits, and at the expense of the government.

. . . It was now apparent that a settlement would be difficult to reach.

A long round of conferences and consultations began. Dr. John Steelman, my assistant, whose specialty was labor problems, held meetings in his office with groups and individuals representing labor, management, and government. The conferees reported to me on their talks and asked my opinion or decision on some point, but no progress was being made. On April 7 the unions announced that they would go out on strike against the steel companies.

I again called in all my principal advisers to decide what steps to take to meet the emergency. Secretary of Defense Lovett said emphatically that any stoppage of steel production, for even a short time, would increase the risk we had taken in the "stretch-out" of the armament program. He also pointed out that our entire combat technique in all three services depended on the fullest use of our industrial facilities. Stressing the situation in Korea, he said that "we are holding the line with ammunition, and not with the lives of our troops." Any curtailment of steel production, he warned, would endanger the lives of our fighting men.

Gordon Dean, chairman of the Atomic Energy Commission, expressed grave concern over the delay which any lack of steel would mean for the major expansion of facilities for atomic weapons production. Henry H. Fowler, Administrator of the National Production Authority, told me that in addition to military equipment and atomic energy construction, power plants, railroad construction, shipbuilding, machine-tool manufacture, and the like, all would come to a halt if the steel mills closed down. He pointed out that it would depend on the inventory situation how soon the steel shortage would make itself felt in the manufacturing plants, and in certain types of ammunition there was virtually no inventory stock on hand.

Secretary of Commerce Sawyer briefed me on the effect a shutdown would have on the several transportation programs. His figures showed that a ten-day interruption of steel production would mean the loss of ninety-six thousand feet of bridge and fifteen hundred miles of highway. He reported that in the event of a steel shutdown only twenty-one of the ninety-eight ships then under construction in American yards could be completed, and thirty-nine others would have to be abandoned entirely. He informed me that the effect on airplane production would be such that Convair and Douglas, for instance, would have to halt their assembly lines within sixty days. There was a danger that some manufacturers would not await the onset of the shortage but would close down as soon as steel production ceased.

Oscar Chapman, Secretary of the Interior, said that the maintenance and expansion of facilities in the petroleum, gas, and electric-power utility fields depended on steel materials. Coal mines and coke ovens require steel for any number of accessory, but essential, uses.

With Dean Acheson I discussed the impact which this threatening paralysis of our defense economy might have on our relations with the rest of the world. Any failure on our part to deliver what we had promised to furnish our allies under the Mutual Defense Assistance Program would seriously undermine their faith in our ability to aid them in critical moments. Russia would be cheered by such evidence of a slowdown in our rearmament. We could not overlook even the possibility that Russia would believe us so weakened by an extended strike as to invite further aggression, and there might be other "Koreas."

All of this presented a very serious picture. The Congress was debating and doing a lot of talking about the steel crisis, and I would have welcomed any practical solution from it. But discussion was not enough. I had to act to prevent the stoppage of steel production, which would imperil the nation. Unless some last-minute effort brought peace and a settlement, I could see no alternative but to order the seizure of the steel mills by the government.

The expression "government seizure" sounds forbidding. Some people believe that seizure means confiscation or expropriation of private property. But what really happens is that the government merely assumes temporary custody of the properties. The very same people responsible for the management before seizure are kept on to continue the management of the mills and plants on behalf of the government. In this way the government can make sure that there is no interruption of production.

Neither management nor labor likes government seizure. They are not supposed to like it, any more than the government likes it, and they should not like it. It is much better for everyone for labor and management to work out their own problems without government interference. But when they reach an impasse that endangers the country, as they did in this case, seizure is an effective way to help bring them to a settlement.

During my occupation of the White House I had been frequently urged by department heads to seize an industry or a plant that was strikebound or threatened with a strike. But except in a few critical instances, I refused to do it. I have always considered seizure a last resort—something the President should turn to only when there appears to be no other way to prevent injury to the national interest, or when it is necessary to protect the whole country.

It was for that reason that I waited until the afternoon of the very last day before the strike was to begin before issuing the seizure order. I spent most of that last day with Dr. Steelman and with Secretary of Commerce Sawyer, whose job it would be to supervise the seized industry. Then, just a few hours before the mills were scheduled to be struck, I issued Executive Order No. 10340 to seize the steel mills, and later in the evening of that same day I addressed the nation by radio, explaining the reason for this action. . . .

Truman's Seizure Speech, 10:30 P.M., April 8[1]

My fellow Americans:

Tonight our country faces a grave danger. We are faced by the possibility that at midnight tonight the steel industry will be shut down. That must not happen. . . .

We do not have a stockpile of the kinds of steel we need for defense. . . . If steel production stops, we will have to stop making the shells and bombs that are going directly to our soldiers at the front in Korea . . . [W]e will have to cut down and delay the atomic energy program . . . [I]t won't be long before we have to stop making engines for the Air Force planes. . . .

I would not be faithful to my responsibilities as President if I did not use every effort to keep this from happening. . . . Therefore, I am taking two actions tonight. First, I am directing the Secretary of Commerce to take possession of the steel mills, and to keep them operating. Second, I am directing the Acting Director of Defense Mobilization to get the representatives of the steel companies and the steel workers down here to Washington at the earliest possible date in a renewed effort to get them to settle their dispute. . . .

[The President then explained that normal collective bargaining

[1] From the text of the President's speech, printed in *The New York Times*, April 9, 1952, p. 16, cols. 2–5.

was not possible in the present national emergency and that wage and price increases were determined at present, under Congressional statute, by "fair, impartial Government boards and agencies." The companies, said the President, have demanded a price increase far beyond what the Government should grant and have refused to pay the just wage increase awarded to the workers.]

I think they realize that the board's recommendations on wages are reasonable, and that they are raising all this hullabaloo in an attempt to force the Government to give them a big boost in prices. Now, what about the price side? Is it true that the steel companies need a big increase in prices in order to be able to raise wages?

Here are the facts. Steel-industry profits are now running at the rate of about $2,500,000,000 a year. The steel companies are now making a profit of about $19.50 on every ton of steel they produce. On top of that, they can get a price increase of close to $3 a ton under the Capehart amendment to the price-control law . . . [If] all the recommendations of the wage board were put into effect, they would cost the industry about $4 or $5 a ton . . . they would still be making profits of $17 or $18 on every ton of steel. . . . During 1947, 1948 and 1949, the three years before the Korean outbreak, steel profits averaged a little better than $11 a ton. . . . The plain fact is— though most people don't realize it—the steel industry has never been so profitable as it is today—at least not since the "profiteering" days of World War I.

And yet, in the face of these facts, the steel companies are now saying they ought to have a price increase of $12 a ton, giving them a profit of $26 or $27 a ton. That's about the most outrageous thing I ever heard of . . . they want to double their money on the deal.

[The President explained that a rise in steel prices would boost the prices of goods "all up and down the line." Furthermore, other industries such as paper, brass, trucking and auto-parts had sought rises and had been turned down. They had "taken 'no' for an answer . . . and kept right on producing."]

But not the steel companies. Not the steel companies. The steel industry doesn't want to come down and make its case, and abide by the decision like everybody else. The steel industry wants something special, something nobody else can get. . . .

You may think this steel dispute doesn't affect you—you may think it's just a matter between the Government and a few greedy companies. But it isn't. If we granted the outrageous prices the steel industry wants, we would scuttle our whole price control program. And that comes pretty close to home to everybody in the country. . . .

[The President then explained why he did not invoke the Taft-Hartley Act, stressing that its procedures "could not prevent a steel shutdown of at least a week or two." In his concluding remarks, the President again called for the companies and union to settle their grievances and for the companies to apply for "whatever price increase they are entitled to by law," thereby composing their differences "in the American spirit of fair play and in obedience to the law of the land."]

The Steel Industry's Response

"The Biggest Lawsuit in Years"

Shortly after the President's speech was completed, the White House issued Executive Order 10340 to govern the seizure. The President rested this action on "the authority vested in me by the Constitution and laws of the United States, and as President of the United States and Commander-in-Chief of the armed forces of the United States." Secretary of Commerce Charles Sawyer, designated as custodian of the companies, sent telegrams to 85 companies appointing the firm's president as Operating Manager for the United States and setting three requirements: that the company fly the American flag, post notices that the plants were in Government possession, and set up account books to keep separate records for the period of "Government operation."

At 11:30 P.M., an hour after the President's address, attorneys for Republic Steel Company and Youngstown Sheet and Tube Company arrived at the Washington home of Federal District Judge Walter Bastian.[1] They handed Judge Bastian a motion for a temporary restraining order, with accompanying applications for a permanent injunction. Judge Bastian replied that he would not act on the motions without hearing from the Government, and he set a hearing for 11:30

[1] According to Clarence Randall, the chief executives of the large steel companies met in New York on April 8 and concluded that seizure was unlikely. This conclusion was based on reports given them by "persons who professed to be close to the administration" and on their own analysis that the consequences of government seizure would be "so monstrous that we persuaded ourselves that it just couldn't happen." It was only when the individual executives learned about eight o'clock that night of President Truman's radio and television speech, Mr. Randall relates, that the company leaders realized seizure was to take place. Clarence B. Randall, *Over My Shoulder*, Little, Brown & Co., Boston, 1956, 213–215.

17

A.M. the following morning. As the lawyers left, one commented to reporters that this was the beginning of the "biggest lawsuit in years."

The morning of April 9, several companies filed motions in Federal District Court, in Washington, for a declaratory judgment and permanent injunction against the seizure as an unlawful act. Identical suits were lodged against Charles Sawyer, as Secretary of Commerce, and as an individual. For the first type, a 60 day summons was drawn, as a suit against "the Government." In the second, a 20 day summons was drawn, as a suit against a private party. Litigation was not, however, the only reply that the companies had prepared.

On April 9, speaking for the steel industry, Clarence Randall, President of Inland Steel, broadcast a nationwide rebuttal to the President's indictment.

Speech of Clarence Randall, April 9 [1]

I am here to make answer on behalf of the steel industry to charges flung over these microphones last night by the man who stood where I stand now. I am a plain citizen. He was the President of the United States. Happily, we still live in a country where a private citizen may look the President in the eye and tell him that he was wrong, but actually it is not the President of the United States to whom I make answer. It is Harry S. Truman, the man, who last night so far transgressed his oath of office, so far abused the power which is temporarily his, that he must now stand and take it. I shall not let my deep respect for the office which he holds stop me from denouncing his shocking distortions of fact. . . .

He has seized the steel plants of the nation, the private property of one million people, most of whom now hear the sound of my voice. This he has done without the slightest shadow of legal right. No law passed by the Congress gave him this power. He knows this, and speaks of general authority conferred upon him by the Constitution. But I say, my friends, that the Constitution was adopted by our forefathers to prevent tyranny, not to create it. . . .

For whom has he done this? Let no American be misled. This evil

[1] From a radio and television broadcast by Clarence Randall, April 9, 1952. Excerpts from text used with permission of Mr. Randall.

deed, without precedent in American history, discharges a political debt to the C.I.O. Phil Murray now gives Harry S. Truman a receipt marked, "paid in full."

He speaks of war. . . . Is your boy making $1.70 an hour in Korea? That is what the steelworkers got before Korea. And this new offer is a dollar a day more in straight pay, or a total package with fringe benefits, that would give the companies new and added costs of three-quarters of a billion dollars.

[Mr. Randall then explained why he considered the decision of the "so-called public members" of the Wage Stabilization Board to be "unreasonable," adding criticisms of the Board's recommendation by members of Congress such as Senator Walter George (Dem.–Georgia) and Rep. Ralph Gwinn (Rep.–N.Y.).]

And heartsick as many Americans were last night at what their President said, they were pained also at what he did not say. . . . He made no mention of the closed shop. . . . Has liberty sunk so low in Harry Truman's scale of values [that he did not think it necessary] . . . to make it clear whether or not he had seized the steel plants in order to compel workers to join a union against their will? . . .

But for downright distortion of fact, Harry Truman was at his magnificent best when he talked of profits in the steel industry. . . . He tossed off vast figures of profits without telling the American people that he meant profits before taxes. He said, for example, "the steel industry makes $19.50 of profit on a ton of steel," and neglected to say that he takes at least two thirds of that away in taxes. Steel companies cannot pay wages and taxes with the same dollars. . . .

The truth is that in terms of net profit, by which I mean the money the company has left after all costs are paid, the steel companies made—per ton—less than one third of the $19.50 that the President talked about. And that was off 15 percent from the preceding year.

The actual cost to the steel companies of the package recommended by the Wage Board is 30 cents per man-hour. But even this is only half of the ultimate cost. When steel wages go up the cost of things that steel companies buy goes up in the same degree. . . . With a wave of his hand, the President tossed this fantastic wage increase aside by saying the steel workers would thus merely be catching up with workers in other industries. Actually . . . since Korea, the cost of living has gone up 11 percent, while the earnings of steel workers have gone up 13½ percent. Does this mean that the steel workers have been unfairly treated?

My time is running out. . . . This is America at the crossroads. To the housewife this means that the whole giddy spiral of inflation starts again. To freedom-loving people it means the closed shop and compulsory unionism. To the business man it is the threat of nationalization. A sad chapter has been written in American history, which must be erased.

The Constitutional Rules

Excerpts from The Constitution of the United States

The steel seizure was not, of course, the first exercise of Presidential power in American history to be challenged as unconstitutional. As a result, a body of constitutional precedent had been accumulated and general lines of Supreme Court response had been drawn. The central source relied on by all the parties, naturally, was the Constitution itself. In the sections relevant to this issue, the Constitution states:

Article I, Section 1. All legislative Powers herein granted shall be vested in a Congress of the United States, which shall consist of a Senate and House of Representatives. . . .

. . . *Section 8.* The Congress shall have Power . . . [here the Constitution lists 17 areas of Congressional jurisdiction, such as the powers to levy and collect taxes, establish post offices, declare war, provide and maintain a Navy, establish rules for naturalization and to establish federal courts below the Supreme Court. An 18th power grants Congress the right to "make all Laws which shall be necessary and proper for carrying into Execution the foregoing Powers. . . ."]

Article II, Section 1. The executive Power shall be vested in a President of the United States of America. . . .

. . . *Section 2.* The President shall be Commander in Chief of the Army and Navy of the United States, and of the Militia of the several States, when called into the actual Service of the United States. . . .

. . . *Section 3*. He shall from time to time give to the Congress Information of the State of the Union, and recommend to their Consideration such Measures as he shall judge necessary and expedient; he may, on extraordinary Occasions, convene both Houses, or either of them, and in Case of Disagreement between them, with Respect to the Time of Adjournment, he may adjourn them to such Time as he shall think proper; he shall receive Ambassadors and other public Ministers; he shall take Care that the Laws be faithfully executed. . . .

Article III, Section 1. The judicial Power of the United States shall be vested in one supreme Court, and in such inferior Courts as the Congress may from time to time ordain and establish. . . .

. . . *Section 2*. The judicial Power shall extend to all Cases, in Law and Equity, arising under this Constitution, the Laws of the United States, and Treaties made, or which shall be made, under their Authority. . . . In all Cases affecting Ambassadors, other public Ministers and Consuls, and those in which a State shall be Party, the supreme Court shall have original jurisdiction. In all other Cases before mentioned, the supreme Court shall have appellate Jurisdiction, both as to Law and Fact, with such Exceptions, and under such Regulations as the Congress shall make.

The Fifth Amendment. No person shall be . . . deprived of life, liberty, or property, without due process of law; nor shall private property be taken for public use, without just compensation.

Prospects for Judicial Review

Although important Supreme Court precedents had been assembled by 1952 on such aspects of Presidential power as removal of executive officers, exercise of delegated rule-making authority, wartime powers, management of public lands, and control over foreign affairs, little law had been laid down as to the "inherent powers" a President could employ without reliance on an express grant in Article II or on Congressional statutes. Particularly undefined were the unspecified powers the President might wield in a situation of national emergency short of war, such as a critical labor crisis. According to Professor Edward Corwin,

Presidents had intervened in major industrial disputes on 24 occasions before 1952 "without specific legal authorization and even to the derogation of law in some instances . . . ." Wilson had taken such action eight times, Harding twice, Franklin Roosevelt eleven times, and Truman twice.[1] These Presidential exertions had not been measured in the Supreme Court for a variety of reasons: because Congress frequently ratified the move by statute and its constitutionality did not have to rest on inherent power; because the labor disputes were settled, or the President returned property, before a test case could reach the Supreme Court, thus causing cases to be dismissed as "moot;" or because the Supreme Court's reluctance to decide such large constitutional questions led the Justices to find non-constitutional grounds on which to dispose of the cases.

In addition to these grounds on which exercises of "inherent power" had been left unreviewed in the past, there were a series of general doctrines which were current in the post World War II setting of judicial review which must have encouraged President Truman and his legal advisors to believe that a Supreme Court ruling on the merits of the seizure would not be likely. First, the Supreme Court's general mood, at least in "economic matters," was one of judicial self-restraint born of the New Deal's struggle with the "Nine Old Men" of the 1930's. Under this outlook, the Justices gave more than lip service to the idea that measures of the elected branches of the Federal Government were entitled to a strong presumption of constitutionality and must clearly offend an express constitutional limitation to be struck down. Coupled with this was the axiom that an offense to the economic or political conceptions of particular Justices was not enough to make out a constitutional violation. Second, the Court had evolved what was known as the "political questions" doctrine, which held that certain questions were within the special competence of the elected branches of the government to decide, or that they were matters of self-regulation for those agencies. In such instances—for example, in cases of recognition of foreign governments—the Court simply refused to intervene.

Related to this doctrine were Supreme Court holdings that the federal courts had no power to enjoin the discretionary acts of the President. Enunciated in the Reconstruction-era case of *Mississippi v. Johnson* (1867), the holding had been based upon the judiciary's belief that it

---

[1] Edward S. Corwin, *The President: Office and Powers*, 4th Rev. Ed., p. 154, New York University Press, 1957. See also Glendon A. Schubert, Jr., *The Presidency in the Courts*, Univ. of Minnesota Press, Minneapolis, 1957.

lacked "power to enforce" obedience on the executive. Once carried out, however, the President's actions were stated in the Johnson case to be "subject to judicial review," and the acts of subordinates of the President might be reached in advance of completion by injunction. What the Johnson case left vague was the question of which were acts of a subordinate and which those of the President.

Finally, the steel dispute arose at a time when the nation was still technically at war with Japan and was fighting a very non-technical police action in Korea. Furthermore, steel production was closely tied to our wide-flung foreign policy commitments. If the judiciary identified the seizure as a military or foreign policy move, this would provide additional grounds for believing that the seizure would be left untouched by the courts. The sort of tender treatment which the President's discretion in foreign policy matters was likely to be accorded had been illustrated just a few years before, in the case of *Chicago and Southern Air Lines v. Waterman S.S. Corp.* (1948). In refusing to review a presidential ruling denying certificates to two airline companies to operate an overseas air route, the Court explained:

The President, both as Commander-in-Chief and as the Nation's organ for foreign affairs, has available intelligence services whose reports neither are nor ought to be published to the world. It would be intolerable that courts, without the relevant information, should review and perhaps nullify actions of the Executive taken on information properly held secret. Nor can courts sit in camera in order to be taken into executive confidence. But even if courts could require full disclosure, the very nature of executive decisions as to foreign policy is political, not judicial. They are delicate, complex, and involve large elements of prophecy. They are and should be taken only by those directly responsible to the people whose welfare they advance or imperil. They are decisions of a kind for which the Judiciary has neither aptitude, facilities nor responsibility and have long been held to belong in the domain of political power not subject to judicial intrusion or inquiry. . . .

At the same time, there was nothing in the post-war setting of judicial review to guarantee that the Court would abstain from judging the validity of the seizure, or that the Justices would uphold the action upon review. Although the formalistic notion of separation of powers which had been used in the 1930's to strike down New Deal measures was no longer in vogue on the Court, the idea of a vital jurisdictional division between executive and legislative authority was still an article of constitutional faith. Operating on the Justices was also the feeling, held by many observers in the 1940's and 1950's, that presidential power had been inflated by depression, war, and international crises into dangerously large proportions and that the judiciary should be zealous to prevent unneeded additions to that power. Finally, the Court had shown a steady disposition to continue its role as balancer of conflicting claims in the federal system, particularly if the issue was permeated by concern for the liberties of the citizen from "arbitrary" control.

In this unusually vague but super-charged context, the seizure was accomplished and the companies went to court.

Round One in District Court

At 11:30 A.M., Wednesday, April 9, the steel companies' motions for a temporary injunction were heard in the Federal District Court for the District of Columbia. The District Courts (84 in the various States, 1 for the District of Columbia, and 3 in the Territories) have from 1 to 18 judges assigned to them and are the tribunals where most cases proceeding through the federal judicial channel will first be heard. The steel case, as usual, was assigned to one of the 15 judges of the District Court who was hearing motions that day, a designation which brought Judge Alexander Holtzoff to the Bench.[1]

The following is a selection from the 46 page transcript of argument before Judge Holtzoff.

Transcript of Proceedings, April 9

YOUNGSTOWN SHEET AND TUBE COMPANY, REPUBLIC STEEL CORPORATION, BETHLEHEM STEEL COMPANY, *et al.*, Plaintiffs,

v.

CHARLES SAWYER, individually and as Secretary of Commerce, Defendant.

Washington, D.C.

Wednesday, April 9, 1952.

---

[1] Judge Holtzoff was born in Riga, Russia in 1886. He received his B.A., M.A. and LL.B. from Columbia University and practiced law in New York city from 1911 to 1924. Between 1924 and 1945, he was Special Assistant to the Attorney General of the United States. In 1945, he was appointed by President Truman to the District Court for the District of Columbia. A Democrat, Judge Holtzoff is an expert and author in the field of federal judicial procedure.

The above entitled actions came on for hearing on motions for temporary injuncton, [*] before the Honorable Alexander Hortzoff . . .

ARGUMENT ON BEHALF OF THE YOUNGSTOWN
SHEET AND TUBE COMPANY, AND THE YOUNGSTOWN
METAL PRODUCTS CO.
[by John J. Wilson, Esq.]

Mr. Wilson: If Your Honor please, several of us, on behalf of the steel companies, would like to present certain matters to Your Honor this morning. [Here, Mr. Wilson summarized the seizure.]

Our position is that there is no power in the President, and no power in Mr. Sawyer, to make the seizure which was made last evening. . . . I do not understand we must resolve to a moral certainty that legal question at this time. I understand the law to be that if we can convince Your Honor that there is reasonable question about the situation, then you will go to the next question, perhaps, of whether there is irreparable injury; and, if so, we hope we can convince you on that.

The Court: Well, there are other factors than irreparable injury; there is a question of balancing equities, when you apply for a temporary restraining order or a preliminary injunction.

*[An injunction is an order issued by a court of equity to prevent an irreparable injury from being done to a person's legal rights, for which money damages would be inadequate compensation. What injuries are irreparable and non-compensable, as the arguments of the Steel case will indicate, is a matter of sharp dispute and will turn largely on the factual circumstances of each situation. Injunctions can be obtained against public officials if their acts are unauthorized or if they are unlawful, as in the case of an unconstitutional action. In the federal courts, Rule 65 of the Federal Rules of Civil Procedure recognizes three types of injunctions: the *temporary restraining order*, which lasts no more than ten days and is intended to preserve the status quo until a full hearing can be held with both parties present, the *preliminary injunction*, which involves a determination of the merits of the controversy and leads to the *permanent injunction*, which is a final disposition of the case ordering the infringing party to do what is required to preserve the complaining party's rights. There is considerable dispute as to which of these injunctive remedies a complaining party may be entitled to at a particular time and how deeply into the merits of an unfolding dispute a court should go in an injunction proceeding rather than a suit at law.]

Mr. Wilson: All right, sir; I will not dispute that with Your Honor at this time. I think, frankly, it is not a question of balancing the equities. I think the equities are 100 percent on our side.

The Court: I am not prejudging that, but I am only suggesting that irreparable damage, or the possibility of it, is not the only matter for the Court to consider. . . .

*   *   *

Mr. Wilson: We point out in the moving papers that not only from the dollar side of things, the conditions which are sought to be imposed upon the steel industry in these cases, and, more particularly, because I am speaking for Youngstown, imposed upon the plaintiff in this case, are so burdensome financially that we will not be able to sustain them without a corresponding increase in price.

The Court: I don't think I can go into that.

Mr. Wilson: I am well aware of that, and I am moving from the motives and the details to a result, which is very crucial.

Another feature is this union shop situation. That can't be measured in dollars-and-cents. That is trying to cram down the throats of the steel industry a method of employer-labor relations, policy-management control contrary to and against the will of the steel companies.

I wanted to reemphasize those things to make this point: We say, that based upon prior experiences in similar situations, more specifically in the coal industry, that when the Government makes a seizure such as this, it then steps in and makes a contract with the union, and it makes a contract with the union which burdens the business of the plaintiff; and it turns out, aside from the question of whether the contract is one which might legally survive the return of the property to the steel company, it turns out, that it is made a condition of return to the steel company. That is to say, we fear it will be made a condition of return, as it was a condition of return in the coal industry.

The Court: Of course, I can't consider that. You are trying to prognosticate the future, what the Government might do at some future time. The mere fact that the Government might do something, which you say would be illegal if it did it, is no reason, in itself, for granting an injunction at this time.

Mr. Wilson: Yes, sir, I think it is, sir, if you will permit me to differ with you, because here, we are here on an application for a temporary restraining order, and we are saying to Your Honor that, "Stay the hand of this defendant from doing that very thing for ten days or twenty days, until you can investigate more thoroughly this problem—perhaps receive an answer from the respondent, and consider the thing materially."

The Court: I would be very glad if you would address yourself to the question as to why the drastic remedy of a temporary restraining order, or a preliminary injunction, is necessary at this particular time. You have just suggested that there should be 20 or 30 days to investigate those matters. Well, why do you need an injunction in the meantime? . . .

Mr. Wilson: I say to Your Honor that the record before Your Honor shows a policy of the Government in previous cases to do the very thing about which I am now complaining, and to saddle the industry with a Government-made contract, and not return the property to industry without the willingness of the industry to accept the Government-made contract.

I say, that if I came before Your Honor today with a motion for a temporary restraining order to enjoin my neighbor from cutting down my tree, if the tree isn't cut down before I come into the courtroom, all I can come in and say is that he has got an ax or a saw, and he is out there hacking away on the trunk of the tree, and that is some kind of reasonable fear; and I say to the Court, in this case, that I do not have to come in with a written letter from Mr. Sawyer in which he says, "The day after tomorrow, I intend to make a contract with the union." I say, the facts speak for themselves. I say, the history of the conduct of the Government in similar matters can be drawn upon by us in this situation to explain the reasonableness of our position. . . .

We point out, in the three paragraphs of paragraph 8 of the affi-
davit, that the defendant and his agents now are in our businesses.
That the defendant and his agents have control of our trade secrets
and methods of doing business, which are confidential with us.

The Court: You don't have that danger, so long as the president
of your company is the operating manager.

Mr Wilson: I say to Your Honor that it is inherent in this situation that Mr. Sawyer, the appointive power, may choose to call upon
a plant today, and call for records. Now, do I have to wait until
that occurs, before I must run down here and ask Your Honor for
temporary relief[?]. . . .

ARGUMENT ON BEHALF OF BETHLEHEM STEEL COMPANY
[by Bruce Bromley, Esq.]

Mr. Bromley: With characteristic keenness and clarity Your Honor
has put two questions to the plaintiffs' side of the table, satisfactory
answers to which I think must be furnished you in order for us to
prevail.

I refer to your suggestion that possibly in a consideration of the
relative equities here, that the damage to the plaintiffs, although it
may be irreparable or at least severe, . . . might be balanced or . . .
even outweighed by damage to our nation as a whole. Now, I assert
that that is not so, and I say that for this reason: There is no
emergency facing this country which has not been created by the
action of our President himself. . . . He said last night:

"I can't go under the Taft-Hartley Act because it might take
me a week or two."

Now, let's examine that. The Taft-Hartley Act requires that a
board of inquiry be convened and that it report the facts to the
President and thereafter the Government should—move against the
union for at least eighty days under the injunctive provision.

Isn't it perfectly plain to any observer that the President could a
week ago, ten days ago—this afternoon, if you please—constitute the

present Wage Stabilization Board, that board of inquiry who could within sixty minutes report to the President what the situation was, and the machinery of that Act be launched on its intended course. . . .

Now, why do we need a temporary restraining order, says Your Honor, and that is the second question, I think closely allied to the first. Well, I had assumed we needed it badly because, as counsel this morning said, if the seizure is unlawful we must content ourselves with a suit against Mr. Sawyer who may not—I hope he has, but who may not have quite enough money to pay our damages.

And Your Honor I thought very properly said, "What about the Tort Claims Act?"

Now, I say to Your Honor that the Tort Claims Act gives us no remedy whatsoever, and I hope I can demonstrate it in this fashion:

First, what is the affirmative grant of jurisdiction against our Government under the Tort Claims Act? Well, that is to be found in the jurisdictional section.

The Court: I am familiar with the Tort Claims Act, quite familiar with it. I participated in drafting it.

Mr. Bromley: Yes, sir, I know you did, but I want to make sure that Your Honor agrees with me that there is no grant under that section of any right to sue Mr. Sawyer.

[The jurisdictional section of the Tort Claims Act reads:]

> "The District Courts shall have exclusive jurisdiction of civil actions on claims against the United States for money damages. . for injury or loss of property, or personal injury, or death caused by the negligent or wrongful act or omission of any employee of the Government while acting within the scope of his office or employment, ..."

Now, if Mr. Sawyer is not lawfully authorized to seize our plants, I submit to Your Honor that he is not acting within the scope of his office and that we have no remedy against the United States Government. And if that is not clear enough, sir, I beg to call your attention to the exception contained in Section 2680 of Title 28 of

the Tort Claims Act, which I think makes assurance doubly sure
that we have no right against the Government, for it says:

"... [The Act] shall not apply to—

(a) any claim based upon an act or omission of an employee
of the Government exercising due care in the execution of a
statute or regulation, whether or not . . . valid, ..."

Now, that is an exclusion, sir, and this executive order under
which Mr. Sawyer purports to act, is a regulation. And all liability
against the Government for any act taken by Mr. Sawyer, whether
that regulation be valid or invalid, is, I think, excluded from the
scope and coverage of the Tort Claims Act.

The Court: I don't understand that an executive order directing
the doing of some specific act is a regulation.

Mr. Bromley: That is a question which must be resolved, and I
have found no decision on it. Because, of course, this Act was passed
to protect people from being run down by mail trucks, not to be
applied in this situation. So it is not surprising that we have no
decision, and I respectfully submit to Your Honor that the broad
language "statute or regulation" should include an executive order
such as this, and I certainly think that it does as a matter of construction, and I certainly think that we would get cold comfort out
of the attempt to assert any right against the Government if it
turned out that Mr. Sawyer's seizure was unlawful. . . .

And now may I impose upon Your Honor to say a word about the
fundamental question of power? And I do that hoping I can make a
little progress, because I think the Government ought to tell Your
Honor today that there is no statutory provision upon which they
can place any reliance. It is perfectly plain that there is in existence
today no statute from Congress which authorizes seizure of our
plants for the purpose of settling a labor dispute—like the War
Labor Disputes Act was, now no longer in existence.

Therefore, they have to go to some other kind of an Act, and I
think they can only go to two such Acts, and I think they should
disavow that either covers, but I must mention, I think in the in-

terest of expedition, the Selective Service Act of 1948 and the Defense Production Act of 1950.

Now, let's take the easiest one first. The War Production Act of 1950 merely authorizes the requisition of supplies or equipment when all other means of obtaining those parts or supplies upon fair and reasonable terms have been exhausted.

It is a sort of condemnation statute. It applies first to personal property, supplies and articles, and then it applies to real estate. But, as to real estate, the only power is to bring a court proceeding of condemnation. So I think you have got to admit at once—and I think Mr. Baldridge should admit at once that he does not place any reliance upon that Act at all.

Now, let's go to the Selective Service Act. Section 18 of that Act, as I read it, provides that if a company gets [a contract] order under that Act and each one of these complaints, may it please Your Honor, before you alleges that no one of these companies has any such order as is provided for by Section 18, and the provision there is that if the President gives an emergency order under this statute for the benefit of the Armed Services or the Atomic Energy Commission, and the contractor fails or refuses—and I submit that means being able to do so—fails or refuses to fill the order, then seizure may take place. . . .

Now, the Constitution, I suppose we have to start off with Article 2, and there are three sections there that might possibly give some grant of power relevant to this situation.

The first one is that the executive power shall be vested in the President. And the second one is that the President shall be Commander-in-Chief of the Army and Navy. And the third one is that he shall take care that the laws be faithfully executed.

I do not believe there is any other section of the Constitution to which my friends can point, and I take it that the one to which they are most apt to point is the one that makes our Chief Executive Commander-in-Chief of the Armed Forces. . . .

What can he do as Commander-in-Chief? Well, first we are not at war with Korea, I assume as lawyers, although to everybody else in this court room we certainly would be.

What about Japan? Your Honor was quite right. We are this very minute in a technical state of war with Japan.

Why? Well, simply because everything having been done by all the ratifying powers in the world, everything having been done by our Senate which has consented and approved ratification, the document which the President must sign is on his desk. He has not signed it.

When he does sign and deposit it, war is over. . . .[*]

So I must frankly say to Your Honor that there is a technical state of war. I think it is about the thinnest and the most technical state of war in which we have ever been, but there it is.

Now, I say to Your Honor that even in time of war the Commander-in-Chief, the President, has no power to seize private property in these circumstances. I think he can only do so, that is, his authority can only be exercised to do so in the area of conflict, or, if outside that area, at a time when the clear and present danger of national disaster is so overwhelming that, as a practical matter, nothing else will satisfy the demands of the safety of our people. And I think a consideration of our brief on that point and the cases in support of it will demonstrate the soundness—

The Court: Of course, as you read the life of Lincoln, he certainly took the position that there is a reservoir of inherent powers in the Presidency because he drew upon that reservoir time and time again.

Mr. Bromley: He did. He stretched [the Constitution's] very sides. There is no doubt about it, and I think it is very interesting now to look back on that, but he did. There can be no doubt about it.

The Court: And Theodore Roosevelt threatened to seize the coal mines, I recall reading, at one time when there was a threatened coal strike.

---

*[President Truman signed the Japanese treaty on April 15, 1952 and the instrument of ratification was deposited by the United States on April 28, with the result that references to the "technical state of war" did not arise again in the litigation.]

Mr. Bromley: Yes.

The Court: Apparently he felt that there was such power.

Mr. Bromley: Yes, my criticism of too much executive power is not confined to the present incumbent alone. I think the fact that Presidents feel sometimes the necessity of this, points to the danger. It is very easy to solve problems in a dictatorial fashion. It is very easy to forget about Congress; it is very easy to say "I alone will do this," but we cannot maintain our existence in safety that way. Some day we will get a fellow who will go far too far and we will end up with a Hitler. . . .

* * *

The Court: Suppose I issue this restraining order and Mr. Sawyer comes in and says, "I am acting pursuant to the direct orders of the President"?

Mr. Bromley: Well, first, if this were a suit against the United States, then I might be in some difficulty, but the law is perfectly clear, Your Honor, and there is a point in our brief which covers that, that a suit in this precise situation against a Cabinet Officer— and mind you, it is not only against him as Secretary; it is against him as an individual. My caption is "Individually, and as"—

The Court: I would not ask the question that I addressed to you if Mr. Sawyer of his own volition, in the exercise of his own discretion, took this action and if you demonstrated that the action was illegal, but he is acting pursuant to a directive of the President, and therefore wouldn't an injunction against him be in effect an injunction against the President?

Mr. Bromley: I think not, sir. I think not. I don't think the President is an indispensable party to this action.

The Court: I don't say that he is, as a matter of form, but I mean in essence and in spirit wouldn't an injunction against him be an injunction against the President?

Mr. Bromley: I do not think it would, sir, under the law.

I approach the problem this way: It certainly is not a suit against the United States.

The Court: No, it is not. I don't think you have to labor that point.

Mr. Bromley: And I do not think it is a suit against the President, although, if it were, I think it would lie. I think a suit against the President under this kind of situation would lie.

The Court: Do you think that the Court has authority to issue an injunction against the President? . . .

Mr. Bromley: Yes, sir.

The Court: I don't know of any case in which that has been done.

Mr. Bromley: I do not at the moment either. But we considered that before we drew our pleadings and came to the conclusion that Your Honor, as a District Judge, possessed that authority. But I do not think it, sir, any more necessary that the action be thought of as an action against the President than an action against a local postmaster to enjoin him from carrying out an order of the Postmaster General can be said to be an action against the Postmaster General.

*   *   *

The Court: I will hear from the Government.

ARGUMENT ON BEHALF OF THE DEFENDANT
[by Holmes Baldridge, Assistant Attorney General of
the United States.]

Mr. Baldridge: May it please the Court, the complainants are here seeking the extraordinary remedy of a restraining order. . . .

Since, in order to secure this extraordinary remedy it is necessary for the complainants to show irreparable injury, we submit in the absence of irreparable injury and in the absence of an adequate remedy at law, they are not entitled to the order, and I should like to address myself first, briefly, to the question as to whether they have made out a case for irreparable injury. . . .

The Court: What do you say about the point made by counsel for the plaintiffs that what they really fear is the possibility—or they call it the probability—that the Government, during the period of

Government operation, may enter into labor contracts with which the companies will be saddled after they resume possession, and which they will consider highly unfavorable to them? . . .

Mr. Baldridge: Based on past histories of seizures of this type, research discloses that in only one instance has the Government ever negotiated a wage contract with the union in a seized plant.

That was the Krug-Lewis agreement, I believe, in 1946.

In all other seizures—and there was one seizure in Lincoln's time of this type, under the general plenary powers of the President, and there was one in Woodrow Wilson's time, and there were twelve in Franklin Roosevelt's time—and in none except the 1946 Krug-Lewis agreement was there any effort nor any agreement consummated in respect to terms and conditions of employment as between the Government, who was operating the plants technically, and the unions.

I submit, Your Honor, that paragraph 3 of the executive order not only permits, but it was deliberately designed to permit, as well as encourage, continued collective bargaining as between the steel plants on the one hand and the unions on the other. . . .

The management is to continue to perform the usual functions of management.

We submit, second, that the request for a temporary restraining order is untimely, not only because there has been no irreparable injury shown, or threatened, but because these complainants have an adequate remedy at law.

This, I submit—and it is our position—is a legal taking under the inherent executive powers of the President and subject to just compensation under the Fifth Amendment to the Constitution in the event damage is suffered and proved by them. . . .

* * *

Now, a word, Your Honor, as to the power of the President to seize under the inherent executive powers. It is our position that this is not the proper time to present that problem. That is a legal problem on the merits and it is going to require more time.

The Court: No, I think it is a proper time. I think that is one of the matters that the Court weighs in determining whether or not to grant a restraining order.

Mr. Baldridge: Well, if there is no irreparable—

The Court: I do not think you should just decline to argue that matter.

Mr. Baldridge: Well, I would like to submit a brief on it, Your Honor.

The Court: No, I am going to decide the matter at the end of this argument. This is an application for a restraining order. I think the application would be defeated if I reserved decision and decided the matter ten days hence.

I think I have to decide the matter today. . . .

Mr. Baldridge: I call Your Honor's attention to Article 2 of the Constitution which provides that the executive power shall be vested in the President of the United States; that the President shall affirm that he will faithfully execute the office and will attest to the best of his ability, preserve, protect and defend the Constitution of the United States; that he shall be Commander-in-Chief of the Army and Navy of the United States; that he shall be the sole organ of the nation in its external relations, and that he shall take care that the laws be faithfully executed.

We submit that these provisions of the Constitution are sufficiently broad that the executive powers vested in the President of the United States is, in itself, a grant to the President of all executive power, not specifically divested by other provisions of the Constitution.

The Court: What is meant by "executive powers," Mr. Baldridge? Isn't it the power to execute statutes?

Mr. Baldridge: Well, among other things it is the power to protect the country in times of national emergency by whatever means seem appropriate to achieve the end.

The Court: Well, how far would you carry that?

Mr. Baldridge: Well, we don't think we have carried it too far in this particular instance, Your Honor. I don't know as I can discuss it—

The Court: Now, you say that this is really a taking by eminent domain. Of course, the Government has the power of eminent domain; the Supreme Court has held that time and time again, but what perturbs me a little bit when you assert this to be a seizure by eminent domain, it was my understanding that eminent domain was a power that has to be exercised pursuant to an Act of Congress.

Mr. Baldridge: We say it is a legal taking, Your Honor, subject to just compensation under the Fifth Amendment. We don't go so far as to take the position that it is a taking under the eminent domain powers.

The Court: Well, what kind of legal taking if not a taking by eminent domain?

Mr. Baldridge: I am not prepared to answer that.

The Court: Very well.

Mr. Baldridge: Now, the complainants have argued, Your Honor, that the Government had an adequate remedy by statute; that they did not have to move under the plenary powers which reside in the executive.

We submit that that is a matter that cannot be inquired into.

The Court: I don't think you need to argue that. It is not for this Court to say which of several courses the President should have pursued. That is for the President. If he has legal power to pursue the course that the President has pursued, the mere fact that he had the choice of some other course is nothing for the Court to pass on.

Mr. Baldridge: We think that is correct, too, Your Honor.

* * *

And just one more word, Your Honor, as to the President's power to seize: I think in the last analysis it is fair to say that magnitude of the emergency itself is sufficient to create the power to seize under these circumstances.

The Court: I think Chief Justice Hughes said in one of his opinions that emergencies do not create power. They may give an occasion for the exercise of power that has been dormant, but they do not create power.

Mr. Baldridge: Well, under our Constitutional system, Your Honor, it seems to me that there is enough residual power in the executive to meet an emergency situation of this type when it comes up.

The Court: I think that whatever decision I reach, Mr. Baldridge, I shall not adopt the view that there is anyone in this Government whose power is unlimited, as you seem to indicate.

Mr. Baldridge: I was not indicating that, Your Honor. I just said I thought that the present emergency presented a sufficiently serious situation that it could be met by the residual powers that reside in the executive.

The Court: Do you rely on the President's powers as Commander-in-Chief? You have not mentioned them at all, except in reading Article 2.

You seem to place more virtue in the first sentence of Article 2 than in the laws constituting him Commander-in-Chief.

Mr. Baldridge: Based upon all the powers that he has as an executive, including the powers that he has by virtue of his position as Commander-in-Chief.

*   *   *

Now, if a temporary restraining order is entered now, that order will have the effect of causing a strike and, as a matter of fact, it would be legalizing a strike by court order.

The Court: No, now, just a moment. You are not suggesting that if this Court issues a restraining order, there will be a strike?

Mr. Baldridge: If a restraining order is issued, then the situation remains, I suppose, in status quo prior to seizure action, and what that means is that you have notice that the union is going out on a strike as of a certain time.

The Court: You mean, in other words, that if I issued a restraining order, the status will revert to what it was before the President's seizure order took effect?

Mr. Baldridge: Yes.
The Court: When was that, 12 o'clock midnight?
Mr. Baldridge: 12:01, I believe.
The Court: I see your point.

·   *   *   *

(There was a brief informal recess, at the conclusion of which the proceedings were resumed as follows:)

Opinion of Judge Alexander Holtzoff, April 9

[The opinion first described the dispute and the seizure.]

". . . An application for a temporary restraining order involves the invocation of a drastic remedy which a court of equity ordinarily does not grant, unless a very strong showing is made for the necessity and the desirability of such action. The application is, of necessity, addressed to the discretion of the Court. It is not sufficient to show that the action sought to be enjoined is illegal. It is, in addition, essential to make a showing that the drastic remedy of an injunction is needed in order to protect the plaintiff's rights.

In arriving at its decision, the Court must arrive at a balance of equities, and consider not only the alleged legality or illegality of the action taken, but also other circumstances that will appeal to the discretion of the Court.

There are several matters that the Court must weigh in this instance. Although, nominally, and technically, the injunction, if granted, would run solely against the defendant, Sawyer, actually and in essence it would be an injunction against the President of the United States, because it would have the effect of nullifying and stopping the carrying out of the President's Executive Order for the seizure of the plants. It is very doubtful, to say the least, whether a Federal Court has authority to issue an injunction against the President of the United States, in person. (The State of Mississippi v. Johnson, 41 Wall. 475.) In that case, Chief Justice Chase made the following statement, at page 500:

"The Congress is the legislative department of the Government. The President is the executive department. Neither can be restrained in its action by the judicial department, though the acts of both when performed are in proper cases subject to its cognizance."

The Court, it seems to me, should not do by indirection what it could not do directly, irrespective of whether the Court has the power so to do. It would seem to me that this is a consideration that should affect the exercise of the Court's discretion.

Another circumstance that must be considered is whether the plaintiffs will sustain irreparable damage if a temporary restraining order were denied. The Court heard counsel at length on this point, because that is a matter that seemed to the Court to be of vital importance. The situation, as it presents itself at this stage, is that the president of each company, and his managerial staff, remain in control and are named as operating agents for the United States. They have not been dispossessed or displaced. They are still in possession and will continue to conduct the company's operations.

True, plaintiffs fear that other drastic steps may be taken which would displace the management or which would supersede its control over labor relations. It seems to the Court that these possibilities are not sufficient to constitute a showing of irreparable damage. If these possibilities arise, applications for restraining orders, if they are proper and well-founded, may be renewed and considered.

On the other hand, to issue a restraining order against Mr. Sawyer, and in effect nullify an order of the President of the United States, promulgated by him to meet a nation-wide emergency problem is something that the Court should not do, unless there is some very vital reason for the Court stepping in.

The Court feels that the balance of the equities is in favor of the defendant, so far as the present application is concerned. This conclusion is fortified by the concessions of Government counsel, to the effect that, in any event, the plaintiffs have an adequate remedy in suits for damages. Government counsel concedes that if, as they say it is, the seizure is lawful and a legal taking of property, a suit for just compensation will lie in the Court of Claims against the United States.

On the other hand, Government counsel further concedes that if the seizure is illegal, an action for damages lies against the United States under the Federal Tort Claims Act. The Court is of the opinion that such actions would lie.

The fact that the plaintiffs have adequate remedies by way of actions for damages, and the considerations already stated, lead to the conclusion that the balance of equities requires a denial of a temporary restraining order. The motion for a temporary restraining order is denied.

Public Opinion and the Congressional Response

Politics, Advertising, and Appropriations

On the morning of April 9, as the District Court hearing was beginning, Congress received from President Truman a message reporting what he had done, explaining the necessity for the action, and agreeing to abide by any Congressional policy drafted to deal with the dispute. The manner in which Truman put this last point to Congress is as follows:

It may be that Congress will deem some other course to be wiser. It may be that the Congress will feel we should give in to the demands of the steel industry for an exorbitant price increase and take the consequences as far as resulting inflation is concerned.

It may be that the Congress will feel the Government should try to force the steel workers to continue to work for the steel companies for another long period without a contract, even though the steel workers have already voluntarily remained at work without a contract for 100 days in an effort to reach an orderly settlement of their differences with management.

It may even be that the Congress will feel that we should permit a shutdown of the steel industry, although that would immediately endanger the safety of our fighting forces abroad and weaken the whole structure of our national security.

I do not believe the Congress will favor any of these courses of action, but that is a matter for the Congress to determine.

It may be, on the other hand, that the Congress will wish to pass legislation establishing specific terms and conditions with reference to the operations of the steel mills by the Government. Sound legislation of this character might be very desirable.

On the basis of the facts that are known to me at this time, I do not believe that immediate Congressional action is essential; but I would, of course, be glad to cooperate in developing any legislative proposals which the Congress may wish to consider.

If the Congress does not deem it necessary to act at this time, I shall continue to do all that is within my power to keep the steel industry operating and at the same time make every effort to bring about a settlement of the dispute so the mills can be returned to their private owners as soon as possible.

The message was inserted in the *Congressional Record* to the accompaniment of general debate on the seizure in both Houses. The first legislative skirmish took place in the Senate over the proper committee to which the President's message should be referred. Senator Styles Bridges (Rep.—N.H.), a strong Truman foe, declared that it should go to the Senate Judiciary Committee to consider whether the President had exceeded his powers, or to the Senate Banking Committee, which had authority over wage and price controls. The chairmen of these committees were conservative Democrats, Pat McCarran of Nevada and Burnett Maybank of South Carolina, respectively, who could be counted on to oppose the presidential seizure. Vice President Alben Barkley, personally pro-labor and an Administration stalwart, ruled as presiding officer of the Senate that this was a labor dispute and the President's message should go to the Senate Labor Committee, where Barkley was confident its reception would be more favorable. A series of Republican speakers—Bridges, Homer Capehart (Ind.), Robert Taft (Ohio), John Bricker (Ohio), and Bourke Hickenlooper (Iowa)—opposed the Barkley ruling, stressing the "illegality" and "usurpation" of the President's action. When Barkley persisted in his ruling, however, Senator Bridges chose to withdraw his motion to overrule the chair and not to force the issue at that moment.

Between April 10 and 15, with bargaining between union and management producing no solution, each legislative day provided more debate on the seizure but no Congressional declaration of any kind. As editorial opinion accumulated—running very heavily against the President's action and criticizing Judge Holtzoff's "timidity"—Congressional critics read denunciatory editorials, attacked the constitutional and political aspects of the move, and challenged the need for the drastic seizure action. Several Congressmen introduced resolutions and bills to resolve the impasse. One of these would have expressed Congress' judgment that the seizure was illegal. Another called for impeachment of the President. Liberal Republicans in the House (Javits, N.Y.) and in the Senate (Morse, Ore.) introduced measures to allow the Government to operate struck plants whose production was essential to national safety and to broaden Government seizure authority in labor disputes. On April 16, seventeen Republican Senators, mostly from the Taft-Conservative wing of the party, presented a resolution calling for an investigation by the Senate Judiciary Committee to determine whether there was any constitutional or statutory authority for Truman's solution of the dispute. (The day before, a Senate Labor and Public Welfare Subcommittee had begun hearings on the President's message and on the Morse bill, S. 2999, to authorize seizure.)

The running of the New Jersey and Pennsylvania presidential primaries during this period made the seizure a general stump topic, with supporters of Senator Taft and General Eisenhower vying with each other to denounce Mr. Truman's "usurpation" most strongly. Senator Estes Kefauver (Dem.—Tenn.) also expressed opposition to the seizure as he moved along the Democratic primary trail.

On April 15, the "Steel Companies in the Wage Case" (350 Fifth Avenue, New York City) placed full page advertisements in newspapers throughout the country. These denounced the "illegal seizure" as having stirred "the greatest Constitutional issue since the Court Packing Plan of 1937," and featured excerpts from 13 representative editorials condemning the President's action as dictatorial. A second advertisement, headed, "A Threat to American Freedom," appeared on April 17, and called for a mass letter-writing campaign to Washington, since "the only recourse is Congress." The same day Steel Union President Philip Murray protested against "the greatest campaign of advertising against the President of the United States and the Government in the history of the country." Speaking before the National Press Club, Murray denounced the fact that taxpayers' money was paying for this campaign, since it would be charged off as a business expense against taxes. After one further ad from the Jones and Laughlin Steel Company on April 18, this particular form of company public relations attack ceased.

April being the month that the Senate was debating the Third Supplemental Appropriations Bill, providing government revenue for the coming fiscal year, Senator Homer Ferguson (Rep.—Mich.) invoked one of the traditional techniques by which Congress controls Presidential policy—the rider to an appropriations act—to attack the steel seizure. (Congresses in the past have used riders to forbid Presidents to expend money in foreign relations with certain nations, to hire employees who believe in overthrowing the government by force and violence, or to dispose of government food surpluses in ways that the Congressmen disapproved.) On April 16, Senator Ferguson put into the hopper an amendment to the Appropriations Bill to forbid the use of any of these funds by the President to carry out seizure of the steel mills. Debate began on April 18 and "threw the Senate into turmoil," according to *The New York Times* report. "Before galleries packed with Easter-week visitors," *The Times* described, "Senators clashed bitterly in shouted debate surcharged with implied threats of Presidential impeachment, on the one side, and challenges to try it, on the other."

The following excerpts from the *Congressional Record* contain the gist of the constitutional argument in the debates.

Debate in the United States Senate, April 18–21[1]

The Acting President pro tempore: The clerk will state the amendment.

The Legislative Clerk: It is proposed to insert the following new section:

"No part of any appropriation contained in this act, or of any funds made available for expenditure by this act, shall be used for the purpose of enforcing Executive Order 10340, dated April 8, 1952, directing the Secretary of Commerce to take possession of and operate the plants and facilities of certain steel companies, or any other order or regulation relating thereto."

Mr. Martin (Rep.): . . . It is not pleasant to deprive a department of appropriations, but that seems to be about the only power we have to keep the departments in line.

Mr. Mundt (Rep.): . . . I believe that this is a good time to make

[1] 98 *Cong. Rec.* 4089–4126, 4130–4155 (82nd Cong., 2d Sess., 1952).

clear to all concerned that if we are to stop socialism in this country, if we are to stop the trend toward dictatorship, we must stop it wherever it reaches out to seize power. . . .

Mr. Humphrey (Dem.): . . . As to the constitutionality of the President's seizure, I was of the opinion that I was elected to the United States Senate, not to the Supreme Court. I know there are undoubtedly persons who have a great ambition to be judges, but there are no judges in this body. . . . Now there is a case pending. The steel companies have jointly pressed suit against the Government. Do not the Senators think it would be well to let the normal procedures of law prevail? Do they not have men who are honorable, trained in the law, and who will be able to defend themselves and their interests? Are there those in this body who believe the courts of the United States are incapable of making an honorable, objective judgment? . . .

Mr. Morse (Rep.): I will summarize my argument of the last hour and a half . . . my first premise, [is] namely: I believe, at least until the United States Supreme Court rules to the contrary, that under the Constitution of the United States a President has broad inherent powers to act in an hour of crisis to protect the security of the country. That is major premise number one.

Major premise number two: He, however, must exercise that power in such a manner as to lead a court to find that it was a reasonable exercise of the power. Anytime he does not do that, I think he would then find himself in difficulty in a court, if the issue could be squarely placed before the court.

Third . . . it becomes a question of fact as to whether, in a particular case, the facts prove the existence of a crisis so serious that immediate action must be taken to protect the security of the Nation. If that is so—and it makes no difference whether it is a steel case, a telegraph case, a copper case, a railroad case, or what manner of case it is—I think the President, in the absence of legislation by the Congress, has the power to take immediate action to protect the national security. . . .

Mr. Hayden (Dem.): . . . If the pending legislative rider is attached to this appropriation bill and likewise to every other appropriation bill . . . absolutely nothing will be accomplished in respect to a final determination of the issue of whether the Constitution confers on the President of the United States any inherent powers which he can use at any time or under any particular circumstances.

Mr. Knowland (Rep.): . . . It seems to me that what the able Senator from Arizona is saying is that the Congress, instead of being one of the coequal branches of the Government, along with the executive and judicial, is in fact a subordinate branch of the Government.

Mr. Hayden: I interpret the amendments in exactly the other way, namely, as taking the position that the Congress is superior to the judicial branch of the Government and is attempting in this bill to state what the Constitution means on the question which is involved. Congress cannot do that.

Mr. Knowland: Does the able Senator from Arizona question that under the Constitution the Congress has control of the public purse?

Mr. Hayden: No, but control of the public purse is not an effective way to answer the question of whether the President of the United States has inherent powers under the Constitution.

Mr. Knowland: Does not the Senator from Arizona agree that this is the first piece of proposed legislation which has been before the Congress since the President's usurpation of power; is it not the first time the Congress of the United States has had an effective way of blocking this usurpation of power; and if we are not to surrender our coequal position in the Government of the United States this is the time and this is the place for the Congress to give a clear warning signal that we do not intend to sit idly by while the President of the United States seeks to seize an industry without authority of law, and perhaps open the door for the complete socialization of the Nation? . . .

Mr. Lehman (Dem.): . . . [E]ven though it be a fact that, as the Senator from California has stated, Congress controls the purse strings, Congress is still not justified in using its power over appropriations in this round-about way, in order to block an emergency action taken by the President—an action which the President of the United States felt to be clearly within his authority, an action whose legality cannot be finally determined until there is a decision by the Supreme Court of the United States. . . .

Mr. Knowland: . . . Congress should be just as zealous to protect the Constitution of the United States as should the other coequal branches of the Government. Otherwise, I think we would be failing in our duty to the United States, for after all, we are Senators of the United States as well as Senators representing particular States. . . .

This morning the President of the United States sent to this body a letter attempting to tell us how we should legislate on the bill which is before the Senate. I think the President is stepping out of his field as the Executive. His job is to see that the laws are faithfully executed, and our job is to pass laws. We are not going to be intimidated by the President of the United States. We are not going to be intimidated by any outside agency into not doing our duty as we see it. We have to follow our conscience. We have to follow our oath of allegiance to the Constitution of the United States and to the people of the United States, whom we represent. . . .

[The President's letter, addressed to Vice-President Alben Barkley, had noted the debate on Senator Ferguson's amendment and had repeated the President's desire to see Congress take action. "But," the President said, "I do not believe the Congress can meet its responsibilities by following a course of negation. The Congress cannot perform its constitutional functions simply by paralyzing the operations of the Government in an emergency." The letter went on to say that Congress was free, of course, to reject the "course of action" taken, but it expressed the President's hope that Congress would pass legislation to deal with the steel dispute itself.]

Mr. Case (Rep.): . . . If there were an emergency of the gravity which the President has suggested, he could have come before the Congress with a special message, as he did in the railway case some years ago, and asked for special legislation. He could have asked the Congress to join him in declaring an emergency, which would authorize seizure or whatever other procedure might grow out of the situation. It seems to me that the Senator [Humphrey] is unduly circumscribing the President when he says that he could merely seize, or operate under the Taft-Hartley law. He could have asked for new legislation. He could have asked the Congress to join with him in measuring the depth of the emergency.

Mr. Humphrey: I thank the Senator from South Dakota. I remind him that negotiations in the steel strike were taking place as late as 11 o'clock on the night of April 8. Three times there had been a postponement of the strike. Frantic efforts had been made by the Conciliation Service and by members of the Wage Stabilization Board, which comprises some of America's finest arbitrators and negotiators in the field of labor-management relations.

The United States Senate was not in session at 11 o'clock on the night of April 8. Even if it had been, we could not have passed a bill in less than 15 minutes. Once the steelworkers had walked out on strike great damage would have been done to the production program.

Surely we would not have had the time to draft intricate legislation in less than 24 hours. I hope we shall never legislate in that manner. . . .

Mr. Case: What [I] . . . suggested awhile ago was that if we are confronted with an emergency which calls for action of this sort the problem should be submitted to Congress. I submit that there was greater violence done to the institutions and traditions of America by the President's action than would have resulted by way of damage to America by not producing steel for a few days. It would have been far safer to have done things in a proper way than to have acted as the President did. . . .

* * *

When the amendment was brought to a vote on April 21, it was carried, 44-31. Although Senator Richard Russell (Dem.—Ga.), himself a critic of the seizure, had urged his fellow Southerners not to show their disapproval by denying funds to the President, 11 Southern Democrats joined the 33 Republicans to impose the rider. The 2 Republicans who voted with the 29 Democrats in opposing the amendment were long standing liberal mavericks, William Langer of North Dakota and Wayne Morse of Oregon. Twenty-two Senators did not vote.

Another Ferguson amendment, which would have denied the use of *any* federal appropriations to operate the seized mills, was not adopted by the Senate.

Court Maneuvers, April 9–24

Disqualification and the Fortunes of Judicial Roulette

On the morning after the seizure announcement, the steel companies had filed their suits in Federal District Court at Washington for a permanent injunction. Following Judge Holtzoff's denial of a temporary restraining order, company counsel appeared at noon on April 10, to argue for a motion to set the date for trial on the injunctions as early as possible. Before counsel could present their arguments, District Judge Walter Bastian announced:

Let me say this Court is going to disqualify itself. I have a very modest portfolio acquired, . . . namely, 30 shares in the Sharon Steel Corporation. While the Sharon Steel Corporation is not a party to either of these suits, its position is similar to those of the other companies which have filed suits and the Court therefore feels it should disqualify himself. I therefore refer this case to Judge Pine, if he could take it, or otherwise to the Assignment Commissioner for re-assignment.

Even though Government and company counsel assured Judge Bastian that they would both consider him disinterested, Judge Bastian said that possession of the stock—worth about $1,000—would embarrass him. "Like Caesar's wife," he explained, "I guess we have got to be above suspicion."

Within ten minutes, counsel were drawn up before Judge David A. Pine. At the opening of the proceedings, Judge Pine declared:

Well, I should make this disclosure to you. My wife is the owner of twenty or twenty-five shares of Bethlehem Steel Company. [Bethlehem was one of the parties in the suits at hand] . . . I suppose this is valued at about a thousand dollars.

53

Now, if you wish to make any point of that, or any of the other counsel wish to make any point of that, why this is the time to do it.

The company and Government attorneys hastened to say that they had no objection, and the argument began. The point of the companies' motion was their desire to have a trial on the merits set down for hearing in the near future, with the suggestion of 20 days. Since the Federal Rules provide a 60 day period for the Government to file its answer when it is sued, Assistant Attorney General Baldridge insisted that he had the right to take that period since this was really a suit against the United States. Judge Pine refused to rule on the question whether Charles Sawyer was a private party (with only 20 days to file an answer) or a Government agent, stating that this was not the proper time to resolve that issue.

At this point, company counsel tried to persuade Mr. Baldridge to agree to file the Government's answer in a "reasonable period." This prompted the following exchange between Baldridge and two lawyers for the companies:

Mr. Jones: May I ask Mr. Baldridge a question? Mr. Baldridge, would you be willing to have this case set down and get your answer in, and have it disposed of, let's say the early part of May, or within thirty days? We don't want to rush you into five days or six days.

Mr. Baldridge: Well, in all frankness, your Honor, this matter is suddenly laid in our laps as counsel for the Government, just as it was with respect to the complainants. It is a matter of tremendous importance. We want to make as thorough a preparation as we can. Until we have studied it a little more, I am not in a position to make any commitment as to an accelerated answer or a trial date other than that provided by the Rules.

Mr. Wilson: I should have thought, your Honor, that the Government of the United States would have known what the law was on this subject before the Executive Order was issued; and they wouldn't have to make their research after the injunction suits were filed. I mean no reflection upon Mr. Sawyer, whom I do not know, but I certainly do regard the attitude of the Department of Justice here today as one of stalling. . . .

At this point Judge Pine broke in and informed counsel:

"Well, under the circumstances, I know of no rule which permits me to advance the case for hearing in its present posture. . . . The Rules anticipate this by providing a remedy, to-wit, a motion for preliminary injunction [which can be heard sooner]."

Company counsel expressed their awareness of that alternative and thanked the Court, with which the hearing ended.

During the next two weeks, United States Steel, Bethlehem, Jones and Laughlin, Armco, E. J. Lavino, Republic and Youngstown Sheet and Tube Companies each filed motions for a preliminary injunction to restrain the Government (Sawyer) from doing "unlawful and un-constitutional acts against the [companies]." The motions were not filed any too soon, from the companies' standpoint. On April 18, Secretary Sawyer announced that the Government planned to take up wage in-creases the following week, an intention he repeated later on the program, "Meet the Press." (One of the companies, Inland Steel, decided to tie another string to its bow and filed suit for an injunction in Federal District Court for Northern Indiana, where Inland plants were located. The Government headed off this action by asking the Court to stay the case pending disposition of the suits being tried at Washington.)[1]

On April 24, proceedings began in Washington before Judge David A. Pine[2] on the motions for a preliminary injunction. The following highlights are from the 147-page transcript of argument held on April 24 and 25.

---

[1] On the crucial importance of maneuvering the best test case into the desired forum at the ideal time before the most favorable judge, see Jerome Frank, *Courts on Trial*, pp. 241–242, Princeton Univ. Press, 1950; Benjamin Twiss, *Lawyers and the Constitution*, Princeton Univ. Press, 1942; Paul A. Freund, *On Understanding the Supreme Court*, p. 77 *et seq.*, Little Brown, Boston, 1951; Jack Peltason, *Federal Courts in the Political Process*, pp. 43–55, Doubleday and Co., Short Studies, New York, 1955.

[2] David Andrew Pine was born in Washington, D. C. in 1891. He graduated from Georgetown Law School in 1913 and became confidential clerk to Attorney General (later Justice) James McReynolds, remaining in the Justice Department and rising to Special Assistant Attorney General. A Democrat, Pine found himself out of a job with the entrance of the Harding Administration in 1921 and he turned to a general law practice in Washington, which he maintained for the next 13 years. In 1934, he was appointed Chief Assistant U.S. Attorney for the District of Columbia, by President Franklin Roosevelt. In 1938, he was promoted to U.S. Attorney and two years later, Roosevelt designated him as a Judge of the United States District Court.

Transcript of Proceedings, April 24–25.

YOUNGSTOWN SHEET AND TUBE COMPANY, *et al.*, Plaintiffs

v.

CHARLES SAWYER, WESTCHESTER APARTMENTS, WASHINGTON D.C.,

Defendant.

motion for preliminary injunction

The Court: . . . Now, in order to avoid repetition so far as that is possible, have counsel [for the steel companies] made any arrangement among themselves for any particular one of them to present the case generally?

Mr. Bromley: Yes, your Honor; I think we have. We have agreed that Mr. Kiendl representing the United States Steel Company should bear the brunt of the argument and make the initial presentation, and the rest of us I take it will confine our remarks thereafter to matters which are not repetitious. . . .

Mr. Kiendl: May it please the Court, this is an application by the United States Steel Company primarily for an injunction restraining what we consider to be the imminent threatened changes in the terms and conditions of employment of a steel employee. . . . This is not in any sense the situation which existed before your colleague, Judge Holtzoff . . . on April 9, 1952.

[Mr. Kiendl discussed the fact that the Holtzoff ruling had rested on the premise that the companies had not shown, as of April 9, that the Government would take steps which would "displace the management or supersede its control over labor relations," thereby creating irreparable damage. However, Mr. Kiendl continued, on April 18, Secretary Sawyer announced publicly that he was going to begin consideration of employment terms, and on April 20, on the television program, "Meet the Press," the Secretary stated positively that there would be "some wage increases granted" and the only decision was how much. In light of this threatened change in conditions, Mr. Kiendl argued that a preliminary injunction was needed. He went on to discuss the injury which would be done by a wage increase, the availability of the Taft-Hartley procedures, and the seriousness of the companies' main contention that the President lacked constitutional power to seize. As he turned to the issue whether an injunction would lie, the following exchanges took place.]

Mr. Kiendl: . . . We submit that the minimum that the plaintiff is entitled to is a preliminary injunction against this threatened change in working conditions, terms of employment, and so forth. . . .

The Court: I thought you were asking for an injunction enjoining Mr. Sawyer from continuing in possession and control of your property.

Mr. Kiendl: . . . I state unreservedly now that what we are trying to accomplish by this motion is to obtain a temporary injunction restraining the Secretary of Commerce from changing the terms and conditions of employment. . . .

The Court: All you ask us, then, is the preservation of the status quo?

Mr. Kiendl: Exactly.

The Court: Is that what the others are asking?

[General nods of approval were made by several other steel counsel]

Mr. Kiendl: Of course, that is what the others are asking.

The Court: Your moving papers ask for everything.

[This point was discussed between the Court and Mr. Kiendl, the latter concluding:]

Mr. Kiendl: . . . I had hoped that I made my reservation clear: We are asking to have the status quo continue until we have a full trial on the merits—and the sooner that can be had and the case decided the happier we will all be. . . .

Mr. Bromley: That is not all that Bethlehem Steel is asking for, your Honor: We have filed a motion for a preliminary injunction and our position is "the whole hog."

The Court: If I should hold that the defendant acted without authority of law, as I understand the law, I should grant a preliminary injunction [against the seizure] unless, in weighing convenience and balancing the equities, I find it would not be equitable to do so.

[At this point, Judge Pine declared a special recess "for a few moments." When the Court resumed, Mr. Kiendl rose to continue his presentation and was interrupted as follows.]

The Court: Wait just a minute. You have an announcement to make before you go on your next point?

Mr. Kiendl: No; Your Honor, I have no announcement to make.

[The Court then specified that before the hearing went further, he wanted Mr. Kiendl and counsel for each of the steel companies to rise and state exactly what relief they were asking for. Mr. Kiendl repeated that he wanted a preliminary injunction to restrain the defendant from altering the terms of employment. One by one, counsel for Bethlehem, Republic, Jones & Laughlin, Youngstown, E. J. Lavino, Armco, and Sheffield Steel Corporations rose and said that they were seeking relief which included an injunction against the seizure itself. In the course of these colloquies, Judge Pine declared: ". . . I can't understand Mr. Kiendl's position when he asks me to find the act illegal, and yet he wants to continue the illegality. That is the reason I was astonished when he told me that that was all you were asking, because it seems inconsistent to me."]

The Court: Is the Government opposed to that, what [Mr. Kiendl asks for]?

Mr. Baldridge: Yes, Your Honor.

The Court: All right. You are opposed to maintaining the status quo?

Mr. Baldridge: Our position is, Your Honor, that Mr. Sawyer has the job of running the steel plants as long as they are in Government possession. . . .

[After Mr. Kiendl concluded his presentation, Mr. Bromley spoke for Bethlehem Steel, and Mr. Day began argument for Republic Steel. Again, the question of the remedy sought was raised by the Court, in response to Mr. Day's statement that he was seeking immediate relief against changes of condition until a hearing on the merits was had.]

The Court: Don't we have to determine the legality or illegality of the seizure?

Mr. Day: I don't think so at this time . . . as I understand the rules of law and procedure applicable here: If Your Honor reached the conclusion that there is a probable and discernible showing here of a lack of power upon the part of the President to issue the order, then you could grant the . . . preliminary injunction prayed for, to the extent of preserving the status quo pending the final determination of this case.

The Court: . . . Well, on a hearing on the merits, what would be argued that isn't being argued today? Anything?

Mr. Day: . . . When this matter was before Your Honor some weeks ago when we all came in . . . and asked that the case be advanced for immediate hearing, Your Honor said, and properly said, that is was not within your power to compel the filing of an answer by the defendant [before the time provided for filing answers by the Rules.] . . . It would seem to me that the ultimate question before the Court on the hearing on the merits is the basic question presented at this time. . . .

The Court: I feel the same way, but I have no power to compel the premature filing of an answer. . . .

* * *

ARGUMENT FOR THE UNITED STATES
[by Holmes Baldridge]

Mr. Baldridge: . . . I assume, at least for the purpose of the oral limitation, that the United States Steel Company for the moment, at least, concedes the legality of the seizure for the purpose of the present hearing.

What the limitation amounts to is that this Court now enjoin any attempt on behalf of the Secretary of Commerce to change, in any way, the terms and conditions of employment, and that means:

First: That the United States Steel Company wants to be free from the effects of the strike;

Second: They want to be free from the possibility of any wage increase;

Third: They want protection in damages for any seizure; **and**

Fourth: Just compensation under the Fifth Amendment **to the** Constitution.

I suggest, Your Honor, that the United States Steel **Company** cannot have its cake and eat it too. In fact, that is what the **oral** limitation of the written motion amounts to. I may add that **Labor** has been damaged by this seizure. The only way in which Labor can make its position known and felt is through the power to strike, **and** that power to strike has been taken away by this seizure. Obviously the plants cannot be turned back to management unless and until the controversy which was immediately responsible for the seizure action of the President has been resolved. If Your Honor should enter a temporary injunction preventing any action by the Secretary of Commerce in changing the terms and conditions of employment, the whole situation would, in effect, remain on dead center. . . .

*   *   *

The Court: Now, you contend that exercising powers where there is no statute makes a case stand on a different plane—a preferred plane?

Mr. Baldridge: Correct. Our position is that there is no power in the Courts to restrain the President and, as I say, Secretary Sawyer is the alter ego of the President and not subject to injunctive order of the Court.

The Court: If the President directs Mr. Sawyer to take you into custody, right now, and have you executed in the morning you say there is no power by which the Court may intervene even by habeas corpus?

Mr. Baldridge: If there are statutes protecting me I would have a remedy.

The Court: What statute would protect you?

Mr. Baldridge: I do not recall any at the moment.

The Court: But on the question of the deprivation of your rights you have the Fifth Amendment; that is what protects you.

I would like an answer to that—what about that?

Mr. Baldridge: Well, as I was going to point out in a little while—

The Court (interposing): I will give you a chance to think about that overnight and you may answer me tomorrow.

Mr. Baldridge: Very well. I won't pursue this point at the moment. . . .

* * *

The Court: . . . I would like cases . . . from you where there is a showing of invalidity of power where the Court must find that the equities when weighed in the balance favor no granting of relief.

Mr. Baldridge: We will submit those.

The Court: I have asked the other side to do it. I have heard of cases on the law, learned argument with respect to them but no cases have been cited to me about it.

Mr. Baldridge: Their memorandum of law mostly were served last night or this morning and we would like to have a reasonable opportunity in which to make answer.

The Court: I do not know what a "reasonable opportunity" means.

Mr. Baldridge: Well, we would like a week if possible.

The Court: These cases involving applications for temporary injunction require speedy action, almost immediate action by the Court.

Now, unless there is an agreement to maintain the status quo I think the parties are entitled to a very prompt decision, and such a decision will be made by me for I will consider this case to the exclusion of everything else working day and night and I will decide it, and that is not consistent with your request for a week's time—

Mr. Baldridge: I cannot make that agreement or promise to maintain the status quo, Your Honor.

The Court: Then I cannot give you the time you ask for. It would not be fair to the other side.

These motions take precedence over all other motions. . . .

The Court: Now, Mr. Attorney General, it is getting near the time when we shall have to stop. I wonder if you would give me such assistance as you can before we stop so that I can think about your

viewpoint overnight, as to your power, or as to your client's power.
As I understand it, you do not assert any statutory power.

Mr. Baldridge: That is correct.

The Court: And you do not assert any express constitutional power.

Mr. Baldridge: Well, Your Honor, we base the President's power on Sections 1, 2 and 3 of Article II of the Constitution, and whatever inherent, implied or residual powers may flow therefrom.

We do not propose to get into a discussion of semantics with counsel for plaintiffs. We say that when an emergency situation in this country arises that is of such importance to the entire welfare of the country that something has to be done about it and has to be done now, and there is no statutory provision for handling the matter, that it is the duty of the Executive to step in and protect the national security and the national interests. . . .

The Court: So you contend the Executive has unlimited power in time of an emergency?

Mr. Baldridge: He has the power to take such action as is necessary to meet the emergency.

The Court: If the emergency is great, it is unlimited, is it?

Mr. Baldridge: I suppose if you carry it to its logical conclusion, that is true. But I do want to point out that there are two limitations on the Executive power. One is the ballot box and the other is impeachment. . . .

The Court: And that the Executive determines the emergencies and the Courts cannot even review whether it is an emergency.

Mr. Baldridge: That is correct. . . .

The Court: Do you have any case of a seizure except a seizure authorized by statute during wartime, which made the statute constitutional?

Mr. Baldridge: Well, we have set out in our brief a number of instances, Your Honor, in which seizure occurred in the absence of statutory authorization.

The Court: I mean where the Courts approved it.

Mr. Baldridge: I do not know of any—

The Court: I do not think a seizure without judicial interference is relevant. The fact that a man reaches in your pocket and steals your wallet is not a precedent for making that a valid act. . . .

* * *

The Court: . . . Let me put a case to you that is not quite so difficult:

Supposing the President should declare that the public interest required the seizure of your home and directed an agent to seize it and to dispossess you: Do you think or do you contend that the court could not restrain that act because the President had declared an emergency and because he had directed an agent to carry out his will?

Mr. Baldridge: I would rather, Your Honor, not answer a case in that extremity. We are dealing here with a situation involving a grave national emergency. . . .

I do not believe any President would exercise such unusual power unless, in his opinion, there was a grave and an extreme national emergency existing.

The Court: Is that your conception of our Government?

Mr. Baldridge: Our conception of the powers of the Executive, Your Honor, is that under the doctrine of separation of powers—which I shall discuss a little more at length after a while—that, except for an occasional overlapping, there have not been and are not any instances of importance where one branch of the Government attempts to encroach upon the power and authority of the other.

The Court: Well, is it not your conception of our Government that it is a Government whose powers are derived solely from the Constitution of the United States?

Mr. Baldridge: That is correct.

The Court: And is it not also your view that the powers of the Government are limited by and enumerated in the Constitution of the United States?

Mr. Baldridge: That is true, Your Honor, with respect to legislative powers.

The Court: But it is not true, you say, as to the Executive?

Mr. Baldridge: No. Section 1, of Article II of the Constitution—

The Court (interposing): Have you read the case of McCullough [sic] v. Maryland lately?

Mr. Baldridge: I have, Your Honor.

Section 1, Article II, of the Constitution reposes all of the executive power in the Chief Executive.

I think that the distinction that the Constitution itself makes between the powers of the Executive and the powers of the legislative branch of the Government are significant and important.

In so far as the Executive is concerned, all executive power is vested in the President.

In so far as legislative powers are concerned, the Congress has only those powers that are specifically delegated to it, plus the implied power to carry out the powers specifically enumerated.

The Court: So, when the sovereign people adopted the Constitution, it enumerated the powers set up in the Constitution . . . limited the powers of the Congress and limited the powers of the judiciary, but it did not limit the powers of the Executive.

Is that what you say?

Mr. Baldridge: That is the way we read Article II of the Constitution.

The Court: I see. . . .

Mr. Baldridge: . . . The plaintiffs argued here that the damage as a result of the seizure has been incalculable. We want to reiterate that the seizure has also taken away from the unions the only weapon they have to enforce what they think are their rights, namely, the right to strike. They are now Government employees and as such, cannot strike. Again, this seizure is not a one-way street. I want to give some figures . . .

We submit, if Your Honor please, that the burden of proof here lies with the plaintiffs to show that there is no power in the Executive to seize. Yesterday the Government was placed on the defensive, and asked to show wherein lies power to seize. We are not the moving parties here. The plaintiffs, the steel companies, have asked Your Honor to enjoin this seizure. It is their duty to make a showing, if they can, that no such power resides. And all they have shown so far is to make oral assertions that no such power exists.

In the Government's memorandum we have analyzed the applicable provisions of the Constitution. We have dealt with customs and usage in so far as the executive and legislative branches of the Government are concerned. And we have given Your Honor the benefit of what case law is available.

I want to point out that whether that be too convincing or not, there is not one single instance in which the courts have enjoined executive power where it was based upon the Constitution and not upon statute.

Now, if the plaintiffs here have such cases, we say let them come up with them. We have not seen them. We have been unable to discover any. . . .

I submit, Your Honor, if the Government is enjoined from taking the action it deems appropriate, that is, effecting an increase in wages and an increase in prices, both of which are contemplated, on the theory that the seizure is or may be unlawful, there is no assurance that the Union will not strike. As a matter of fact there have been three wild-cat strikes already, under the seizure. Under the circumstances if the seizure were declared unlawful, through the issuance of an injunction, the Union may well feel free to strike. . . .

Hence, Your Honor, we say that an injunction against the wage increase may well create a worse situation than that which exists at the present time because it would give rise to the immediate possibility of a strike and,—against that, if such a situation occurred, the legal situation would be so clouded that it would be difficult for anyone to work out a remedy.

We think, Your Honor, that upon a balancing of all the equities this Court should not throw this matter into further confusion but should withhold relief, if any be warranted to the plaintiffs, until a final decision on the merits of the case.

White House Anxiety and Judge Pine's Thunderbolt

Amending Mr. Baldridge

While the arguments were taking place before Judge Pine, Congress continued to debate and hold hearings on the steel seizure dispute. On April 24, the House of Representatives voted an investigation of the Wage Stabilization Board by the House Labor Committee, to probe whether the Board's recommendations had violated national labor policy as set forth in the Taft-Hartley Act. Also on April 24, a Subcommittee of the Senate Judiciary Committee, chaired by Willis Smith (Dem.— N.C.), launched hearings on the legality of the President's seizure order. On the floor of the two houses, impeachment bills multiplied, defenders of the President became more harassed, and the debate took on a decidedly shriller tone. It was clear that opponents of the President's seizure had received soundings of barbershop reactions and had found, as did the opinion polls, that Mr. Truman was in one of his periodic lows in public esteem.

At such a stage, as students of Mr. Truman's behavior had observed before, the President could be expected to give as well as he was getting. When his press conference opened on April 24, the President told reporters that a "lot of hooey" was being handed out about the steel seizure, in an attempt to portray him as having exceeded his powers. In reply to a reporter's question whether he felt there were any limits on the President's emergency powers, Truman replied:

Well, . . . you better read your history and find out. There are a lot of Presidents who have had to make decisions in emergencies, and if you read history you will find that they had to make them, but you will find it did not hurt the Republic but made the Republic better.

Asked to specify, the President cited Jefferson's purchase of Louisiana, Tyler's agreement to the annexation of Texas, Polk's annexations, Secretary of State Seward's purchase of Alaska, and Lincoln's Civil War actions. When questioned whether he should not have asked for legal sanction from Congress, Truman answered that he had asked Congress twice but all he seemed to be getting was advice that he had "done wrong" and threats that he might be impeached.

On April 25 and 26, newspapers throughout the nation carried accounts of Assistant Attorney General Baldridge's statements that the President's powers were not limited by the Constitution. As criticism of this statement mounted, the White House took frantic steps to correct the formulation of the Government's position. Sunday afternoon, April 27, Charles S. Murphy, the President's personal counsel, put in a long distance telephone call to a World War I pilot named Casey Jones. Jones, one of sixteen-hundred correspondents on the seizure, had written the President a letter on April 8, asking five questions about the seizure. Murphy told Jones that the President was going to reply to his letter and asked permission to make the reply public. This was given, and the press, on Monday morning, April 28, featured the President's letter. After explaining why profits before taxes had been the proper figure to use in judging the companies' capacity to pay, and discussing the union shop, the Taft-Hartley Act, and the Wage Board's recommendations, Truman declared:

The powers of the President are derived from the Constitution, and they are limited, of course, by the provisions of the Constitution, particularly those that protect the rights of individuals.

But, the President told Jones, nothing in the Constitution required him to endanger national security by letting the steel mills shut down at this moment. A similar declaration that the Government was not claiming any "residuum of powers outside of the Constitution inherent in his position as Chief of State . . ." was written into the brief that the Government filed with Judge Pine.

The Administration was still worried about Baldridge's argument at the Pine hearing and rightly so, since this had become the keynote of anti-seizure publicity directed at the public. On April 28, Senator Hubert Humphrey (Dem.—Minn.) emerged from a conference with the President and told reporters that Truman had pointedly declared, "I am a constitutional President." Senator Humphrey said that the President was concerned about statements which seemed to claim for him powers outside the Constitution. To reporters, and again in the Senate, Humphrey stated that Baldridge's comments were bad law and "a great disservice to the President," a view which was echoed by Senator Wayne Morse.

Meanwhile, an inner struggle seemed to be going on over a question of tactics to pursue in the District Court. According to a later account in *The New York Times,* Baldridge had advised C. D. Williams, General Counsel of the Department of Commerce, on April 25, that it would be a mistake for the Government to grant a wage increase while the case was pending. Baldridge felt that it would be strategically wiser to stipulate to Judge Pine that no change of conditions would be effected. Williams agreed. On April 26, learning that no action had been taken to this effect by the Justice Department, Williams asked that this be done. It never was, and reporters from *The Times* were unable to ascertain whether the failure was due to "fumbling, buck-passing, indecision at a high level, or a deliberate high-level decision to withhold the assurance."[1] From later developments the last alternative seems to be the most likely explanation.

One thing which was presented to Judge Pine—as events transpired it reached him just a few hours before he announced his decision—was a "Supplemental Memorandum" from the Justice Department. "We feel," the Government's memo said, "that a further statement is justified and perhaps necessitated by misunderstandings which may have arisen during the course of oral argument." The memo explained:

At no time have we urged any view that the President possesses power outside the Constitution, and our brief, filed with the court, is clear on that point. On the contrary, we have urged that the President must act within the Constitution, specifically Article II. . . . If the court understood us to say more, we respectfully ask that this memorandum be accepted as the accurate statement of our views.

The disclaimer, if it would have had any effect at all, came too late. To a packed courtroom on April 29, Judge Pine read his opinion:

Opinion of Judge David Pine, April 29

[The opinion first reviewed the facts and legal proceedings to date.] . . . [It] should be noted that, although there is no law of the case

[1] *The New York Times,* May 9, 1952, p. 16, col. 1.

rule in interlocutory orders in this jurisdiction, these cases are in a materially different posture than they were when Judge Holtzoff of this court refused a temporary restraining order in respect of several of them.

The fundamental issue is whether the seizure is or is not authorized by law. In my opinion, this issue should be decided first, and that I shall now do.

There is no express grant of power in the Constitution authorizing the President to direct this seizure. There is no grant of power from which it reasonably can be implied. There is no enactment of Congress authorizing it. On what, then, does defendant rely to sustain his acts? According to his brief, reiterated in oral argument, he relies upon the President's "broad residuum of power" sometimes referred to as "inherent" power under the Constitution, which, as I understand his counsel, is not to be confused with "implied" powers as that term is generally understood, namely, those which are reasonably appropriate to the exercise of a granted power.

This contention requires a discussion of basic fundamental principles of constitutional government, which I have always understood are immutable, absent [sic] a change in the framework of the Constitution itself in the manner provided therein. The Government of the United States was created by the ratification of the Constitution. It derives its authority wholly from the powers granted to it by the Constitution, which is the only source of power authorizing action by any branch of Government. It is a government of limited, enumerated, and delegated powers. The office of President of the United States is a branch of the Government, namely, that branch where the executive power is vested, and his powers are limited along with the powers of the two other great branches or departments of Government, namely, the legislative and judicial.

The President therefore must derive this broad "residuum of power" or "inherent" power from the Constitution itself, more particularly Article II thereof, which contains that grant of Executive power. . . .

The non-existence of this "inherent" power in the President has been recognized by eminent writers, and I cite in this connection the unequivocal language of the late Chief Justice Taft in his treatise entitled "Our Chief Magistrate and His Powers" (1916) wherein he says: "The true view of the Executive function is, as I conceive it, that the President can exercise no power which cannot be fairly and reasonably traced to some specific grant of power or justly implied and included within such express grant as proper and necessary to its exercise. Such specific grant must be either in the Federal Constitution or in an Act of Congress passed in pursuance thereof. There is no undefined residuum of power which he can exercise because it seems to him to be in the public interest, and there is nothing in the Neagle case and its definition of a law of the United States, or in other precedents, warranting such an inference. The grants of executive power are necessarily in general terms in order not to embarrass the Executive within the field of action plainly marked for him, but his jurisdiction must be justified and vindicated by affirmative constitutional or statutory provision, or it does not exist."

I stand on that as a correct statement of the law . . . [Judge Pine then refuted, to his satisfaction, the cases and historical incidents cited by the Government.]

Enough has been said to show the utter and complete lack of authoritative support for defendant's position. That there may be no doubt as to what it is, he states it unequivocally when he says in his brief that he does "not perceive how Article II [of the Constitution] can be read . . . so as to limit the Presidential power to meet all emergencies," and he claims that the finding of the emergency is "not subject to judicial review." To my mind this spells a form of government alien to our constitutional government of limited powers. I therefore find that the acts of defendant are illegal and without authority of law.

I shall next turn to defendant's claim that the courts are without power to negate executive action of the President. Defendant relies on the case of Mississippi v. Johnson, 4 Wall. 475, where the Supreme

Court held that the Judiciary would not attempt to control the President. But in this case the President has not been sued. Charles Sawyer is the defendant, and the Supreme Court has held on many occasions that officers of the Executive Branch of the Government may be enjoined when their conduct is unauthorized by statute, exceeds the scope of constitutional authority, or is pursuant to unconstitutional enactment. Larson v. Domestic and Foreign Commerce Corp., 337 U.S. 682. Land v. Dollar, 330 U.S. 371. Philadelphia Co. v. Stimson, 223 U.S. 605. Lee v. United States, 106 U.S. 196. . . .

Taking up the next point, namely, that the courts will not interfere in advance of a full hearing on the merits except upon a showing that the damage to flow from a refusal of temporary injunction is irreparable and that such damage outweighs the harm which would result from its issuance, I first find as a fact, on the showing made and without burdening this opinion with a recital of facts, that the damages are irreparable. As to the necessity for weighing the respective injuries and balancing the equities, I am not sure that this conventional requirement for the issuance of a preliminary injunction is applicable to a case where the Court comes to a fixed conclusion, as I do, that defendant's acts are illegal. On such premise, why are the plaintiffs to be deprived of their property and required to suffer further irreparable damage until answers to the complaints are filed and the cases are at issue and are reached for hearing on the merits? Nothing that could be submitted at such trial on the facts would alter the legal conclusion I have reached. But assuming I am required to balance the equities, what is the situation in which I find this case? I am told by defendant of the disastrous effects on our defense efforts and economy if an injunction should be granted, because it would automatically be followed by a crippling strike; and I am asked to weigh that damage against the incalculable and irreparable injuries to plaintiffs' multi-billion-dollar industry, if I should refuse to issue it. Assuming the disastrous effects on the defense effort envisioned by the defendant, that can come about only in case of a strike, and that presupposes that the United Steel Workers will strike notwithstanding the damage it will cause our defense effort. It also presupposes that the Labor Management Relations Act, 1947. is inadequate when it has not yet been tried, and is the statute provided by Congress to meet just such an emergency. And it further presupposes, as defendant apparently does, that, this statute being inadequate, Congress will fail in its duties, under the Constitution, to legislate immediately and appropriately to protect the nation from this threatened disaster. I am unwilling to indulge in that assumption, because I believe that our procedures under the Constitution can stand the stress and strains of an emergency today as they have in the past, and are adequate to meet the test of emergency and crisis.

Under these circumstances I am of the opinion that, weighing the injuries and taking these last-mentioned considerations into account, the balance is on the side of plaintiffs. Furthermore, if I consider the public interest from another viewpoint, I believe that the contemplated strike, if it came, with all its awful results, would be less injurious to the public than the injury which would flow from a timorous judicial recognition that there is some basis for this claim to unlimited and unrestrained Executive power, which would be implicit in failure to grant the injunction. Such recognition would undermine public confidence in the very edifice of government as it is known under the Constitution. . . .

[Judge Pine then found that money damages would be inadequate, and that there could be no recovery for the companies under the Tort Claims Act.]

Counsel will submit, with all due speed, orders in accordance herewith.

Round Two: Into the Court of Appeals

Press and Congressional Reaction to the Pine Ruling

At the announcement of Judge Pine's decision, the United Steel-workers of America called a strike to take effect immediately. Newspaper editorial reaction, in keeping with the overwhelmingly anti-Truman response to the seizure, was highly complimentary to the District Court ruling. "His would-be majesty Harry S. Truman got his claws seriously clipped yesterday by Federal Judge Pine," the N.Y. Daily *News* reported happily. "Majestic principles" enunciated with "refreshing candor and courage," wrote the Hartford *Courant*. To the Charleston *News & Courier*, the Pine decision "restored hope of constitutional government in the United States," and to the good-grey paper, *The New York Times*, the decision was in keeping with "the spiritual necessities of our day." In agreement with these evaluations were comments from the Washington *Times-Herald*, St. Louis *Globe Democrat*, Miami *Herald*, Boston *Globe*, Minneapolis *Tribune*, Atlanta *Constitution*, San Francisco *Chronicle*, and *New York Herald Tribune*.[1]

By the time of the Pine decision, possibly 95% or more of the press had condemned the seizure editorially. A search of the Appendix to the Congressional *Record*, where sheafs of editorials were inserted, provides an anti-Truman roster which reads like a Who's Who of American Daily Journalism and includes papers with Democratic and Independent editorial labels as well as Republican: the *Christian Science Monitor*, Washington *Post*, Detroit *Free Press*, Boston *Herald*, Philadelphia *Inquirer*, Baltimore *Sun*, Richmond *News-Leader*, Indianapolis *News*,

[1] These are collected at 98 *Cong. Rec.* 4647 (82nd Cong., 2d Sess., 1952) and citations to a large number of further editorials are found in the *Index*, 98 *Cong. Rec.* 402.

Cleveland *Plain Dealer*, Newark *Star-Ledger*, Chicago *Daily News*, Charlotte *Observer*, Los Angeles *Times*, Pittsburgh *Post-Gazette* and dozens of others. The rural press was planted firmly alongside its metropolitan brothers, as indicated by the stand of papers such as the Ashtabula (Ohio) *Star-Beacon*, Zeeland (Michigan) *Record*, and Palestine (Texas) *Herald-Press*.[1] Senator Wayne Morse, one of the President's most determined and resourceful defenders, was able to insert in the record only one pro-Truman editorial from the St. Charles (Missouri) *Daily Banner*. This "ganging up" on the President by press and commentators was attacked by Senator Morse, Senator Hubert Humphrey, and other liberals[2] with no effect whatever on the continuing newspaper hostility.

Most Congressmen, judging by the reaction on the floor of Congress, approved of the Pine ruling, and Congressional developments multiplied in its aftermath. On April 30, the Republican Policy Committee in the Senate issued a statement that the President should invoke the Taft-Hartley Act's "cooling-off" provisions before Congress should pass any new legislation dealing with the steel dispute. Rep. Howard W. Smith (Dem.—Va.) introduced a bill to permit federal courts to appoint receivers for unions and companies when strike disputes affecting the health and safety of the nation lasted longer than the 80 day Taft-Hartley period. This was filed as an amendment to the Selective Service Act, then under consideration by Congress, and was sent to the House Armed Forces Committee, where Chairman Carl Vinson (Dem.—Ga.) began the fourth set of hearings relating to the steel case. Only three of the hearings continued after April, however, since the Senate Judiciary Subcommittee postponed its hearings on the legality of the seizure after the Pine ruling was delivered on April 29. (The Subcommittee never resumed its hearings. Instead, the full Judiciary Committee, without public hearings, approved a resolution of its chairman, Senator McCarran, proposing a constitutional amendment to bar presidential seizure of private property.) The three other hearings ran along during May while Congressional floor attention was given to other matters. Wage Stabilization Board Chairman Nathan Feinsinger, Price Stabilizer Ellis Arnall, U.S. Steel Vice President John A. Stephens, Industry WSB Member John C. Bane Jr., Philip Murray of the CIO, Secretary of Defense Robert Lovett, Secretary of Labor Maurice Tobin, the President of the National Association of Manufacturers, the legislative

[1] *Ibid.*
[2] 98 *Cong. Rec.* 5754–5755; *Appendix*, A 2788.

representative of the AFL, and several other witnesses went before the Senate Labor Subcommittee and gave expert advice. Much the same set of witnesses, with a few additions or subtractions, appeared before the House Labor Committee and the House Armed Services Committee. The committees, as had been predicted, came up with very different recommendations. The Armed Services Committee, impressed with solid labor opposition to the Smith "receivership" bill, took no action on his proposal but let it wither unreported. The Senate Labor Subcommittee approved the Morse bill to authorize presidential seizure under certain procedures, and this measure, along with a committee bill, S3407, received approval by the full committee. The House Labor Committee voted, 16-5, that the Wage Stabilization Board should be abolished.

At a White House strategy meeting held after the Pine opinion, government advisors decided to carry the case up on appeal, by going before the Federal Court of Appeals for the District of Columbia to ask for a stay of Judge Pine's order returning the mills to private management. (There are 11 Courts of Appeals throughout the country, to which rulings of the District Courts are appealed except in certain special instances where Congress authorizes direct review of District Court decisions by the Supreme Court. Each Court of Appeals has from 3 to 9 judges and cases are usually heard by 3 judges as a panel. In important cases, the Court of Appeals may sit *en banc*, with all its judges present.)

At the Department of Justice Building, a team of eight lawyers went to work on the evening of April 29. Writing and dictating in relays to a team of six stenographers preparing the Government brief went on until 4 A.M.[1] On the morning of the 30th, Government lawyers appeared before Judge Pine to go through the customary form of asking him to reverse himself, by issuing a stay pending appeal. Pine refused and the case was transferred immediately to the Federal Court of Appeals. A hearing began the same afternoon before the nine circuit judges sitting *en banc*, Chief Judge Stephens and Associate Judges Edgerton, Clark, Miller, Prettyman, Proctor, Bazelon, Fahy and Washington. Twenty lawyers appeared for the companies and three for the Government (Acting Attorney General Perlman, Mr. Baldridge, and Assistant Attorney General Marvin Taylor).

In his opening for the Government, Baldridge recited the facts of the case to date and told the judges that the situation was now just where it was on the night of April 8. What the Government was asking, in this crisis, was for the Court of Appeals to stay the District Court

[1] *The New York Times,* May 4, 1952, IV, p. 1, col. 1.

order so that the Government could remain in possession of the plants while it petitioned the Supreme Court to by-pass Court of Appeals review and hear an appeal from the Pine decision immediately. The following exchanges and argument ensued:

Transcript of Proceedings, April 30–May 1

CHARLES SAWYER, Appellant

v.

UNITED STATES STEEL COMPANY,

et al., Appellees

Application FOR STAY PENDING

APPEAL FROM ORDER GRANTING

PRELIMINARY INJUNCTION.

Judge Bazelon: What assurance will there be that the men will go back to work?

Mr. Baldridge: There is no assurance. . . . We are asking you, your Honors, to put the Government back in possession of the steel mills and we hope that the Union will go back to work. If it does not, of course, the Government has open to it the injunctive procedures that it can use, that is, the Government can proceed against the Union in the same manner as it did, with the approval of the Court in the case of United States vs. United Mine Workers of America, 330 U.S. 258. . . . That action would not be under the Taft-Hartley Act. . . .

Judge Bazelon: But you say that you have no assurance that the men will go back to work.

Mr. Baldridge: That is correct; we do not. We hope the Union will cooperate. . . .

The Chief Judge (Harold Stephens): I understand you to say that you ask for a stay order that you may have an opportunity to apply to the Supreme Court for a writ of certiorari. If that application . . . should be refused . . . you intend to have the matter heard in this Court on the merits, and, if the application for certiorari is granted . . . you intend to have the case heard on its merits in the Supreme Court. Is that a correct statement of what you are saying?

Mr. Baldridge: Correct.

The Chief Judge: . . . In refreshing my recollection, I find that title 28, Section 2101 of the [Federal] rules . . . states that:

"In any case in which the final judgment or decree of any court is subject to review by the Supreme Court on writ of certiorari, the execution and enforcement of such judgment or decree may be stayed for a reasonable time to enable the party aggrieved to obtain a writ of certiorari from the Supreme Court. . . ."

I am asking you this: Now that you have applied, is it not more appropriate for this Court to defer to the Supreme Court on the matter of a stay so that the Supreme Court can hear argument on the probability of reversal and the balance of conveniences and so forth. . . . You are, when it boils down, asking us to take perfunctory action, are you not?

Mr. Baldridge: I do not like to put it that way. We think that this is the most expeditious way in which we can get the matter disposed of. . . .

* * *

Mr. John J. Wilson, for Youngstown Sheet & Tube Co.: . . . Obviously, the Government in this case has sought to get a stay from this Court solely by reason of coming in here and saying they have been enjoined below and that they are taking an appeal from the action of the lower court and that, therefore, they want a stay until they can get to the Supreme Court.

They want to deprive this Court of weighing the seriousness of the question that is before the Court; they want to deprive this Court of the opportunity to weigh and balance the equities. . . . They admit the strike and they admit that they have no assurance, and give this Court no assurance, that the men will go back to work if the stay for which they ask is granted. . . .

Mr. Wilson went on to maintain that the Government would not be able to get an injunction to require work continuance within the time required for application on a writ of certiorari. He felt the Court should "weigh the same considerations as it would have if the case were here on its merits, instead of acting as a mute conduit. . . ."

Several judges then asked Mr. Wilson to discuss the issue as to whether this was a suit by the companies against "the sovereign" or against Mr. Sawyer as an individual, particularly in relation to the case of Larson v. Domestic and Foreign Commerce Corp., 330 U.S. 682 (1949). Mr. Wilson gave his view that the present suit was against an individual "trespasser" and was maintainable under the precedents.

Mr. Wilson: . . . Now, if the United States, if the Government, is serious about wanting to stop the strike, if it puts its efforts to work as assiduously and arduously toward that end, instead of burning the midnight oil to get applications for stay orders ready, why don't they get the injunction ready? They had eight to ten hours, more than that, to get the injunction ready. . . .

Shorter arguments were made by other company counsel in opposition to the grounds of the Government's applications for stay. Interpretation of the meaning of Federal Rule, Title 28, Section 2101 was further discussed.

Mr. Philip Perlman, for the Government: . . . Although we do not at the moment argue that the opinion of the lower Court is in error, you ask: What are we doing here? You ask: Why appeal, why ask for a stay since you are not attacking the order? Of course, we attack the opinion. Of course, we want the order of the lower Court reversed—it ought to be reversed and will be reversed. That is the reason we are here. . . .

I want you to remember that Pewee Coal Company case. It is a case like this one, where the President of the United States, in the absence of any statutory authority, seized the mines, and, after all the noise and excitement created in this country had been heard, during the past week, you would think the present President of the United States has done something unknown in this country and something that no President of this nation ever did do before. . . .

And Judge Pine—read the opinion! He does not cite precedents of things done by other Chief Executives of this nation! They don't mean anything to him! He said that six wrongs do not make one right. Why, Judge Pine held in his opinion that the Emancipation Proclamation was illegal, and I guess that we will go back and have our slaves tomorrow because Judge Pine said so. He invalidated, in that decision, the act of every President taken at the time of national danger and crisis. . . . We are asking you to stay that order! Stay it—every minute counts. . . . We know that if you sign the kind of an order that we have submitted to this Court then the whole country will know that the order of Judge Pine has been stayed.

Mr. Perlman then explained that he was seeking a stay only until the application for a writ of certiorari was acted upon by the Supreme Court. Once the Supreme Court granted that petition, Mr. Perlman said, the Supreme Court "would assume jurisdiction over the case."

Judge Prettyman: The suggestion is that the stay be granted until four-thirty o'clock on Friday afternoon and, if the petition is filed prior to that time, then until such time as the petition gets attention by the Supreme Court and is acted on. . . .

Mr. Bromley: Do I understand that it will be conditioned on the rates of pay or terms of employment here remaining in status quo; that Mr. Sawyer will not feel himself at liberty to do us this irreparable injury?

Mr. Pearlman: The Government of the United States is responsible for any loss or damage that occurs in that circumstance. . . .

Judge Bazelon: You have an assurance by the Government. Can you go along on that with the Government?

Mr. Bromley: No, of course not. That could not bind the Government. The Tort Claims Act could not do it, and no Attorney General and no court could do that. . . .

At 6:09 P.M., the Court rose for a recess to consider its decision. On reconvening at 6:50 P.M., the Chief Judge announced that the Court was divided in its views and that the majority opinion would be announced by Judge Edgerton.

Judge Edgerton: . . . In order fully to preserve the jurisdiction of the Supreme Court and of this Court in these controversies, it is

Ordered by the Court that the orders of the District Court granting the preliminary injunctions in these causes be, and they are hereby, stayed until 4:30 o'clock p.m., Daylight Saving Time, on Friday, May 2, 1952, and, if petitions for writs of certiorari in these cases have then been filed in the Supreme Court, then until the Supreme Court acts upon the petition for writs of certiorari; and, if the petitions for writs of certiorari be denied, then until the further order of this Court.

The Chief Judge: Chief Judge Stephens and Circuit Judges Clark, Wilbur K. Miller, and Proctor are of the opinion that the Government has made no showing whatever which would justify this Court in staying Judge Pine's orders.

At 10:30 A.M. the following day, Thursday, May 1, counsel for the steel companies filed applications to attach to the stay order a condition that nothing be done to cause irreparable injury to the steel owners. In opening the proceedings and allotting three-quarters of an hour for argument to each side, Chief Judge Stephens commented: "There is obviously considerable feeling and heat that is generated in the course of the conduct of this matter. The Court will greatly appreciate it if the arguments on both sides will be made in a temperate manner . . . and it will not be necessary to raise one's voice or indulge in too many gesticulations."

Mr. Horace C. Westwood, on behalf of United States Steel Co.: . . . Our position, your Honors, is that unless the condition we propose be attached to the stay there will be neither protection of the rights of appellees or preservation of the status quo, pending review by the Supreme Court of the United States or after by this Court if the Supreme Court of the United States does not review it.

The condition we propose has been stated in our application and I shall not repeat it: It is simply designed to prevent the appellant from himself making a change in the terms and in the conditions of employment . . . except with the consent of appellee concerned, or alternatively, except in accordance with a collective bargaining agreement between such appellee and its employees. . . .

[If the Government is left free to alter the terms and it adopts the recommendations of the Wage Stabilization Board] it would mean, in the case of my client, United States Steel Company, increased wage costs which, in 1952, would amount to $100,400,000, and, in 1953, would amount to $141,000,000. . . . But, further than that and of fundamental importance, from the standpoint of the interests of the appellees, is that if the minute terms and conditions of employment are prescribed by appellant, there is irreparable and final damage, there is a condition destroyed that never will be retrieved, and that is the bargaining position which the appellees presently enjoy vis-a-vis the Union.

There followed a lengthy discussion and cross-questioning about the effect of the Pewee Coal Company case upon the liability of the Government to pay damages to the steel companies.

After several other company counsel had made substantially the same arguments as Mr. Westwood, Judge Prettyman asked company counsel whether, if the condition asked for were granted, they would agree to file their answer to the Government's petition for certiorari by noon of Saturday, May 3. This was agreed to after a conference among company lawyers, and the companies closed their presentation.

Mr. Perlman, for the Government . . .

Judge Miller: . . . Are you able to say to us whether or not Mr Sawyer has already issued an order changing the terms and conditions of employment? If Mr. Sawyer has done so, it may be that we have nothing further to consider.

Mr. Perlman: Mr. Sawyer has not done so, if your Honor please. . . . These fears seem to be conjured up in the minds of counsel while there is, actually, no basis for them. . . . Today, what they are asking the Court to do is to put the companies in a better position than they were in before the contract. They can sit there as long as they can maintain the situation that they seek to have the Court create, and the employees will be paid under the 1950 contract, if they work at all, and the companies will have nothing to worry about; they won't even have to make an increase, not even the increase that they themselves suggested. . . .

Judge Prettyman: My difficulty with the proposition that you have just advanced is this, Mr. Solicitor General: You said that if the Government, as such, is in possession of the plants during the period of the stay, it could be in a position to bargain, or what have you.

Mr. Perlman: Yes, your Honor.

Judge Prettyman: . . . Now, you come in asking for an indefinite stay, and the Court declined to give you that.

Mr. Perlman: That is right.

Judge Prettyman: Now, the Court inquired yesterday as to whether a stay which would permit you to get to the Supreme Court would take care of the emergency situation you pictured yesterday.

Mr. Perlman: Yes, your Honor.

Judge Prettyman: . . . Now, since the Government [was granted a stay in order to get to the Supreme Court] . . . how can you say that you should between now and the next day or so, while you are getting to the Supreme Court, . . . be put in full possession of the properties in question, and possessed of all the rights connected with such a possession. . . . We cannot overlook the fact that there has been a court order which ordered the Government to relinquish the possession of these properties. . . .

Mr. Perlman: Your Honor, I am trying to tell the Court that I cannot speak for the President of the United States and that I cannot speak for Mr. Sawyer. For myself, [I say] . . . we have a conditional stay at the moment and until we meet that condition, the condition on which the stay was granted, I certainly would not agree to changing the order of things.

The Chief Judge: But you are not willing to give us assurance. . . .

Mr. Perlman: . . . I don't want any statement that I make here to be misrepresented to the men. We want the men back, and we will do all that we can, properly, to get them back.

I did not want to say it but I will tell you now: Nothing will be done until the petition for certiorari is filed. I did not want to say that, but I say that. . . .

Judge Miller: . . . But when you have met that condition, by filing a petition for certiorari, then you would feel that [Mr. Sawyer] is free, under the stay, to prescribe different terms and conditions of employment if he saw fit to do so. . . .

Mr. Perlman: That is exactly correct. . . . If we assume that Mr. Sawyer would not exceed, in any way, the recommendations made by the Wage Stabilization Board, then any change he would make would be within the amount already offered by the companies for that period of time. . . .

At noon, the Court recessed. Returning at 1:30, the Court was again declared to be in division. Judge Edgerton announced the majority ruling which denied the application to attach a condition to the stay order. Chief Judge Stephens, for the same dissenters as the previous day, indicated their view that a condition such as that urged by the companies should have been imposed.

The same day, May 1, President Truman announced he would do whatever was "necessary" to get the mills going again. That evening he appealed to Philip Murray to call off the strike, asking him to appear with six company presidents at the White House on Saturday morning, May 3. Murray accepted the President's plea and the strike was postponed on May 2. On the same day, the Court of Appeals issued a memorandum explaining the stay decision.

Opinion of the Court of Appeals, May 2

Edgerton, Prettyman, Bazelon, Fahy and Washington, Circuit Judges: The order entered by this court on April 30, 1952, was designed, as it recited, to preserve the jurisdiction of the United States Supreme Court and of this court over the controversies here presented, pending appeal.

The District Court thought that there was "utter and complete lack of authoritative support" for the Government's position, and that the steel companies would suffer irreparable injury by any continuance of Government possession of the mills.

The Supreme Court said as long ago as 1871:

". . . Extraordinary and unforeseen occasions arise, however, beyond all doubt, in cases of extreme necessity in time of war or of immediate and impending public danger, in which private property may be impressed into the public service, or may be seized and appropriated to the public use, or may even be destroyed without the consent of the owner. . . . Exigencies of the kind do arise in time of war or impending public danger, but it is the emergency, as was said by a great magistrate, that gives the right, and it is clear that the emergency must be shown to exist before the taking can be justified. Such a justification may be shown, and when shown the rule is well settled that the officer taking private property for such a purpose, if the emergency is fully proved, is not a trespasser, and that the government is bound to make full compensation to the owner." *United States v. Russell*, 13 Wall. 627–8 (U.S. 1871).

Only last year the Supreme Court held that "the United States became liable under the Constitution to pay just compensation" for a taking under circumstances closely parallel to those of the present case. *United States v. Pee Wee Coal Co.*, 341 U.S. 114, 117.

In the case before us the Chief Executive took possession of the steel plants as President and as Commander-in-Chief. When that action was challenged, his delegated representative—the Secretary of Commerce—submitted to the court, in the form of affidavits of the Secretary of Defense and other officials primarily responsible for the national security, the evidence which they said "fully proved" the emergency.

Under these circumstances, the cases we have cited, and many others, indicate there is at least a serious question as to the correctness of the view of the District Court to which we have referred.

The Supreme Court has said an appellate court is empowered "to prevent irreparable injury to the parties *or to the public* resulting from the premature enforcement of a determination which may later be found to have been wrong." *Scripps-Howard Radio v. Comm'n*, 316 U.S. 4 at 9. (Emphasis added.) *See also Virginia R. Co. v. Federation*, 300 U.S. 515, 552.

This case was before the District Court upon a motion for a preliminary injunction. Upon such a motion, the Supreme Court has ruled:

". . . Even in suits in which only private interests are involved the award is a matter of sound judicial discretion, in the exercise of which the court balances the conveniences of the parties and possible injuries to them according as they may be affected by the granting or withholding of the injunction. . . .

"But where an injunction is asked which will adversely affect a public interest for whose impairment, even temporarily, an injunction bond cannot compensate, the court may in the public interest withhold relief until a final determination of the rights of the parties, though the postponement may be burdensome to the plaintiff." *Yakus v. United States,* 321 U.S. 414, 440.

In the affidavits in this record, defense officials are emphatic that continued production of steel is of vital importance to the national security, and submit data in support of that view. On the other hand, the companies may suffer monetary loss. But as to this the Government concedes that any such loss will be compensable under the Constitution, and the Supreme Court cases above cited support that view. Upon these considerations, we think that the preliminary injunction issued by the District Court must be stayed as we have ordered.

Chief Judge Stephens and Circuit Judges Clark, Wilbur K. Miller and Proctor dissent from the foregoing opinion.

James Reston, Foreign Policy Implications of a Strike[1]

There is no time that can be described as ideal for a steel strike, but this particular walkout at this particular time is calculated to cause more trouble in the field of foreign policy than almost any other imaginable.

In Korea the truce talks have reached a most delicate phase. After months of wrangling the long catalog of grievances on both sides

[1] *The New York Times,* May 1, 1952, p. 24, col. 3.

has been reduced to three points on which the Western powers have proposed to compromise.

This compromise is under consideration not only in Panmunjom but also in Moscow itself, and the chances of a settlement are certainly not going to be improved by the prospect of a prolonged strike in this country's steel industry, which furnishes the basic power for the entire Allied rearmament program.

A similar situation exists in Germany. There the success of the Allied rearmament effort and the prospect of bringing the West German Federal Republic into the North Atlantic defense system have produced a turn in Soviet policy.

For the first time since the end of World War II the Kremlin has embarked on a series of reckless promises in an attempt to block West Germany's alliance with the West. The Germans have been offered "unity," a national army and the withdrawal of the Soviet Army in return for a policy of German neutrality.

At the same time, the Western powers have offered to end West Germany's occupation status, to make Germany part of the first great experiment in the formation of a European army and to cooperate with the new International coal and steel organization under the Schuman Plan—which is within weeks of receiving its final parliamentary ratifications.

In short, at the particular moment when the steel crisis hit, many governments in both Europe and Asia were confronted with decisions in which the dependability of American leadership and the American economy was a vital factor. . . .

Last January, the United States and Britain negotiated a raw material agreement during the visit of Prime Minister Winston Churchill to Washington. At that time this country promised to deliver 1,000,000 tons of steel, scrap and pig iron to Britain during this calendar year in return for British tin and rubber. . . . Obviously, a prolonged steel strike would wreck this program. . . .

Of all these situations, however, the Korean is perhaps the most sensitive to economic and political strife in the United States. This country has offered to make one or two concessions to the Communists for a truce, but it also has demanded a deal on the prisoners of war issue that is not easy for the Kremlin to accept. . . . For the Communists to admit that 60,000 of their soldiers [refuse to return to North Korea and China] would not precisely fit the Kremlin's propaganda line that the Communist world is a sort of poor-man's heaven. Therefore, any development that offers the Kremlin hope of trouble in the United States is calculated to make them hesitate about accepting this country's compromise. . . .

At the Threshold of the Supreme Court

Dueling in the Petitions for Certiorari

With a deadline of 4:30 P.M., May 2, for the filing of papers seeking review in the Supreme Court, Government lawyers went to work preparing their petitions for certiorari. (The Supreme Court hears cases under its appellate jurisdiction in three classes. Cases "on appeal" are decisions from state or federal courts which Congress has specified must be heard by the Supreme Court because of the nature of the issue involved, as where a state court has held a federal law invalid or where a federal court has declared an Act of Congress unconstitutional. Cases heard "on certification" are those in which certain questions of law are sent to the Supreme Court from the Federal Court of Claims or Federal Courts of Appeals. Finally, and the most numerous class, are cases arising "on certiorari," where the Supreme Court selects from the flood of cases brought to it each year those which raise important federal questions which the Justices feel should be clarified. A vote of four Justices is sufficient to have certiorari granted, and if three Justices feel very strongly about the case, it is customary to let it be heard. Only 10% of the applications for certiorari are granted in a typical year.) In the steel dispute, two cases were filed asking for certiorari. In "No. 745, Charles Sawyer, Secretary of Commerce, Petitioner v. The Youngstown Sheet and Tube Co., et al., Respondents," the Government asked the Supreme Court to review Judge Pine's injunction order. In "No. 744, Youngstown Sheet and Tube Co. et al., Petitioners v. Charles Sawyer, Respondent," the companies, even though winning parties in the District Court, asked for certiorari to be granted and for an order to be issued forbidding changes in condition if a stay of the Pine ruling should be granted.

Since the Government and the companies had been filing briefs and memoranda steadily since April 9—first with Judge Holtzoff, then Judge Pine, and then in the Court of Appeals—preparation of the petitions for certiorari required only an expansion of their previous papers. The basic sections of the petition—much like that of the brief once the case is accepted by the Supreme Court—include a summary of the matter involved, a description of the jurisdiction of the Supreme Court to review the judgment below, the legal questions presented, the constitutional and statutory provisions involved, the reasons why certiorari (or relief) should be granted, and supporting arguments. In its petition, the Government outlined the grave national peril created by a strike, argued that the District Court had erred in deciding the constitutional issue, and maintained that—if the constitutional issue were to be reached—the President's action was fully supported by law and precedent. The petition included a strong paragraph denying that the Government was arguing "from expediency" or that the President "possesses unlimited powers." It also challenged Judge Pine's resort to "immutable" constitutional principles, branding this "a discredited technique of constitutional interpretation" and one which "brushed aside more than 100 years of constitutional precedent." In a footnote to this argument, the Government linked Judge Pine neatly to his first employer; "Prophecies . . . of 'impending legal and moral chaos' upon failure rigorously to limit the power of the Federal Government by such 'immutable' principles have often been made in connection with attacks upon Congressional enactments of social legislation in the recent past. See, e.g., Mr. Justice McReynolds, dissenting, in the Gold Clause Cases, 294 U.S. 240, 361, 381."

The Companies' petition, in No. 744, supported the Pine ruling as correct and proper, urged its confirmation by the Supreme Court, and asked that the mills be returned to private hands while the case was pending. Should the Government be allowed to remain in possession, however, the companies urged that a condition be imposed that no changes in wages or working terms be permitted. It was on this point that the sharpest exchange came between the Government and the Companies at this stage of the proceedings. Each side filed a Memorandum to the petition of the other for certiorari. The Government's Memorandum stated:

The plaintiffs [Companies] . . . argue at some length . . . that in the event this Court should continue the stay granted by the Court of Appeals, it should modify its terms so as to include an injunction against the Secretary of Commerce restraining him from putting into effect any changes in the terms and conditions of employment.

We are informed that Mr. Philip Murray, president of the United Steel Workers of America, C.I.O., has this morning ordered the steel workers back to work, and that the workers are returning to work. Accordingly, it would appear that the interruption of vitally needed steel production, which was averted by the President's Executive Order but which then began immediately after the filing of Judge Pine's opinion, is over and production is being resumed. Any change in the nature of the stay now in effect would probably result in a new crisis, with danger of still another interruption. Accordingly, we earnestly urge that the stay granted by the Court of Appeals be continued without change by this Court. . . .

In the event that any departure from the terms of stay approved by the Court of Appeals should be considered by this Court, we request the privilege of a hearing.

This was echoed in a Memorandum filed by the United Steel Workers of America, C.I.O., as *amicus curiae*. (This is a "friend of the court" who may be permitted to file a brief, with the consent of both parties, in order to protect some interest of the "friend" or to present arguments which might not otherwise be brought forward. An American Legion Post was refused permission to file an *amicus curiae* brief supporting seizure.) The Union Memo said as to a conditioned stay:

We respectfully suggest to this Court that the companies are suggesting action to the Court which would constitute an intervention on the side of the companies in their dispute with the Union. It would give the companies temporary relief both against a strike and against an increase in wages, relief which the companies will have no right to receive even if they are completely successful in this litigation. And it will give the companies this relief at the sole expense of the employees whom the Union represents.

The companies assert that the *status quo* should be maintained. But a stay order modified as requested by the companies would not preserve the *status quo*. It would effectively destroy the Union's right to bargain on wages—a right which the Union possessed before the seizure, which it possessed after the seizure and which it will possess when this litigation is terminated. Judge Pine's order did not destroy that right. A stay of that order will not destroy it. But an order that no changes in wages and working conditions be made *pendente lite* will destroy it. It will maintain the status of the companies by destroying the status of the Union. This is hardly a maintenance of the *status quo*.

The companies' reply to both Government and Union was as follows:

The first and longest step in the contrary course of procedure proposed on behalf of Mr. Sawyer is the issuance of an unconditioned stay. That is the step which would free Mr. Sawyer from all legal restraint for months to come. If that stay is issued, as prayed, Mr. Sawyer will then seek to appropriate the respondents' private funds to grant the Union whatever wage and other concessions he sees fit and to impose on the respondents a new pattern of employment conditions which cannot be undone. This record shows clearly that he threatens to take precisely that course, and that that is the reason that he prays for the stay.

If that long step is taken by this Court, then even if this Court proceeds promptly to a decision of this legal and Constitutional controversy, it will be unable effectively to dispose of this case as law and justice may require. Inevitably the respondents would suffer grievous and irreparable injury.

Mr. Sawyer's petition wholly abandons the groundless claim of his counsel in the District Court that if his acts are invalid the steel companies have a remedy under the Federal Tort Claims Act.

And the concession of Mr. Sawyer's counsel in the District Court that the steel companies would have no right to sue for damages in the Court of Claims for the damaging consequences of his acts (if they are not the acts of the United States because invalid) is not modified in Mr. Sawyer's petition. On the contrary Mr. Sawyer's counsel carefully—indeed adroitly—refrains from questioning the authority of *Hooe v. United States*, 218 U.S. 322, 335–336 (1910); *United States v. North American Transportation & Trading Company*, 253 U.S. 330 (1920); and *Larson v. Domestic and Foreign Commerce Corp.*, 337 U.S. 682, 695 (1949). Those three cases stand squarely for the principle that no suit will lie in the Court of Claims for compensation for an *illegal* taking. . . .

The only possible argument against attaching the condition—demanded by every consideration of equity toward the steel companies for whose funds Mr. Sawyer is even now reaching to placate the Union—is that the Union will strike against a stay so conditioned. In his memorandum in response to the petition in No. 744 counsel for Mr. Sawyer lays it down bluntly that "Any change in the nature of the stay now in effect would probably result in a new crisis, with danger of still another interruption." (Memorandum on behalf of Respondent in No. 744 . . .). A suggestion that this Court should not do equity because a powerful Union might strike against this Court's action has implications hardly less grave than the basic Constitutional issue in Mr. Sawyer's seizure.

The petitions and memoranda were filed on May 2. At 10 A.M. on May 3, President Truman met in the Cabinet Room of the White House with leaders from the union and the companies. With a "grim expression," the President read a statement announcing that "Monday morning or as soon as we can get ready," the Government was going to order changes in the terms of employment. As for price increases, the companies would get whatever they were "entitled to" under law. With this, the President told the representatives that he "wanted action" and that he was leaving them to bargain over the steel issues. Seven hours later, the Supreme Court issued its ruling on the petitions for certiorari:

Order of the Supreme Court, May 3

JOURNAL OF SATURDAY, MAY 3, 1952

Present: Mr. Chief Justice Vinson, Mr. Justice Black, Mr. Justice Reed, Mr. Justice Frankfurter, Mr. Justice Douglas, Mr. Justice

Jackson, Mr. Justice Burton, Mr. Justice Clark, and Mr. Justice Minton.

The order of the District Court entered April 30, 1952, is hereby stayed pending disposition of these cases by this Court. It is further ordered, as a provision of this stay, that Charles S. Sawyer, Secretary of Commerce (respondent in No. 744 and petitioner in No. 745) take no action to change any term or condition of employment while this stay is in effect unless such change is mutually agreed upon by the steel companies (petitioners in No. 744 and respondents in No. 745) and the bargaining representatives of the employees.

Memorandum by Mr. Justice Burton with whom Mr. Justice Frankfurter concurred:

The first question before this Court is that presented by the petitions for a writ of certiorari bypassing the Court of Appeals. The constitutional issue which is the subject of the appeal deserves for its solution all of the wisdom that our judicial process makes available. The need for soundness in the result outweighs the need for speed in reaching it. The Nation is entitled to the substantial value inherent in an intermediate consideration of the issue by the Court of Appeals. Little time will be lost and none will be wasted in seeking it. The time taken will be available also for constructive consideration by the parties of their own positions and responsibilities. Accordingly, I would deny the petitions for certiorari and thus allow the case to be heard by the Court of Appeals. Such action would eliminate the consideration here of the terms of the stay of the order of the District Court heretofore issued by the Court of Appeals. However, certiorari being granted here, I join in all particulars in the order of this Court, now issued, staying that of the District Court.

Parties and Friends Before the Bar

With the Justices having agreed to eliminate argument in the Court of Appeals and with a ruling expected before the Supreme Court recessed in June, the companies saw to it that the bargaining talks collapsed at once. Since a settlement would mean that the Supreme Court would not rule on the validity of the seizure, the last thing that the companies wanted was to arrive at a bargain which would cause to be dismissed as moot a case so favorably shaped from their point of view. For his part, Philip Murray announced that a strike would not be called while the case was pending.

The Court set oral argument for May 12, allotting five hours to the presentation, two and a half for each side. Ordinarily, oral argument consists of one hour or less for each party. The Steel Workers Union was allowed time to present argument as *amicus curiae*, as were counsel for three railway unions who wanted to argue against the seizure. (President Truman had seized the railroads in 1950 to avert a general railway strike, reciting his powers under the Railway Labor Act of 1916 and also his powers "as President." The railway unions, whose members had been working two years without a wage increase, were permitted to enter the steel seizure litigation to protect their rights in several pending cases challenging the railway seizure.)

In Supreme Court cases, briefs are filed with the Clerk of the Court before oral argument commences. These briefs are a blend of case precedents, legislative and constitutional interpretation, political and policy arguments, and historical surveys, and usually conclude with sweeping invocations of moral authority. Since these documents represent substantial research and offer argumentation by distinguished counsel, the briefs are a primary source of information for the Justices. (A comparison of the summary of the emergency in the Government's steel seizure brief with Chief Justice Vinson's discussion of this issue in his opinion discloses a close similarity.) In other cases, the briefs do not approach the eventual opinion in depth of research and fineness of statement. In the steel case, the two main briefs sparkled with discussions of Magna Carta, the Ship Money Case in 17th Century England, debates at our Constitutional Convention, President Lincoln's policies during the Civil War, Theodore Roosevelt's "Stewardship Theory," and a general assortment of quotations from former Attorneys-General, Presidents, and even professors of political science. The companies' brief made repeated use of the statements Mr. Baldridge had made in District Court, while the Government included its (by now standard) disclaimer, denying that it was asserting unlimited powers for the President.

The Government's brief was 175 pages long. The Youngstown, Republic, Armco, Bethlehem, Jones and Laughlin, U. S. Steel, and E. J. Lavino Companies filed a joint brief of 104 pages. An additional 53-page brief was submitted for Armco and Sheffield and another of 11 pages for the Lavino Company (Lavino argued that it was not a steel producer at all and should not have been seized.) The Steel Workers Union and the Railway Unions each filed briefs, 27 and 59 pages respectively, taking opposite sides of the constitutional argument.

Reprinted below are the "Argument" sections of the Table of Contents from the Government and company briefs, and excerpts from their discussion of the *inherent powers* issue.

For the Companies: Inherent Powers

ARGUMENT:

POINT I—

POINT IV—

The preliminary injunctions were providently issued by the
District Court...................................... 86

POINT V—

This is not a suit against the President; and the District
Court had jurisdiction to grant the requested injunctions.. 90

CONCLUSION 97

* * *

POINT II. [OF THE COMPANIES' BRIEF]

E. The Seizure Cannot be Justified by Any Claim of an "Aggregate of Powers" or by Isolated Instances of Past Executive Action Which Were Never Legally Challenged.

At the argument before Judge Pine Mr. Sawyer's counsel argued
squarely that the President had both an unreviewable discretion to
decide whether an emergency existed and an unlimited power to
deal with it (*cf. supra*, pp. 27–29). In his concluding statement the
following colloquy occurred:

"*The Court*: Well, we have had crises before in this country,
and we have had governmental machinery that was adequate to
cope with it.

You are arguing for expediency. Isn't that it?

Mr. Baldridge: Well you might call it that if you like. *But we
say it is expediency backed by power*" (R. 420).

Although counsel in their petition for certiorari now expressly
repudiate this appalling claim (the assertion of which fully justified
the strong language of Judge Pine's opinion), their basic argument
remains unchanged.

Despite the fact that the memorandum filed on behalf of Mr.
Sawyer in the District Court, and his petition for certiorari here,
pay lip service to the requirement that the President's power must be
found somewhere in the Constitution, the argument below proceeded specifically, and the argument here proceeds by necessary

implication, upon the nebulous theory of a "broad residuum of powers" in the President and of his "aggregate" of powers.

In essential analysis, this theory boils down to a claim that executive action which is not authorized under any specific provision of the Constitution or any law of the United States, and is indeed inconsistent with every specific existing statute, somehow achieves validity when all provisions of the Constitution and statutes are considered together.

We respectfully submit that the Executive Order and action purportedly taken thereunder, being without authority under any constitutional or statutory provision, cannot be validated by the application of labels such as "broad residuum" or "aggregate" of powers.

Closely related to the foregoing contention is the suggestion that the Executive Order and Mr. Sawyer's action are justified by various instances in which Presidents in the past have apparently acted without constitutional or legislative authority. For example, the memorandum in the District Court lists 12 properties seized by President Roosevelt prior to the passage of the War Labor Disputes Act under his purported powers as President. For a variety of reasons, the lawfulness of none of these seizures was ever put to judicial test.

It must also be emphasized that, despite the extended parade of citations presented in the opposing memorandum below, there is no judicial authority supporting the actions here attacked. It would unduly extend this brief to consider individually every case advanced. Brief consideration of a few random examples, however, demonstrates the complete lack of precedent or support for the present action.

1. Counsel referred below (see p. 57 of their Memorandum) to *United States v. Pewee Coal Co., Inc.*, 341 U.S. 114 (1951), as confirming the existence of a constitutional power in the President to seize property during a national emergency. This assertion was made in the face of the incontrovertible fact that the legality of the taking— i.e., the question of the power of the Executive to seize the property— was not an issue in the case, as specifically stated by the Court of Claims. See *Pewee Coal Co. v. United States*, 88 F. Supp. 426, 430

(Ct. Cls. 1950). The briefs of both parties in the *Pewee* case were in complete agreement that the legality of the seizure was not in issue; and on the argument before Judge Pine Mr. Sawyer's counsel so conceded (p. 184).

2. The cases cited involving seizures of facilities during wartime (*e.g. Ken-rad Tube and Lamp Corp. v. Badeau*, 55 F. Supp. 193 (W.D. Ky. 1944), although presented as justification for inherent executive power to take property, actually involved seizures made under the specific authority of the War Labor Disputes Act, as Judge Pine pointed out (R. 71).

3. Counsel now assert (petition for certiorari in No. 745) that the principles embodied in the decision below, if contemporaneously applied, would have gone so far as to prevent President Jefferson from making the Louisiana Purchase and President Lincoln from issuing the Emancipation Proclamation. This is sheer nonsense.

All that President Jefferson did was to negotiate a treaty on April 30, 1803 (8 Stat. 208) with the Government of France. That treaty under accepted constitutional principles did nothing more than give the President an option to buy Louisiana, subject to ratification by the Senate and to the appropriation of the purchase price by both Houses. The conditions of the option were duly fulfilled. The Senate ratified the treaty on October 20, 1803. On October 31, 1803 both Houses authorized the President to occupy the Louisiana territory pursuant to the treaty; and ten days later they appropriated the necessary sums for payment (2 Stat. 245–265).

The Emancipation Proclamation (12 Stat. 1267, 1268) was purely a war measure, *flagrante bello*. It recited that it was to operate solely against enemy property in Confederate territory. The Supplemental Proclamation of January 1, 1863 (12 Stat. 1268), by which the original Proclamation was put into effect, specifically excepted all of Tennessee and West Virginia as well as portions of Louisiana and Virginia then occupied by Federal troops. Slaves in those areas, as well as in the border States (Kentucky, Delaware, Maryland and Missouri), did not receive their legal freedom until the Thirteenth

Amendment. The Proclamation of January 1, 1863 recited that it was "a fit and necessary war measure for suppressing said rebellion" (12 Stat. 1268). Constitutionally, it was no different from Sherman's destruction of property in enemy territory on his march to the sea.

4. In their petition for certiorari Mr. Sawyer's counsel cite among the "precedents" of Executive action "the seizure by President Lincoln during the Civil War of the railroads and telegraph lines between Washington and Annapolis". This seizure, again, was made *flagrante bello* at a time in early 1861 when the area in question was actually in the theatre of hostilities and the capital itself was in danger of being isolated. Congress subsequently passed a statute which in effect ratified this seizure and specifically gave the President control of all railroads and telegraph lines. The Act in terms provided that it was to remain in force only so long as was "necessary for the suppression of this rebellion". (Act of Jan. 31, 1862, c. 15; 12 Stat. 334).

5. Mr. Sawyer's counsel below, citing from Corwin's *The President: Office and Powers*, p. 190, finds support for his action in President Theodore Roosevelt's "stewardship theory" as exemplified by his consideration of the possible seizure of coal mines during a strike to prevent a coal shortage. Counsel neglected to point out, however, that Corwin in the very next paragraph of his study had this to add:

"One fact 'T.R.' omits to mention, and that is that Attorney General Knox advised him that his 'intended' step would be illegal and unconstitutional. For some reason the opinion is still buried among similar arcana of the Department of Justice" (p. 191).

Past executive acts of doubtful validity can furnish no support for sustaining the Executive Order and defendant's past and threatened actions. As a recent commentator observed:

"Acts based on this law of necessity and assumed probability of excuse or of subsequent ratification do not pretend to be supported by constitutional authority and are, of course, of no value

as precedents establishing the existence of constitutional power."
Whyte, *The War Powers of the President*, (1943) Wis. L. Rev.
205, 211–212.

There would be no more dangerous principle—nor one more
foreign to the Constitution—than a rule that past illegality can
through some legerdemain serve as authority to legalize present illegality.

Indeed, if Executive construction is to be accorded any validity,
a most recent example is directly in our favor. During the coal strike
of 1950 the President invoked the Labor Management Relations Act;
and on March 3, 1950, he sent a message to Congress reciting the
steps taken *and specifically requesting Congressional authorization
for the seizure of the coal mines.*[1]

Mr. Sawyer's counsel now claim that the President has, and has
always had, an "inherent power" to effect seizures. In their memorandum before Judge Pine (p. 60–A) they went so far as to assert
that this "inherent power" could not be diminished or limited by
Congress. The fact that the present Chief Executive, in an almost
identical recent situation, thought it necessary to ask Congressional
authorization for seizure seems clearly inconsistent with the existence
of any such "inherent power".

For the Government: Inherent Powers

ARGUMENT

[1] The message appears in 96 Cong. Rec. 2774–2775 (1950). It concludes with:
"The coal industry is a sick industry. Temporary seizure by the Government,
though it may be necessary under present circumstances, cannot produce a cure.
I am recommending seizure authority because I believe we now have no alternative.
But I urge that it be accompanied by a positive and constructive effort to get at the
root of the trouble. This is in the interest of the men who work the mines. It is
equally in the interest of their employers. Above all, it is in the interest of the
American people.

*I urge the Congress, therefore, to act immediately on legislation to authorize the
Government to take possession of and operate the mines,* and then to turn its attention to legislation looking toward a solution of the basic difficulties of the coal
industry." [Footnote in the Brief, emphasis that of the company counsel.]

* * *

[FROM THE GOVERNMENT'S BRIEF]

II. B. THE PRESIDENT, WITHOUT SPECIFIC STATUTORY AUTHORITY, MAY
    SEIZE PROPERTY TO AVERT CRISES DURING TIME OF WAR OR
    NATIONAL EMERGENCY, SUBJECT TO THE PAYMENT OF JUST
    COMPENSATION

The real question here, therefore, is whether seizure was a means
available to the President, in the exercise of his constitutional
powers, to meet the pressing emergency which faced the nation. On
this issue, ample support is to be found in executive and legislative
precedent for the President's action. Moreover, there is direct judicial recognition of executive seizure as a means of meeting emergency
situations.

1. *Executive construction.*—During the Revolution and the War
of 1812 there were numerous instances of taking of property for the
benefit of the armed services by military officers. While the exact
nature of these takings is seldom clear from the available records,
most of them appear to have been based entirely on executive
authority. The records show that during the Revolution, the buildings of Rhode Island College, as well as other buildings throughout
the country, were taken over for use as hospitals and barracks. Other
instances were the taking of wagons, horses, and slaves required for
public service. During the War of 1812 the property of traders at
Chicago was taken to prevent its falling to the enemy, rope walks
at Baltimore were destroyed for the same purpose, a house was taken
to hold military stores and was later blown up to prevent those
stores falling to the enemy, and, in Louisiana, General Jackson freely
took plantations, fencing, and supplies as the emergency dictated.
By the close of the War of 1812, it was firmly established that prop-

erty could be taken in wartime emergencies as an exercise of independent executive power.

More pertinent parallels in history are found during the administrations of Presidents Lincoln, Wilson, and Franklin D. Roosevelt.

The first discovered instance of a taking by order of the President himself, as distinguished from a taking by a subordinate military official, occurred in the first year of the Civil War. On April 27, 1861, Secretary of War Cameron, at the direction of the President, issued a declaration taking over the railroads and telegraph lines between Washington and Annapolis.

Confronted with secession, President Lincoln exercised greater executive power than had been exercised by any previous President. His most dramatic act of executive taking was his Emancipation Proclamation of January 1, 1863, an action resting exclusively on his constitutional powers as Commander-in-Chief. . . .

Following the precedent set by President Lincoln, Wilson, too, exercised his constitutional powers to seize the property of the Smith & Wesson Company on August 31, 1918. . . .

The most recent and extensive exercise of the executive power to seize property without statutory authority occurred during the administration of President Franklin D. Roosevelt. On twelve occasions prior to the enactment of the War Labor Disputes Act on June 25, 1943 (57 Stat. 163, 50 U.S.C. App. 1501–1511), which authorized the seizure of plants, President Roosevelt issued Executive Orders taking possession of various companies when it appeared that a work stoppage would seriously impede operations. The first seizure occurred as much as six months prior to Pearl Harbor, and a total of three plants were seized before our entry into the War.

Although other Presidents apparently did not have the occasion to meet crises of the magnitude and complexity here presented, brief mention should be made of the following incidents of a similar nature which illustrate the views of others who have occupied the office. President Hayes, in connection with the railway strike of 1877 and on other occasions, did not hesitate to make drastic use of his constitutional powers, including the use of troops. Corwin, *op. cit. supra*, (1948), p. 164. Again, in 1894 President Cleveland, over the objection of the Governor of Illinois, sent troops to Chicago in connection with the Pullman strike in order to remove obstructions to interstate commerce and the passage of mails. President Cleveland proclaimed that this action was taken for the purpose of enforcing the faithful execution of the laws of the United States and the protection of its property and removing obstructions to the United States mail. An injunction in connection with the strike was sustained in the *Debs* case, 158 U.S. 564, and the use of troops in that instance was approved by the Court as an exercise of the President's constitutional powers to enforce the Federal laws. 158 U.S. 564,582. Similarly, President McKinley dispatched troops to Idaho in 1899 to suppress the disturbances resulting from a strike of lead and silver miners. Berman, *Labor Disputes and the President* (1942), Ch. II. In 1902, Theodore Roosevelt seriously considered taking possession of the Pennsylvania coal mines during a strike in the mines to prevent a coal shortage. The taking never became necessary because the dispute was settled. 20 *Works of Theodore Roosevelt*, p. 466; Corwin, *op. cit. supra*, (1948), p. 190. Later in his administration, he withdrew from private entry "pending legislation" many parcels of land for forest and coal reserves although the pertinent statutes authorized withdrawal only of lands in which mineral deposits had been found. Corwin, *op. cit. supra*, (1948), p. 147. President Taft, despite his expression of views as an academic matter, did not hesitate to take similar action, in the teeth of existing statute, as a matter of executive power, based on usage. *United States v. Midwest Oil Co.*, 236 U.S. 459. And President Harding, like his predecessors, employed troops to quell the West Virginia Mine disorders of 1921. Berman, *op. cit. supra*, pp. 210–213.

2. *Legislative construction.*—As noted above, the first discovered instance of a Presidential taking was Lincoln's seizure, through his Secretary of War, of the railroad and telegraph lines between Washington and Annapolis in 1861. In January 1862, legislation was

enacted which confirmed the Presidential power to take over any railroad or telegraph line in the United States and provided penalties for interference with their operation by the Government (12 Stat. 334). Throughout the debates on the proposed legislation, virtually every Senator and Representative who addressed himself to the subject either assumed or declared that the President had the inherent constitutional power to take the railroads and telegraph lines if he thought it necessary in the exercise of his war powers. The supporters of the bill advocated its passage as a declaration of existing law and as a means of providing a rigorous system of penalties. . . .

The legislative history of the War Labor Disputes Act of June 25, 1943 (57 Stat. 163, 50 U.S.C. App. 1501–1511) is strikingly similar. On June 9, 1941, as noted above, p. 109, the President took possession of the North American Aviation plant at Inglewood, California, to end an interruption of production caused by a strike. On June 10, 1941, Senator Connally offered a virtually identical proposal as an amendment to S. 1524, a bill amending the Selective Service Act in certain respects wholly unrelated to the present litigation (87 Cong. Rec. 4932).

As with the Civil War Congress, discussed above, it was again generally recognized in consideration of the bill that the President already had full constitutional power to take the actions contemplated by the Act. . . .

3. *Judicial precedent.*—Even were there no direct judicial authorities, we believe that these historical precedents would be sufficient support for the President's action here. As Mr. Justice Holmes has cogently observed, "a page of history is worth a volume of logic." *New York Trust Co. v. Eisner,* 256 U.S. 345, 349. Contrary to plaintiffs' assertions that these precedents prove a usage but do not establish its validity, "even constitutional power, when the text is doubtful, may be established by usage." *Inland Waterways Corp. v. Young,* 309 U.S. 517, 525. "Both officers, law-makers and citizens naturally adjust themselves to any long-continued action of the

Executive Department—on the presumption that unauthorized acts would not have been allowed to be so often repeated as to crystallize into a regular practice. That presumption is not reasoning in a circle but the basis of a wise and quieting rule that in determining the meaning of a statute or the existence of a power, weight shall be given to the usage itself—even when the validity of the practice is the subject of investigation." *United States v. Midwest Oil Co.,* 236 U.S. 459, 472–473; *United States v. Macdaniel,* 7 Pet. 1, 13–14.

In any event, direct judicial recognition of the executive power to seize property to avert a crisis in time of war or national emergency is not lacking. . . .

Indeed, judicial controversy in this area has not been over the question whether the power to take exists but whether just compensation was required in view of the circumstances of the taking. In the analysis which follows we shall show (1) that the pertinent cases all hold that the executive may, without statutory authorization, employ seizure as a means of averting impending crisis; (2) that the power to seize is of two types, one based on the police power and the other in the nature of eminent domain; (3) that the police power seizure, which is not involved in this case, does not require compensation; (4) that the eminent domain taking, which is here involved, requires necessity and the payment of just compensation but can be exercised without regard to its physical relation to the field of battle; and (5) that since the owner suffers no greater injury from a taking under the eminent domain power than any other person whose property is taken by the usual legislative-judicial eminent domain process, a lesser degree of necessity justifies eminent domain takings as contrasted with police power seizures. . . .

In short, at the turn of the century, the existence of executive power to seize private property during time of war or national emergency was firmly established, not only as a matter of executive construction and usage and legislative approval, but also by judicial decision. Viewing this history negatively, the executive power was frequently used and never stricken down. We know of no case which denied the existence of this power nor any instance in which a responsible majority of either House of Congress questioned its existence. Rather, as we have shown, it was always recognized that the executive does have the power and controversy arose only over the question whether a right to just compensation flowed from the circumstances surrounding the taking.

The *Russell* case, if it stood alone, would, we submit, sustain the President's action here. This Court squarely held there that in time of "immediate and impending public danger . . . private property may be impressed into the public service . . . no doubt is entertained that the power of the government is ample to supply for the moment the public wants in that way to the extent of the immediate public exigency" (13 Wall. at 627–628). And, on the bare statements of the Assistant Quartermasters who commandeered the ships that they were taken because of "imperative military necessity," the Court held the takings to be lawful. Certainly, as we have shown above, pp. 9–15, 28–49, the present public danger is at least as "immediate and impending."

. . . But the *Russell* case, and the others discussed above, do not stand alone. Since the turn of the century, there has been continued judicial recognition of the President's constitutional powers in this area. . . . And a recent decision of this Court indirectly confirms the existence of a constitutional power in the President, in the nature of eminent domain, to seize property during time of war or national emergency. *United States v. Pewee Coal Co., Inc.,* 341 U.S. 144.

As in the instant suit, the *Pewee* case involved a nonstatutory seizure by executive order of the coal mines on May 1, 1943, to avoid a nation-wide strike of miners (Executive Order 9340, 8 F.R. 5695). Although no question was raised by the parties as to the validity of the seizure (see 115 C. Cls. 626, 676), the issue whether the seizure was an eminent domain taking within the meaning of the Fifth Amendment was squarely joined. It was the Government's position that the seizure did not constitute a taking within the meaning of the Fifth Amendment but that the seized property was merely in the custody of the Government, as would be property under conservatorship or temporary receivership, and Pewee was not, therefore, entitled to just compensation. The Court rejected the Government's argument. The Court was divided on the question of the measure of just compensation, but it was unanimously of the opinion that there had been a taking of Pewee's property which would require the payment of just compensation under the Fifth Amendment whenever loss is suffered. Although the Court did not expressly so state, it is implicit in the decision in that case that there had been a valid exercise of executive power in the nature of eminent domain or requisition. See *supra*, pp. 67–68. . . .

In the light of these authorities, there is no basis for Judge Pine's reference to "the utter and complete lack of authoritative support for defendant's position" (R.73). Contrast the opinion of the Court of Appeals below (per Circuit Judges Edgerton, Prettyman, Bazelon, Washington, and Fahy) (R. 447–448).

May it Please the Court

Socrates and the Justices

Although the briefs contain as thorough and as powerful a statement as counsel can prepare, there are usually points which the Justices will want explained further or about which they want to question the lawyers directly. These questions and explanations are exchanged in oral argument before the full Court, a scene in which the American judicial process mounts its maximum panoply.

Precisely at the stroke of noon, Monday through Thursday, the dark red velour curtains at the end of the Supreme Court Room part and three little groups enter: the Chief Justice and the two Senior Associates each leading two of their colleagues onto the raised platform where the Court sits. All persons in the room are standing and the Crier of the Court announces: "Oyez, Oyez, Oyez! All persons having business before the Honorable, the Supreme Court of the United States, are admonished to draw near and give their attention, for the Court is now sitting. God save the United States and this Honorable Court." ("*From* this Honorable Court" was the New Deal jest during the Court-crisis of the 1930s.) The Justices take their seats—each a large leather chair selected personally in the style and color preferred by the individual Justice—and the Court is in session. Behind the Justices are four massive marble pillars; a large clock hangs on a chain between the two center-pillars. Seated to the Court's right are the pages and Clerk; to the Court's left is the Marshal. Tables placed directly in front of the Bench are for counsel arguing the case at hand, the Government to the Court's left if it is a party to a suit. Behind the tables is a section for the Bar and a general section for the public. In separate areas to the right and left of these sections are places for the press and distinguished visitors, the latter often filled with Ambassadors, Congressmen, and Cabinet officers on days when an important opinion is expected or when a celebrated case is being argued. All the furnishings of the Courtroom are mahogany. Along the sides are 24 columns of Italian Sienna marble set in double rows, with carved marble panels over them. The west wall, for example, has panels depicting "Justice," "Divine Inspiration," "Powers of Evil," "Corruption and Slander," "Deceit and Despotic Power," and "Powers of Good." In the rear of the room is a place where visitors being conducted on tours through the building can stand and observe the Court for a few minutes before relinquishing this observation post to the next sight-seeing party.

If it is not Monday and there are no opinions left to read, new members of the Bar of the Supreme Court will be admitted, the lawyers in the first case to be argued that day will take their places at the counsel tables, and argument begins. The attorney representing the "moving party" will step to the lectern, pronounce the traditional lawyer's opening, "Mr. Chief Justice, May it Please the Court . . .," and will launch into his presentation. (The time given counsel, as we have seen, varies with the case. In the early days of the Supreme Court, arguments ran as long as 14 days and a four-day solo performance by giants such as Daniel Webster or William Pinkney was not unusual. Today the Court allows 30 minutes for cases on the Summary Docket, 45 minutes for cases on Certification, and 1 hour for ordinary cases on Appeal or Certiorari, with extentions in special circumstances.)

A large clock located in front of counsel (over the heads of the Justices) keeps him informed of his progress. When five minutes remain, the Marshal flashes a red light on the speaker's lectern. When the full time has been consumed, a white light is flashed and counsel must stop, whether he has finished or not; if he continues, the Chief Justice will usually stop him in the middle of a sentence with the comment "Time has expired." The Court can extend time for argument or ask questions beyond the time designated, of course, just as it can stop counsel before his time has run out with the command, "The Court does not desire to hear further argument in this matter." The role of spectators in the Courtroom has been pleasantly expanded in recent years by the introduction of microphones for the counsel and each of the Justices. Previously, plagued by atrocious acoustics, spectators missed hearing the argument more often than not.

Oral argument before the Supreme Court is essentially a Socratic dialogue between counsel and the Justices. Rather than sit silently while counsel sweep through prepared texts, the Justices listen for a polite period (which may be very short) and then break in to ask counsel question after question about his case. These will relate to the applicability of a precedent he is citing in support of his position, his characterization of the facts, or his reading of Congressional intent in a statute, and will include long hypothetical questions testing the limits of the argument being urged upon the Court. The questions vary in tone, naturally, with the personality of the Justice and his blood-pressure reaction to the particular case. Justice Frankfurter, a devoted supporter of the questioning process, fires on counsel as though they were students reciting at his former Harvard Law School seminar. Justice Tom Clark rarely interrupts counsel for questioning. All the questions, and the manner in which they are put, are watched closely by lawyers and reporters as possible guides to a Justice's thinking.

While the argument and questioning proceed, the Bench is a constant stir of activity. The Justices, much to the consternation of counsel arguing their first case in the Supreme Court, will conduct lengthy whispered conversations with their colleagues, thumb through the record, call their clerks to them for instructions, send pages on errands, write memos, occasionally doze, and generally operate as a Court "at work" rather than "at attention." Oral argument runs from 12 to 2 P.M., when the Court "rises" for a half-hour lunch period, the Justices usually lunching together during this hurried repast. Resuming at 2:30 P.M., argument will be heard until 4:30 when the Justices promptly retire. If a Justice desires an additional memorandum on a point being argued by counsel, this may be called for in a supplementary brief or a typed statement. When the time allotted for an argument has ended, the Chief Justice thanks the counsel and they leave the table, to be replaced by the lawyers in "No. 321" or "No. 463," who open their arguments without delay. By a custom which indicates the weight which the Court attaches to oral argument, a Justice who is ill and has to miss an argument does not participate in the decision of the case, even though he has mastered the briefs and record and is an expert in that branch of law. Another indication of the importance of oral argument is that the Court votes on the cases at its conference the same week that they have been argued, so that the oral presentation is fresh in the Justices' minds.

In the steel dispute, counsel for the companies was John W. Davis, a Wall Street lawyer, former Solicitor General of the United States, presidential candidate of the Democratic Party in 1924, and a veteran of hundreds of arguments before the Supreme Court. Appearing for the Government was Philip Perlman, a former newspaperman and Baltimore lawyer who had been Solicitor General of the United States since 1947 and was Acting Attorney General in the Spring of 1952. As we will see from reports and transcripts of the oral argument, Mr. Perlman was a skilled and learned lawyer but he found himself not without troubles on the afternoons of May 12 and 13.

Reports and Transcript of Oral Argument, May 12–13

The New York Times and Associated Press[1]
ACCOUNTS OF THE FIRST DAY OF ORAL ARGUMENT, MAY 12

The court, convening promptly at noon, disposed of motions to admit lawyers to practice. The Chief Justice then announced several decisions.

The courtroom was quite inadequate to accommodate the throng that queued up hours before noon. The 300-plus seats in the main part of the great marble chamber were strictly rationed, as were the limited number of chairs for members of the press, who were assigned to spaces between the pillars at one side of the room. Lawyers and members of Congress had first call on the seats. About forty lawyers, who were "of counsel" for the companies, squeezed into the space in front of the railing and to the right of members of the court. Mr. Perlman had fewer associates with him. The rule against standing during sessions of the court was relaxed and this permitted about 200 more to witness the proceedings. Hundreds more stood outside the chamber.

Mr. Davis, distinguished 79-year-old New Yorker . . . opened the argument at 12:24 P.M. His dark attire, relieved only by the stripes in his necktie, and a three-pointed handkerchief in his breast pocket, contrasted with his snowy hair and eyebrows and pale skin. He wore a sack coat instead of the cutaway that Mr. Perlman and many other lawyers still wear at the bar of the nation's highest court. . . .

Mr. Davis used few dramatic gestures. He referred occasionally to a large, loose-leaf notebook on the lectern in front of him; he

[1] *The New York Times*, May 13, 1952, p. 14, cols. 2–7.

put on glasses to glance at his notes and sometimes did not bother to remove them as he addressed himself directly to the court.

He spent the first fifteen minutes reciting the history of the controversy up to date. . . . He spent another fifteen minutes citing the property seizure statutes that existed over the years, pausing once in this recital to remark, "I trust I am not unduly wearing the patience of the court." He said his conclusions from the seizure review were that the seizure power was drawn from legislative sources, and that this power had been granted grudgingly, if at all, and for limited periods and with clear safeguards.

Mr. Davis then turned to the Taft-Hartley Act, declaring that the President "may or may not resort to that." But he said that the fact of its existence did not permit the President the option of seizure to prevent a strike, because Congress enacted this provision for just such emergencies.

The steel industry's lawyer tore into the Government's argument that one reason for not using the Taft-Hartley Act was the procedural delay incident to getting an anti-strike injunction. He cited the case of a longshoremen's strike where a Taft-Hartley injunction was issued on the fourth day of the proceedings under the act. "Neither the military nor the economic structure of the country would have fallen" in that time, Mr. Davis declared.

Turning to the constitutional question, Mr. Davis cited a Supreme Court ruling of 1871 in the case of United States against Russell. There the court said that in cases of extreme necessity in time of war or of immediate and impending public danger, private property could be impressed into the public service, but "the public danger must be immediate, imminent, and impending, and the emergency in the public service must be extreme and imperative, and such as will not admit of delay or a resort to any other source of supply." After thus quoting from the decision, Mr. Davis said, "I don't know how the English language could provide a better catalogue of adjectives" to indicate the requirements of immediacy before such extreme power could be invoked.

He also attacked what he said was a Government claim that the President was the sole judge of the existence of an emergency and the remedy, and denied the contention of the Government lawyers that the steel industry could sue for damages and collect any so proved from the United States Treasury. "That is a gesture so generous it is quite appealing," the New Yorker said. But, he added, the "Department of Justice cannot give to the court what the court is forbidden to entertain."

[The Associated Press account of Mr. Davis' argument noted at this point an argument directed at the contention in the Government's brief that Judge Pine's reliance upon "immutable principles" represented "a discredited technique of constitutional interpretation." Mr. Davis commented: "Is it or is it not an immutable principle that our Government is one of limited powers? Is it or is it not an immutable principle that we have a choice tripartite system of legislation, execution and judgment. Is it or is it not an immutable principle that the powers of government are based on a government of laws and are not based on a government of man. You cannot dispose of those immutable principles merely by a seizure of this kind. . . ."]

Nearing the end of his argument, Mr. Davis tossed his notebook upon the table at his side. Then, in a low, grave voice, he referred to "the words that Jefferson wrote in the Kentucky Resolution, which in a sentence sums up the theory . . ." that those who occupy public office, however lofty, are servants of the people. The quotation as he gave it was: "In questions of power, let no more be said of confidence in man, but bind him down from mischief by the chains of the Constitution."

Mr. Davis spoke for about eighty-five minutes [with few questions from the Justices during his presentation], which leaves him a little more than an hour for rebuttal tomorrow.

Mr. Perlman began speaking at 1:50 P.M. [According to a selection from the Associated Press account, he began by saying: "Your

Honors have just listened to an eloquent argument, an argument that is designed to turn the minds of this court away from the facts in this case and away from the reasons which prompted the President of the United States to take the action that he did. Very little if anything was said to the court about the condition in the world today, about the struggle in which this nation is engaged, and practically nothing at all about the necessity, the vital necessity, to keep the plants owned by the plaintiffs here in operation without interruption of any kind. And it is argued that your Honors should practically ignore that situation and pass on some Constitutional interpretation of the powers that the President exercised. . . ."]

[Mr. Perlman] was reviewing the early facts of the case when the gavel banged for luncheon promptly at 2 o'clock. He was cut off in the middle of a sentence. The court was just as prompt in resuming at 2:30. At 4:30, the appointed quitting hour, some of the court members got up and left, even as one of their colleagues was still questioning Mr. Perlman. . . .

ACCOUNT OF MR. PERLMAN'S QUESTIONING BY THE JUSTICES,
MAY 12 AND 13, AND ARGUMENT BY
MR. GOLDBERG, MAY 13[1]

Mr. Perlman told how, after the President seized the steel plants, he sent a message to Congress telling them of what he had done and inviting legislation so that his action would be ratified or rejected or some other method proposed. He told how 12 days later, the Chief Executive sent Congress another similar message and that over a month has elapsed since the original message was sent and Congress has taken no action.

Mr. Justice Reed: "How would they reject it?"

Mr. Perlman: "By passing an act or resolution, or they could terminate it."

Mr. Justice Jackson: "If he has inherent power, how could they do that?"

[1] From *United States Law Week*, May 20, 1952. Used with permission of the publisher, Bureau of National Affairs, Washington, D. C.

Mr. Perlman: "The President told Congress he would abide by any decision Congress would make."

Mr. Justice Burton: "But by that time the law suits were pending; doesn't that explain why Congress didn't act?"

Mr. Perlman: "I don't think so. They could avoid it by acting on the President's suggestion. He told them he would abide by any action they took."

Mr. Justice Douglas: "Do you concede power in Congress to overrule the President?"

Mr. Perlman: "I don't concede the power. He told them he would turn back if they said so."

Mr. Justice Frankfurter: "Are you suggesting that the fact that Congress didn't act has legal significance; that Congress approved that action?"

Mr. Perlman: "I think it could be inferred that they were content to let the President's action stand."

Mr. Perlman . . . pointed out that when the President acted, he was exercising power vested in him by the Constitution and many acts of Congress and by treaties which have been entered into with other nations. He cited the North Atlantic Pact, the Mutual Security Act, and the Defense Production Act. These laws and treaties and others are practically without precedence in this nation in time of peace.

Mr. Justice Douglas: "All this means that someone should do something but doesn't advance your argument that the President should."

Mr. Perlman explained that all of these statutes are aimed at mobilizing the assets of the entire nation, and that these are the reasons why he acted.

Mr. Justice Reed: "Do you stand on any statute as giving the President authority?" . . .

Mr. Perlman: "We rely on the Constitution and on the other acts which give him power. We concede that seizure was not pursuant to the [Defense Production] Act. I will come to that."

Mr. Justice Black: "Do you depend on it [the Defense Production Act] to supply power to do what was done here?"

Mr. Perlman: "We think the power is in the Constitution and that Congress by the passage of two statutes has provided authority—"

Mr. Justice Black: "Then the Government is not depending solely on the Constitution but is also relying on statutes."

Mr. Perlman: "We are depending upon the Constitution. But we call the Court's attention to statutes authorizing a taking." He explained further that where such authority exists a suit can be brought for damages in the Court of Claims.

Mr. Justice Douglas: "That merely goes to the remedy."

Mr. Perlman: "Yes."

Mr. Justice Burton: "Would you dispute that the provisions of Taft-Hartley were intended to govern this situation?"

Mr. Perlman: "No, we don't say it is not applicable. It could have been used in December." He explained that the President obtained more than Taft-Hartley gave by the procedure which he followed.

* * *

Mr. Perlman then began discussing the power given the President in Article II of the Constitution. He reminded the Court of Chief Justice Taft's discussion in the Myers case, 272 U.S. 52, upholding the President's right to remove an official, and the broad view of the President's powers taken there.

Mr. Justice Frankfurter: "Then they took it back."

Mr. Perlman agreed that in Humphrey's case, 295 U.S. 602, they reached a different conclusion but he contended there are conflicting views as to whether Humphrey's overruled Myers.

At this point, MR. PERLMAN referred to MR. JUSTICE JACKSON's book, "The Struggle for Judicial Supremacy." As MR. JUSTICE FRANKFURTER asked MR. PERLMAN for further information, MR. JUSTICE JACKSON quipped: "JUSTICE FRANKFURTER hasn't read the book."

Mr. Perlman: "I would like to take this opportunity to recommend it to him."

The next argument made by MR. PERLMAN concerned previous

executive seizures. He noted that they dated back to the Revolutionary War. MR. JUSTICE BURTON wanted to know whether there were any statutory provisions which could have been followed in these seizures, and MR. PERLMAN replied that in some cases there were none.

Mr. Justice Douglas: "Were these war power cases?"

Mr. Perlman: "Some of them were." President Lincoln seized the railroad between Washington and Annapolis and the telegraph lines in the absence of any statutory authority, he stated. He also adverted to President Wilson's seizure of property without statutory authority in the Smith and Wesson case.

Mr. Justice Frankfurter: "There was a statute but he didn't follow it."

Mr. Perlman then referred to the North American Aviation Company seizure by President Roosevelt before Pearl Harbor. There was no statutory authority and merely threats of war, he said.

Mr. Justice Jackson protested that the North American case was not a precedent for the action taken in the steel seizure. He pointed out that North American was under direct contract to the Government, and none of the steel companies are. The Government owned the materials and machinery, and the strike was a strike against the terms of the contract then in force. Here, there is a legitimate labor dispute. North American was a strike against the Government policy of lend-lease. The Communist pickets wouldn't admit employees to the plant; and the owners all but acquiesced in the seizure. They said they were at their wit's end. "I don't believe it is a precedent for this seizure; I don't want it laid at my door."

Mr. Perlman: "Your Honor, we lay a lot of it at your door. The principles which you laid down are applicable here." He read a long quotation from the opinion of MR. JUSTICE JACKSON (then Attorney General) upholding the North American seizure.

As he finished, MR. JUSTICE JACKSON stated: "You stopped too soon." He described the situation as an insurrection. MR. PERLMAN insisted that MR. JUSTICE JACKSON's language upheld the seizure.

Mr. Justice Frankfurter: "He was not 'His Honor' when he said it."

* * *

As MR. PERLMAN adverted to the court's power to review the President's action, MR. JUSTICE DOUGLAS asked: "I thought you said this Court couldn't review the emergency."

Mr. Perlman: "No, sir. And our brief doesn't say that."

Mr. Justice Frankfurter objected to being compelled to "sit in judgment on an appraisal of the situation made by the President."

Mr. Perlman: "Our position is that the courts have a right to determine whether there is a reasonable basis for it."

Mr. Justice Clark also questioned *Mr. Perlman* about the Court's position in reviewing the fact situation. He concluded: "How can we pass on whether the remedy is equal to the emergency or whether the emergency is equal to the remedy?"

Mr. Justice Douglas asked *Mr. Perlman* on what the Government was relying.

Mr. Perlman: "We are relying on every single law passed in recent years dealing with the emergency."

Mr. Justice Douglas: "Would you mind giving me just one law this seizure helped to enforce?"

Mr. Perlman: "The Defense Production Act."

Mr. Perlman referred to the seizures made by President Roosevelt before enactment of the War Labor Disputes Act, nine of which he contended were made without express statutory authority of any kind.

Mr. Justice Jackson interrupted, stating: "Since I'm interpleaded as a defendant let me remind you of the circumstances." He then discussed the factual situations prevailing at the time those seizures were made, contending that they were distinguishable from the seizure in the instant case. . . .

Mr. Perlman turned to other arguments against the injunction. First, that the plaintiffs have an adequate remedy at law. He again pointed out that recovery was allowed in the Pewee Coal case where the seizure took place without authority of a statute.

Mr. Justice Reed: "Doesn't that case assume that the seizure was valid?"

Mr. Perlman: "In the Pewee case, that point was not contested." He also suggested that if it had been thought that the Government was not liable because of illegality, it would probably have been urged. This is the same kind of seizure, he argued, and the Government's liability has been established by that case.

He then adverted to Hurley v. Kincaid, 285 U.S. 95. There, recovery of damages was permitted where a statute authorized seizure but the statutory procedure was not followed.

The Solicitor General passed to his second point. He contended that the plaintiffs failed entirely to show irreparable injury and emphasized that under the Executive Order management remains the same and nothing was to be disturbed.

The Chief Justice: "Could that procedure be changed by the Secretary?"

Mr. Perlman: "Frankly, it is proposed to change working conditions. That is the only basis for their claim. It may or may not cause them damage; if it does, the Government is in back of any damage."

The Chief Justice: "How would you determine the damages with increase in wages?" The Chief Justice added that this question arose in Pewee but was not decided. . . .

Mr. Perlman concluded by saying that in each case as it arises the Court will determine whether or not damages are suffered. . . .

Mr. Justice Frankfurter and *Mr. Perlman* then discussed the seizure power in the Defense Production Act. *Mr. Perlman* indicated that the seizure provision there would have taken too long. *Mr. Justice Frankfurter* disagreed. As they continued to discuss the procedure provided by the Act, *Mr. Justice Frankfurter* said: "You seize before you start condemnation."

Mr. Perlman: "That is what I've tried to tell the Court about Hurley v. Kincaid." He pointed out that two statutes, the Defense Production Act and the Selective Service Act of 1948, authorize seizure. As the discussion continued about the right to seize under the two Acts, *Mr. Perlman* repeated: "All I say is that the two statutes give the Government authority to acquire property. They make it clear that there is a liability on the part of the Government. We cite them for that one point."

At another point, *Mr. Perlman* said that seizure was "the only manner in which the Chief Executive could assure the continued production of steel necessary for the whole war effort; and we are at war."

Mr. Justice Jackson: "Hasn't the President expressly disclaimed this and called it a police action?"

Mr. Perlman: "You can say without fear of contradiction—"

Mr. Justice Jackson: "That it looks like a war?"

Mr. Perlman: "That we are under war conditions."

Mr. Justice Frankfurter: "But yesterday in answering *Justice Douglas* you emphasized that you were not using war powers. Now you say you are not exercising war powers but we are in a war."

Mr. Perlman: "The Executive Order said the President was taking a step (seizure) as commander-in-chief of the Army and Navy."

Mr. Justice Frankfurter: "But he is that during the most peaceful era in our country's history."

Mr. Perlman: "Unfortunately, we do not happen to be in such an era."

* * *

On rebuttal, *Mr. Davis* stated that the steel companies did not concede that the President must choose between Taft-Hartley and the Defense Production Act; nor did they concede that one is a substitute for the other. He stated that the President didn't intend to exclude Taft-Hartley when he called conferences under the Defense Production Act.

As to irreparable injury, he continued, it is the anticipated and threatened injury which equity is empowered to prevent. He emphasized that the Secretary of Commerce intended to change working conditions. What injury could be more irreparable, he continued, than to oust an owner and use his funds to pay an obligation the Secretary has no power to contract.

Arthur J. Goldberg, of Washington, D.C., representing the United Steelworkers of America, appeared as [friend of the Court]. He argued that under the circumstances of this case, where the principal objectives of the Taft-Hartley procedure had already been accomplished by use of the Defense Production Act procedure through the Wage Stabilization Board, the President's refusal to invoke the Taft-Hartley emergency procedures was fully justified. He urged that a court of equity to which any request for a Taft-Hartley injunction would have been addressed would have refused to issue it. This point was material, he told the Court, to refute the company's contention that there was no emergency while the Taft-Hartley Act procedure remained unutilized.

Mr. Justice Burton asked *Mr. Goldberg* whether it made a difference that the Board had made a recommendation and *Mr. Goldberg* pointed out that in that respect it went beyond Taft-Hartley, "which might have helped."

Mr. Justice Burton: "It may have hurt."

Mr. Goldberg: "It may." . . .

Another point pressed by *Mr. Goldberg* was that what is involved is not a labor dispute. It is a dispute between industry and the Government as to the price regulations of the Government. The gist of this argument was that industry wouldn't grant the wage increase unless they received the right to increase prices. He also pointed out that the moment the steel companies were assured by the stay that the Government couldn't raise wages, "we couldn't bargain with them." He also stated that the union does not "look with pleasure" on Government seizure. . . .

As *Mr. Goldberg* concluded his argument, he expressed the hope that an early decision would be reached.

Mr. Justice Jackson: "I think it is important that no false hopes be raised on that score and that your people understand the problem. It frequently happens—I myself have changed my opinion after reading opinions of the other members of this Court. And I am as stubborn as most. But I sometimes wind up not voting the way I voted in conference because the reasons of the majority didn't satisfy me. I would oppose handing down any decision in this case until the opinions are ready because the opinions are even more important than the decisions."

As *Mr. Goldberg* indicated agreement, *Mr. Justice Jackson* added: "This is not something that may be decided in the light of one day's discussion. The arguments may just begin when counsel stops."

Nine Men at Work

How the Supreme Court Reaches Decisions

As Justice Jackson said, the Court's argument begins where that of counsel ends. Each Friday at 11 A.M. (before the accession of the present Chief Justice on Saturday at noon), the Justices meet in the Conference Room of the Supreme Court. In keeping with one of the Court's bits of protocol, the Justices shake hands with one another on entering, to help smooth any ruffled feelings which may have arisen from debates at the last Conference or disagreements in opinions. Once the Conference has begun, secrecy of the proceedings is assured by a rule that the door must remain locked and no-one else may enter. (If a message has to be transmitted, the junior Justice goes to the door, knocks for the Marshal, and passes it through. Justice Charles E. Whittaker is thus referred to by Washington reporters as "the highest paid messenger in town.")

The Conference proceeds into Friday evening and will continue on Saturday if enough business has accumulated. The Court first determines which opinions are ready to be announced the following Monday and takes a final vote on them. Then petitions for certiorari and appeal papers are considered, along with miscellaneous motions such as a handwritten plea for habeas corpus from an inmate of a federal prison who alleges poverty and claims that his conviction was constitutionally unfair. Finally, the Justices discuss and vote on the cases which were argued during that week or which are brought back to the Conference from previous weeks for additional discussion.

Presiding at the Conference is the "Chief," as his colleagues call him. He notes each case in a padlocked Docket Book, recording the number and title of the case, the voting on it, to whom the opinion is assigned, and the date on which the opinion was announced. (Each of the Associates may keep docket books if he desires and some do, preserving their contemporary reflections on the power of their own reasoning and the peculiar obtuseness of disagreeing brethren.) The Conference gets much of its character from the personality and administrative talent of the Chief. He presents each case, giving a short statement of its facts and the legal issues as he sees them, and he moves the discussion along as each Associate speaks, in order of seniority. If the Chief Justice is well prepared and presides effectively, cases can be aired and positions debated without undue heat and bickering. Chief Justice John Marshall was a master chairman in the days when the Justices all boarded together in the same Washington inn, ate at common table, and sipped the Court's specially imported Madeira. In more modern times, Melville Fuller and Charles Evans Hughes earned reputations as skilled presiding officers. To see Hughes conduct the Conference, Justice Frankfurter recalled, "was like witnessing Toscanini lead an orchestra."[1] Edward D. White and Harlan Stone, on the other hand, were weak at the Conference, with the result that discussions lengthened and argument thickened without real reward to the collegial process. Stone, for example, never had Hughes' knack of saying, at the right moment, "Brethren, the only way we are going to settle this is by voting." An idea of the necessity for such management of discussion can be had by anyone who reads biographies of the Justices and obtains descriptions of the clashes between Oliver Wendell Holmes and John Marshall Harlan, Pierce Butler's sometimes savage thrusts at Louis D. Brandeis, and the barely-repressed antagonism between Hugo Black and Robert Jackson.

Once the votes are called for, the newest Justice votes first and the ballots proceed by juniority. After all the cases for that week have been disposed of, the Conference is concluded. At this point, the Chief Justice retires to his suite to decide which Justice will be assigned to write the opinion of the Court in each case. This selection, one of the main ways in which the Chief Justice can place his stamp on constitutional law during his tenure, may be based on a variety of factors—sharing the work load, recognizing a particular Justice's expertise in a subject, choosing a spokesman who will present a delicate ruling to the public with maximum appeal, and finding the Justice who will carry the most colleagues with him when the argument is put into type. If the Chief Justice is not with the majority in a case, the senior Associate assigns the opinion. If more than one Justice is dissenting and there is to be an opinion for the group,

[1] Quoted in *The New York Times*, December 1, 1957, VI, p. 53, col. 4.

the senior Justice among the dissenters decides who shall write this. Each Justice is free to suggest to the Chief (or the assigning Associate) some reason why he feels another Justice than he should write the opinion and even more rarely, why a colleague assigned to the case should not write that opinion, but such responses are quite unusual.

After the assignments have been made, the Justices retire to their three-room suites (one oak-panelled study for the Justice, one room for the secretary, and one for the law clerks) to draft the opinions. (This is usually done during the two-week recess which follows each two weeks of hearing arguments, an alternating schedule which the Court follows during its yearly session, October to June. About 25–30 cases will be heard each two weeks, some 1,000 cases will be passed upon each year, and 150–200 opinions will be written.) Once the opinion is drafted, it is set in type and proofs are printed in the Court's basement printing plant, under tight "security" procedures. The proofs are then circulated to each Justice, including the dissenters in the case, and the writer awaits "returns." These may be simply a sentence stating agreement or disagreement, or a short compliment scrawled across the back of the proof: "good law," "unanswerable," or "exceptionally well done." Sometimes the comments become light and playful. The first Justice Harlan noted gaily on an opinion of Chief Justice Morrison Waite, "I see nothing wrong with this except the law which it announced."[1] This was an art at which Oliver Wendell Holmes was unsurpassed: "Yes—twice if I can get in two votes," he wrote on one proof. "Yes, with humility," he noted to Chief Justice Hughes in one return, "I now see what you have been about when I was giving parties their constitutional right to jaw while I slept." On another Hughes opinion Holmes wrote, "Wee—Mussoo— I float in a fairy bark to the bight and serenely anchor there with you."[2]

Frequently, the returns will suggest detailed changes in argument, or even style. The writer can disregard such recommendations, but if he does so, he may lose the vote of that Justice, and possibly his majority, since no-one is committed to maintain the original vote he had cast in Conference. Polishing the opinions is therefore a process of group adjustment, in which the Justice assigned the opinion to write must shape his statement to the wishes of his colleagues or risk separate concurrences or even defections to the minority. Holmes was particularly sad at having to

[1] Morrison R. Waite Papers, Cincinnati, Ohio.

[2] Merlo J. Pusey, *Charles Evans Hughes*, vol. II, pp. 286–287, The Macmillan Co., N.Y., 1951.

give up his biting phrases and capsule statements to suit his associates. "The boys generally cut one of the genitals out of mine," he wrote a friend.[1] Drafts of dissenting opinions will also be circulated, and the writer for the majority may add paragraphs to take into account arguments made by the dissenters. In one instance, dissenting Justice Stephen J. Field made a telling point in his draft only to find that Justice Horace Gray, for the majority, was persuaded by the criticism to withdraw the weak argument. Field demanded of the Chief Justice that the argument be replaced or else he would tell the story of its disappearance in his dissent anyway. Gray had to put the statement back.[2]

When all the returns are received and a final draft is circulated, the Justice will report to the Conference that "No. 590" is ready to "come down." A final vote will be taken, after which no change of position is permitted.

Monday is the Court's time for reading opinions. ("Black Monday" has been the cry of court critics. New Dealers so referred to May 27, 1935, when several key Roosevelt measures were struck down; and Southern segregationists so characterize May 17, 1954, when separate-but-equal public school facilities for Negroes were declared unconstitutional.) The Justices arrive at the Robing Room a few minutes before noon, hands are shaken all around, the Court is entered at 12 sharp, new attorneys are admitted, and the Chief Justice nods to one of the Associates, who will declare, "I have for announcement the judgment of the Court in the Fry Case, No. 8." The individual Justice decides whether to read the opinion in its entirety (as some do with all their opinions) or to deliver an extemporaneous summary of the points. When all the concurrences and dissents are read in an important case, the sunlight may be gone from the Courtroom entirely; opinions in the *Insular Cases* of 1901 took 6 hours to deliver and if opinions in a large number of cases are read, the reading will go into Tuesday and as long thereafter as may be necessary. The extemporaneous summaries, particularly the dissents, are often more impassioned than the content of the opinion in its written form. Justice James McReynolds ended a dissent against a ruling upholding a New Deal measure with the cry: "The Constitution, as we know it, is dead. This is Nero at his worst." The summaries are not reported by the Court, though, and are taken down only by newsmen looking for colorful statements to put into their stories of opinion day.

[1] *Ibid.*, p. 286.
[2] J. C. Bancroft Davis Papers, Library of Congress, Washington, D.C.

A Profile of the Court

The purpose of the Conference debates, the individual assignments, the collegial editing, and the re-assessment at conferences is to provide the best procedure for judging cases. Judge Curtis Bok has observed that judging represents "the play of an enlightened personality within the boundaries of a system."[1] To follow this play, the student of the constitutional process looks for the interaction in each case of the Justice's personal views on the subject, his fidelity to the Court's case precedents in that area, and his definition of the proper role for the judiciary in this context. In the *Youngstown* case, an attempt to predict the way each Justice would vote, based upon the three elements just noted, might well have produced a six-man majority for upholding—or at least not interfering with—the President's seizure action. Justice Hugo Black and William O. Douglas, in their personal views, were known to be New-Fair Dealers, appreciative of labor unions, and lacking in warmth toward big business. Justice Tom Clark and Chief Justice Fred Vinson were Truman appointees and former members of the Cabinet who had displayed their judicial support for the President's measures on many occasions. Justice Felix Frankfurter was devoted to a firm philosophy of judicial self-restraint and avoidance of unnecessarily large constitutional rulings, which pointed toward a possible disagreement with the Pine ruling. Justice Robert Jackson had written eloquent opinions as Attorney General in 1940 and 1941 interpreting President Roosevelt's powers in broad terms.

Unhappily for those who wish to predict decisions of the courts, judicial values, as Professor Paul Freund has said, "come not single file but in battalions." Along with a pro-union outlook may go a deep allegiance to separation of powers. Although he believes in a philosophy of judicial self-restraint, a Justice may feel that a "clear violation of the Constitution should not be sanctioned by the judiciary. A Justice appointed by a President whose actions have been challenged may feel that his reputation for independence as a judge is at stake in a decision. And a judge who is a political liberal may also be deeply opposed to extension of the "military" authority of a President as Commander-in-Chief, particularly in light of the long cold war vistas.

To appreciate the *Youngstown* case fully, then, one should have a thorough knowledge of the legal doctrines and judicial philosophy of each of the Justices as background for understanding his position in the case. Space permits, however, only brief biographical sketches.

Curtis Bok, *Backbone of the Herring*, p. 9., Alfred A. Knopf, N. Y., 1941.

THE JUSTICES IN THE STEEL SEIZURE CASE

FRED M. VINSON

Dem.; appointed by Truman. Born 1890, father, the town jailor. Centre College, Kentucky; Centre Law School. Gen'l practice, Louisa, Ky. 1911; City Atty, 1913; Cmwlth Atty, 1921; U.S. Congressman, 1922–28, 1930–38, a tax expert with a "100% pro labor record"; Judge, U.S. Ct. of Appeals, 1938–43; Dir., 3 war agencies, 43–45; Sec'y of Treasury, 1945–46. "Underneath a New Deal veneer," wrote *Newsweek*, Vinson is "an orthodox Southern Democrat." General position within the Supreme Court: Conservative toward civil liberty claims, Moderate Conservative in business regulation and labor cases.

HUGO BLACK

Dem.; appointed by Roosevelt. Born 1886, father ran a small general store. One year, Birmingham Med. Coll.; U. of Ala. Law School. Gen'l and labor practice, Birmingham, Ala., 1907–27 (police court judge 1910–11, county solicitor 1915–17); U.S. Senator, 1927–1937, one of the leading Southern populists in the Senate during the Hoover era and a New Deal stalwart after 1933, a critical investigator of utility companies, sponsor of pro-labor legislation, and outspoken opponent of the "old" Supreme Court's favoritism to property rights and "disregard" of "human rights." General position within the Supreme Court: Left-Liberal toward civil liberty claims, Left-Liberal in business regulation and labor cases.

STANLEY K. REED

Dem.; appointed by Roosevelt. Born 1884, father a well-to-do doctor. Yale; Columbia Law School. Gen'l practice, Ky. 1910–29 (Dem. member of Ky. Legisl. 1912–16); Gen'l Counsel, Fed. Farm Bur., 1929–32; Gen'l Counsel, R.F.C., 1932–35; Solicitor General, 1935–38, arguing key New Deal cases before the Supreme Court involving the N.R.A., A.A.A., T.V.A. and other legislation. "Slow and serious," a "craftsman without passion," have been comments describing Reed. General position within the Supreme Court: Moderate Conservative toward civil liberty claims, Moderate Conservative in business regulation and labor cases.

FELIX FRANKFURTER

Independent; appointed by Roosevelt. Born 1882; father a retail merchant in New York. C.C. N.Y.; Harvard Law School. U.S. Ass't Dist. Atty, N.Y. 1906–10, acquiring there a "fastidious regard for procedural regularity"; law officer, Bur. of Insular Affairs 1911–14; administrative posts in Depts. of War and Labor; Sec'y and Counsel, President's Mediation Comm. 1914–18; Chm., War Labor Policies Bd., 1918; Professor, Harvard Law School, 1919–1939. From that post, Frankfurter "radiated his influence on the world"—as counsel in labor and social welfare legislation cases and civil liberty trials, as a founder of the *New Republic* and American Civil Liberties Union, as a top advisor to F.D.R. and a recruiter of New Deal talent, as a correspondent with leading government and intellectual figures in this country and abroad, and as the author of highly influential books and articles on the Supreme Court. General position within the Supreme Court: Moderate Liberal toward civil liberty claims, Moderate Liberal in business regulation and labor cases.

WILLIAM O. DOUGLAS

Dem.; appointed by Roosevelt. Born 1898, father an itinerant Presbyterian preacher. Whitman Coll.; Columbia Law School. Lawyer in a Wall Street firm, 1925–27, "to study the natives"; Professor of Law, Columbia, 1927; Professor of Law, Yale, 1928–1936, earning a national reputation for writing and teaching on corporations, bankruptcy, and business regulation; Member, S.E.C., 1936–37, Chm. 1937–39, reorganizing the N.Y. Stock Exchange, revising codes of security issues, and acting as one of F.D.R.'s inner advisors on business and trustbusting. An outspoken liberal, outdoor sports enthusiast, and author of numerous books on widely ranging subjects. "I am really a pretty conservative sort of fellow from the old school," Douglas once said, and then explained, "perhaps a school too old to be remembered. . . ." General position within the Supreme Court: Left-Liberal toward civil liberty claims, Left-Liberal in business regulation and labor cases.

ROBERT H. JACKSON

Dem.; appointed by Roosevelt. Born 1892, father a farmer. One year Albany Law School; Gen'l practice, specializing in "small corporation" business, Jamestown, N.Y., 1913–34; Gen'l Counsel, Bur. of Internal Revenue 1934–36; Ass't Atty General, 1936–38; Solicitor General, 1938–39; Atty General, 1940–41, one of the keenest spokesmen before the Sup. Ct. and Congress for the New Deal legal position. "I am always suspicious of eternal verities," Jackson once commented, "The ultimate test of the Constitution is not doctrinal, but administrative." General position within the Supreme Court: Moderate Liberal toward civil liberty claims, Moderate Conservative in business regulation and labor cases.

HAROLD H. BURTON

Rep.; appointed by Truman. Born 1888, father Dean at M.I.T. Bowdoin; Harvard Law School. Utility company lawyer and member of corporation-law firms, Cleveland, 1912–35; "reform" Mayor of Cleveland, 1935–40; U.S. Senator from Ohio, 1940–45, a close friend of Senator Truman and member of his War Investigating Committee, strong internationalist and moderate-liberal Republican. "My position," Burton once commented, "is center." General position within the Supreme Court: Conservative toward civil liberty claims, Conservative in business regulation and labor cases.

SHERMAN M. MINTON

Dem.; Truman apptee. Born 1890. Father a farmer. Ind. U.; Yale Law School. Law practice in Indiana and Florida, 1916–33; counselor to "Little New Deal" Administration of Gov. McNutt of Indiana; U.S. Senator, Indiana, 1934–41, a committed New Dealer, Chm. of Senate Lobby Investigating Comm., critic of the Sup. Ct.'s anti-New Deal decisions and supporter of the Court-reform plan; defeated for re-election, 1940; Admin. Asst. to the President, 1941; Judge, U.S. Ct. of Appeals, 1941–49. Never considered a "crusader," Minton was described as "mellowing considerably" as an Appeals Judge. General position within the Supreme Court: Conservative toward civil liberty claims, Conservative in business regulation and labor cases.

TOM C. CLARK

Dem.; appointed by Truman. Born 1889, father an attorney; U. of Texas; U. of Texas Law School. General practice, Dallas, 1922–27; Civil D.A. for Dallas Cty, 1927–32; returned to practice; entered U.S. Dept. of Justice, 1937, serving in the divisions of War Risk Insurance, Anti-Trust, and War Frauds, working closely during 1942–43 with the Truman Committee; Asst Atty General in charge of Criminal Division, 1943–45; U.S. Atty General, 1945–49. Noted for his "folksy" manner and hard working habits, Clark once told a reporter, "I have to work long hours because I'm not as smart as some other fellows." General position within the Supreme Court: Conservative toward civil liberty claims, Moderate Conservative in business regulation and labor cases.

The Setting of the 1951 Term of Court

Another useful bit of background information for the Steel Case was the relation of the seizure dispute to the bulk of cases the Court decided in 1952 and the general grouping of the Justices in these instances.

The Term of Court which ran from October 1951 to June of 1952 was distinguished for the number of public-law issues which the Justices chose to rule upon rather than deflect. Some idea of the range and importance of the cases can be gained by listing just a few of the questions presented: hidden microphoning by F.B.I. agents,[1] proper bail for West Coast Communist leaders indicted under the Smith Act,[2] deportations of resident aliens for previous Communist Party membership,[3] New York's loyalty program for public school teachers,[4] an Illinois law punishing libellous statements against religious and racial groups,[5] the status of movies and movie censorship under the First Amendment,[6] privacy from recorded commercials for riders of District of Columbia buses,[7] released-time programs of religious education for public school children,[8] "stomach pumping" by California police to regain evidence swallowed by a criminal on arrest,[9] a Missouri statute requiring employers to give paid time off on election day,[10] agreements between a white union and a railroad to exclude Negroes from "brakemen's posts,"[11] the percentage of discount to retailers allowed under the Robinson-Patman Act,[12] the contempt convictions imposed upon lawyers for the Communist Party defendants in the *Dennis* trial,[13] a taxpayer's duty to report his blackmail profits as taxable income,[14] and the standing of parents and taxpayers to challenge Bible-reading in New Jersey public schools.[15]

In all, 200 cases were decided on the merits during the Term, out of 1,207 cases disposed of.[16] Most cases, therefore, were handled by denial of certiorari or dismissal of appeal. Of the cases determined on their merits, 83 received signed opinions, seven were given *per curiam* treat-

---

[1] On Lee v. United States, 343 U.S. 747 (5–4 decision).
[2] Stack v. Boyle, 342 U.S. 1 (unanimous with concurrences).
[3] Harisiades v. Shaughnessy, 342 U.S. 580 (6–2 decision).
[4] Adler v. Board of Education, 342 U.S. 485 (6–3 decision).
[5] Beauharnais v. Illinois, 343 U.S. 250 (5–4 decision).
[6] Joseph Burstyn, Inc. v. Wilson, 343 U.S. 495 (unanimous with concurrences).
[7] Public Utilities Commission v. Pollak, 343 U.S. 451 (7–1 decision).
[8] Zorach v. Clauson, 343 U.S. 306 (6–3 decision).
[9] Rochin v. California, 342 U.S. 165 (unanimous with concurrences).
[10] Day-Brite Lighting, Inc. v. Missouri, 342 U.S. 421 (8–1 decision).
[11] Brotherhood of Railroad Trainmen v. Howard, 343 U.S. 768 (6–3 decision).
[12] F.T.C. v. Ruberoid Co., 344 U.S. 470 (7–1 decision).
[13] Sacher v. United States, 343 U.S. 1 (5–3 decision).
[14] Rutkin v. United States, 343 U.S. 130 (5–4 decision).
[15] Doremus v. Board of Education, 342 U.S. 429 (6–3 decision).
[16] See the Tables and Summaries, 66 Harvard Law Review 177–181 (1952).

ment (a short unsigned opinion "by the Court"), and the remainder were disposed of by order. Taken as a group, the cases determined on the merits at this Term showed that the operative core of the Court's majority were the four Truman appointees, Chief Justice Vinson, and Justices Tom Clark, Harold Burton, and Sherman Minton, with one or more of three Roosevelt designees, Justices Stanley Reed, Felix Frankfurter and Robert Jackson, joining to provide a majority (often with a concurring opinion) in the bulk of the cases. The remaining Roosevelt Justices, Hugo Black and William O. Douglas, cast the most dissenting votes (50 and 43 respectively); Justice Clark found it necessary to break with the majority only once in the course of the year.

Decision Monday, June 2, 1952

While the Nation Waited

While the Supreme Court was preparing its opinions, the political side of the dispute continued to unfold. Vice President Alben Barkley and Secretary of Labor Maurice Tobin told the Steel Workers at their national convention on May 14 that the Administration supported the Union's drive to win all that the Wage Stabilization Board had promised. By a unanimous vote, the Convention determined to strike if the Supreme Court returned the plants to the companies. (Two days later, Philip Murray explained that this resolution was not meant as an attempt to intimidate the Supreme Court since that august body was "not subject to pressure.")

Speaking to the Americans for Democratic Action Convention on May 18, President Truman charged that the steel companies wanted a strike. When asked at his weekly press conference on May 22 about his view of presidential powers, President Truman said that he possessed inherent powers which he could not be deprived of by either Congress or the Supreme Court, although he would abide by the Court's decision as to the steel mills. (Later, a "high administration spokesman" clarified this. The President, he said, meant that the Supreme Court passes on particular cases but wouldn't question the general powers of the President in an emergency. The President himself, this spokesman said, had been somewhat uncertain as to whether his inherent powers extended to the steel case but he had been forced to take action by the crisis and had asked Congress to resolve the uncertainty.) Also on May 22, President Truman announced the settlement of the railway dispute of 1950 and the return of the railroads to their owners. By this time, the Gallup Poll showed that 43% of their national sample disapproved of the steel seizure, 35% approved and 22% had no opinion. The Gallup figures also confirmed Truman's analysis that lower income groups were supporting him, since a separate poll of manual workers showed 40% approval to 37% disapproval.

On June 2, 20 days after the close of oral argument, the Supreme Court handed down its ruling. The Court convened at noon and Chief Justice Vinson announced that the admission of attorneys would be deferred until later. Justice Hugo Black began reading the majority opinion at 12:01, holding that the seizure was unlawful. The Black opinion was followed by a 30 minute recitation by Justice Frankfurter, concurring. (In the course of his reading, typical of the asides in oral delivery, Justice Frankfurter commented on the dissenter's use of a quotation from a 1914 brief by John W. Davis, then Solicitor General of the United States, upholding seizure power. Said Frankfurter: "I don't understand the relevance of quoting the brief of a lawyer in a case . . . with the well-known astigmatism of advocates.") The other concurring opinions were read, then Chief Justice Vinson read his opinion for the three dissenters. During his delivery, Vinson referred to the pro-seizure views of Jackson and Clark when they had been Attorneys-General, remarking that he "supposed" it was "evidence of strength" to depart in this case from the views they "ordinarily" held as to presidential powers. Reading of the Vinson opinion continued past the luncheon hour and ended at 2:35, when the Court recessed. Within minutes, news of the seizure's invalidation was on the radio and the afternoon editions carried the headlines across the nation.

Opinions of the Justices

THE YOUNGSTOWN SHEET AND TUBE COMPANY,

et al., PETITIONERS,

v.

CHARLES SAWYER.[1]

June 2, 1952

MR. JUSTICE BLACK delivered the opinion of the Court.

We were asked to decide whether the President was acting within his constitutional power when he issued an order directing the Secretary of Commerce to take possession of and operate most of the

[1] Since the various opinions in this case fill 131 pages in the *United States Reports*, it has been necessary to present them in edited form. For the full texts, see 343 U.S. 579–710 (1952).

nation's steel mills. The mill owners argue that the President's order amounts to law-making, a legislative function which the Constitution has expressly confided to the Congress and not to the President. The Government's position is that the order was made on findings of the President that his action was necessary to avert a national catastrophe which would inevitably result from a stoppage of steel production, and that in meeting this grave emergency the President was acting within the aggregate of his constitutional powers as the Nation's Chief Executive and the Commander in Chief of the Armed Forces of the United States. . . . [Here Justice Black sketched the history of the steel dispute, the seizure, and the court proceedings.]

Two crucial issues have developed: *First.* Should final determination of the constitutional validity of the President's order be made in this case which has proceeded no further than the preliminary injunction stage? *Second.* If so, is the seizure order within the constitutional power of the President?

I.

It is urged that there were non-constitutional grounds upon which the District Court could have denied the preliminary injunction and thus have followed the customary judicial practice of declining to reach and decide constitutional questions until compelled to do so. On this basis it is argued that equity's extraordinary injunctive relief should have been denied because (a) seizure of the companies' properties did not inflict irreparable damages, and (b) there were available legal remedies adequate to afford compensation for any possible damages which they might suffer. While separately argued by the Government, these two contentions are here closely related, if not identical. Arguments as to both rest in large part on the Government's claim that should the seizure ultimately be held unlawful, the companies could recover full compensation in the Court of Claims for the unlawful taking. Prior cases in this Court have cast doubt on the right to recover in the Court of Claims on account of properties unlawfully taken by government officials for public use as these properties were alleged to have been. See *e.g., Hooe v. United States,* 218 U.S. 322, 335–336; *United States v. North American Co.,* 253 U.S. 330, 333. But see *Larson v. Domestic & Foreign Corp.,* 337 U.S. 682, 701–702. Moreover, seizure and governmental operation of these going businesses were bound to result in many present and future damages of such nature as to be difficult, if not incapable, of measurement. Viewing the case this way, and in the light of the facts presented, the District Court saw no reason for delaying decision of the constitutional validity of the orders. We agree with the District Court and can see no reason why that question was not ripe for determination on the record presented. We shall therefore consider and determine that question now.

II.

The President's power, if any, to issue the order must stem either from an act of Congress or from the Constitution itself. There is no statute that expressly authorizes the President to take possession of property as he did here. Nor is there any act of Congress to which our attention has been directed from which such a power can fairly be implied. Indeed, we do not understand the Government to rely on statutory authorization for this seizure. There are two statutes [The Selective Service Act of 1948 and the Defense Production Act of 1950] which do authorize the President to take both personal and real property under certain conditions. However, the Government admits that these conditions were not met and that the President's order was not rooted in either of the statutes. The Government refers to the seizure provisions of one of these statutes (§201 (b) of the Defense Production Act) as "much too cumbersome, involved, and time-consuming for the crisis which was at hand."

Moreover, the use of the seizure technique to solve labor disputes in order to prevent work stoppages was not only unauthorized by any congressional enactment; prior to this controversy, Congress had refused to adopt that method of settling labor disputes. When the Taft-Hartley Act was under consideration in 1947, Congress rejected an amendment which would have authorized such governmental seizures in cases of emergency. Apparently it was thought that the technique of seizure, like that of compulsory arbitration, would interfere with the process of collective bargaining. Consequently, the plan Congress adopted in that Act did not provide for seizure under any circumstances. Instead, the plan sought to bring about settlements by use of the customary devices of mediation, conciliation, investigation by boards of inquiry, and public reports. In some instances temporary injunctions were authorized to provide cooling-off periods. All this failing, the unions were left free to strike if the majority of the employees, by secret ballot, expressed a desire to do so.

It is clear that if the President had authority to issue the order he did, it must be found in some provisions of the Constitution. And it is not claimed that express constitutional language grants this power to the President. The contention is that presidential power should be implied from the aggregate of his powers under the Constitution. Particular reliance is placed on provisions in Article II which say that "the executive Power shall be vested in a President . . ."; that "he shall take Care that the Laws be faithfully executed"; and that "he shall be Commander in Chief of the Army and Navy of the United States."

The order cannot properly be sustained as an exercise of the President's military power as Commander in Chief of the Armed Forces. The Government attempts to do so by citing a number of cases upholding broad powers in military commanders engaged in day-to-day fighting in a theater of war. Such cases need not concern us here. Even though "theater of war" be an expanding concept, we cannot with faithfulness to our constitutional system hold that the Commander in Chief of the Armed Forces has the ultimate power as such to take possession of private property in order to keep labor disputes from stopping production. This is a job for the Nation's lawmakers, not for its military authorities.

Nor can the seizure order be sustained because of the several con-

stitutional provisions that grant executive power to the President.
In the framework of our Constitution, the President's power to see
that the laws are faithfully executed refutes the idea that he is to
be a lawmaker. The Constitution limits his functions in the law-
making process to the recommending of laws he thinks wise and the
vetoing of laws he thinks bad. And the Constitution is neither silent
nor equivocal about who shall make laws which the President is to
execute. The first section of the first article says that "All legislative
Powers herein granted shall be vested in a Congress of the United
States. . . ." After granting many powers to the Congress, Article I
goes on to provide that Congress may "make all Laws which shall be
necessary and proper for carrying into Execution the foregoing
Powers and all other Powers vested by this Constitution in the
Government of the United States, or in any Department or Officer
thereof."

The President's order does not direct that a congressional policy
be executed in a manner prescribed by Congress—it directs that a
presidential policy be executed in a manner prescribed by the President. The preamble of the order itself, like that of many statutes,
sets out reasons why the President believes certain policies should be
adopted, proclaims these policies as rules of conduct to be followed,
and again, like a statute, authorizes a government official to promul-
gate additional rules and regulations consistent with the policy proclaimed and needed to carry that policy into execution. The power
of Congress to adopt such public policies as those proclaimed by the
order is beyond question. It can authorize the taking of private
property for public use. It can make laws regulating the relationships
between employers and employees, prescribing rules designed to settle
labor disputes, and fixing wages and working conditions in certain
fields of our economy. The Constitution does not subject this law-
making power of Congress to presidential or military supervision or
control.

It is said that other Presidents without congressional authority
have taken possession of private business enterprises in order to settle

labor disputes. But even if this be true, Congress has not thereby lost its exclusive constitutional authority to make laws necessary and proper to carry out the powers vested by the Constitution "in the Government of the United States, or any Department or Officer thereof."

The Founders of this Nation entrusted the lawmaking power to the Congress alone in both good and bad times. It would do no good to recall the historical events, the fears of power and the hopes for freedom that lay behind their choice. Such a review would but confirm our holding that this seizure order cannot stand.

The judgment of the District Court is

Affirmed.

MR. JUSTICE FRANKFURTER, concurring. . . .

Although the considerations relevant to the legal enforcement of the principle of separation of powers seems to me more complicated and flexible than may appear from what MR. JUSTICE BLACK has written, I join his opinion because I thoroughly agree with the application of the principle to the circumstances of this case. Even though such differences in attitude toward this principle may be merely differences in emphasis and nuance, they can hardly be reflected by a single opinion for the Court. Individual expression of views in reaching a common result is therefore important. . . .

[O]ur first inquiry must be not into the powers of the President, but into the powers of a District Judge to issue a temporary injunction in the circumstances of this case. Familiar as that remedy is, it remains an extraordinary remedy. To start with a consideration of the relation between the President's powers and those of Congress—a most delicate matter that has occupied the thoughts of statesmen and judges since the Nation was founded and will continue to occupy their thoughts as long as our democracy lasts—is to start at the wrong end. A plaintiff is not entitled to an injunction if money damages would fairly compensate him for any wrong he may have suffered. The same considerations by which the Steelworkers, in their brief *amicus*, demonstrate, from the seizure here in controversy, consequences that cannot be translated into dollars and cents, preclude a holding that only compensable damage for the plaintiffs is involved. Again, a court of equity ought not to issue an injunction, even though a plaintiff otherwise makes out a case for it, if the plaintiff's right to an injunction is overborne by a commanding public interest against it. One need not resort to a large epigrammatic generalization that the evils of industrial dislocation are to be preferred to allowing illegality to go unchecked. To deny inquiry into the President's power in a case like this, because of the damage to the public interest to be feared from upsetting its exercise by him would in effect always preclude inquiry into challenged power, which presumably only avowed great public interest brings into action. And so, with the utmost unwillingness, with every desire to avoid judicial inquiry into the powers and duties of the other two branches of the government, I cannot escape consideration of the legality of Executive Order No. 10340. . . .

The issue before us can be met, and therefore should be, without attempting to define the President's powers comprehensively. I shall not attempt to delineate what belongs to him by virtue of his office beyond the power even of Congress to contract; what authority belongs to him until Congress acts; what kind of problems may be dealt with either by the Congress or by the President or by both, cf. *La Abra Silver Mine Co. v. United States*, 175 U.S. 423; what power must be exercised by the Congress and cannot be delegated to the President. It is as unprofitable to lump together in an undiscriminating hotch-potch past presidential actions claimed to be derived from occupancy of the office, as it is to conjure up hypothetical future cases. The judiciary may, as this case proves, have to intervene in determining where authority lies as between the democratic forces in our scheme of government. But in doing so we should be wary and humble. Such is the teaching of this Court's rôle in the history of the country. . . .

The question before the Court comes in this setting. Congress has frequently—at least 16 times since 1916—specifically provided for executive seizure of production, transportation, communications, or storage facilities. In every case it has qualified this grant of power with limitations and safeguards. This body of enactments—summarized in tabular form in Appendix I—demonstrates that Congress deemed seizure so drastic a power as to require that it be carefully circumscribed whenever the President was vested with this extraordinary authority. The power to seize has uniformly been given only for a limited period or for a defined emergency, or has been repealed after a short period. Its exercise has been restricted to particular circumstances such as "time of war or when war is imminent," the needs of "public safety" or of "national security or defense," or "urgent and impending need." The period of governmental operation has been limited, as, for instance, to "sixty days after the restoration of productive efficiency." Seizure statutes usually make executive action dependent on detailed conditions: for example, (a) failure or refusal of the owner of a plant to meet governmental supply needs or (b) failure of voluntary negotiations with the owner for the use of a plant necessary for great public ends. Congress often has specified the particular executive agency which should seize or operate the plants or whose judgment would appropriately test the need for seizure. Congress also has not left to implication that just compensation be paid; it has usually legislated in detail regarding enforcement of this litigation-breeding general requirement.

Congress in 1947 was again called upon to consider whether governmental seizure should be used to avoid serious industrial shutdowns. Congress decided against conferring such power generally and in advance, without special congressional enactment to meet each particular need. Under the urgency of telephone and coal strikes in the winter of 1946, Congress addressed itself to the problems raised by "national emergency" strikes and lockouts. The termination of war-time seizure powers on December 31, 1946, brought these matters to the attention of Congress with vivid impact. A proposal that the President be given powers to seize plants to avert a shutdown where the "health or safety" of the nation was endangered, was thoroughly canvassed by Congress and rejected. No room for doubt remains that the proponents as well as the opponents of the bill which became the Labor Management Relations Act of 1947 clearly understood that as a result of that legislation the only recourse for preventing a shutdown in any basic industry, after failure of mediation, was Congress. Authorization for seizure as an available remedy for potential dangers was unequivocally put aside. . . . But it is now claimed that the President has seizure power by virtue of the Defense Production Act of 1950 and its Amendments. And the claim is based on the occurrence of new events—Korea and the need for stabilization, etc.—although it was well known that seizure power was withheld by the Act of 1947, and although the President, whose specific requests for other authority were in the main granted by Congress, never suggested that in view of the new events he needed the power of seizure which Congress in its judgment had decided to withhold from him. The utmost that the Korean conflict may imply is that it may have been desirable to have given the President further authority, a freer hand in these matters. Absence of authority in the President to deal with a crisis does not imply want of power in the Government. Conversely the fact that power exists in the Government does not vest it in the President. The need for new legislation does not enact it. Nor does it repeal or amend existing law. . . . The Defense Production Act affords no ground for the suggestion that the 1947 denial to the President of seizure powers has been impliedly repealed, and its legislative history contradicts such a suggestion. Although the proponents of that Act recognized that the President would have a choice of alternative methods of seeking a mediated settlement, they also recognized that Congress alone retained the ultimate coercive power to meet the threat of "any serious work stoppage." . . . In considering the Defense Production Act Amendments, Congress was never asked to approve—and there is not the slightest indication that the responsible committees ever had in mind—seizure of plants to coerce settlement of disputes. . . .

It is one thing to draw an intention of Congress from general language and to say that Congress would have explicitly written what is inferred, where Congress has not addressed itself to a specific situation. It is quite impossible, however, when Congress did specifically address itself to a problem, as Congress did to that of seizure, to find secreted in the interstices of legislation the very grant of power which Congress consciously withheld. To find authority so explicitly withheld is not merely to disregard in a particular instance the clear will of Congress. It is to disrespect the whole legislative process and the constitutional division of authority between President and Congress.

The legislative history here canvassed is relevant to yet another of the issues before us, namely, the Government's argument that overriding public interest prevents the issuance of the injunction despite the illegality of the seizure. I cannot accept that contention. "Balancing the equities" when considering whether an injunction should issue, is lawyers' jargon for choosing between conflicting public interests. When Congress itself has struck the balance, has defined the weight to be given the competing interests, a court of equity is not justified in ignoring that pronouncement under the guise of exercising equitable discretion.

Apart from his vast share of responsibility for the conduct of our foreign relations, the embracing function of the President is that "he shall take Care that the Laws be faithfully executed. . . ." Art. II, §3. The nature of that authority has for me been comprehensively indicated by Mr. Justice Holmes. "The duty of the President to see that the laws be executed is a duty that does not go beyond the laws or require him to achieve more than Congress sees fit to leave within his power." *Myers v. United States,* 272 U.S. 52, 177. The powers of the President are not as particularized as are those of Congress. But unenumerated powers do not mean undefined powers. The separation of powers built into our Constitution gives essential content to undefined provisions in the frame of our government.

To be sure, the content of the three authorities of government is not to be derived from an abstract analysis. The areas are partly interacting, not wholly disjointed. The Constitution is a framework for government. Therefore the way the framework has consistently operated fairly establishes that it has operated according to its true nature. . . . In the *Midwest Oil* case lands which Congress had opened for entry were, over a period of 80 years and in 252 instances, and by Presidents learned and unlearned in the law, temporarily withdrawn from entry so as to enable Congress to deal with such withdrawals. No remotely comparable practice can be vouched for executive seizure of property at a time when this country was not at war, in the only constitutional way in which it can be at war. It would pursue the irrelevant to re-open the controversy over the constitutionality of some acts of Lincoln during the Civil War. See J. G. Randall, Constitutional Problems under Lincoln (Revised ed. 1951). Suffice it to say that he seized railroads in territory where armed hostilities had already interrupted the movement of troops to the beleaguered Capitol, and his order was ratified by Congress.

The only other instances of seizures are those during the periods of the first and second World Wars. In his eleven seizures of industrial facilities, President Wilson acted, or at least purported to act, under authority granted by Congress. Thus his seizures cannot be adduced as interpretations by a President of his own power in the absence of statute.

Down to the World War II period, then, the record is barren of instances comparable to the one before us. Of twelve seizures by President Roosevelt prior to the enactment of the War Labor Disputes Act in June, 1943, three were sanctioned by existing law, and six others were effected after Congress, on December 8, 1941, had declared the existence of a state of war. In this case, reliance on the powers that flow from declared war has been commendably disclaimed by the Solicitor General. Thus the list of executive assertions of the power of seizure in circumstances comparable to the present reduces to three in the six-month period from June to December of 1941. We need not split hairs in comparing those actions to the one before us, though much might be said by way of differentiation. Without passing on their validity, as we are not called upon to do, it suffices to say that these three isolated instances do not add up, either in number, scope, duration or contemporaneous legal justification, to the kind of executive construction of the Constitution revealed in the *Midwest Oil* case. Nor do they come to us sanctioned by long-continued acquiescence of Congress giving decisive weight to a construction by the Executive of its powers.

A scheme of government like ours no doubt at times feels the lack of power to act with complete, all-embracing, swiftly moving authority. No doubt a government with distributed authority, subject to be challenged in the courts of law, at least long enough to consider and adjudicate the challenge, labors under restrictions from which other governments are free. It has not been our tradition to envy such governments. In any event our government was designed to have such restrictions. The price was deemed not too high in view of the safeguards which these restrictions afford. I know no more impressive words on this subject than those of Mr. Justice Brandeis:

> "The doctrine of the separation of powers was adopted by the Convention of 1787, not to promote efficiency but to preclude the exercise of arbitrary power. The purpose was, not to avoid friction, but, by means of the inevitable friction incident to the distribution of the governmental powers among three departments, to save the people from autocracy." *Myers v. United States,* 272 U.S. 52, 240, 293. . . .

MR. JUSTICE DOUGLAS, concurring. . . .

We . . . cannot decide this case by determining which branch of government can deal most expeditiously with the present crisis. The answer must depend on the allocation of powers under the Constitution. That in turn requires an analysis of the conditions giving rise to the seizure and of the seizure itself.

The relations between labor and industry are one of the crucial problems of the era. . . . The method by which industrial peace is achieved is of vital importance not only to the parties but to society as well. A determination that sanctions should be applied, that the hand of the law should be placed upon the parties, and that the force of the courts should be directed against them, is an exercise of legislative power. In some nations that power is entrusted to the executive branch as a matter of course or in case of emergencies. We chose another course. We chose to place the legislative power of the Federal Government in the Congress. The language of the Constitution is not ambiguous or qualified. It places not *some* legislative power in the Congress; Article I, Section 1 says "All legislative Powers herein granted shall be vested in a Congress of the United States, which shall consist of a Senate and House of Representatives."

The legislative nature of the action taken by the President seems to me to be clear. When the United States takes over an industrial plant to settle a labor controversy, it is condemning property. The seizure of the plant is a taking in the constitutional sense. *United States v. Pewee Coal Co.*, 341 U.S. 114. A permanent taking would amount to the nationalization of the industry. A temporary taking falls short of that goal. But though the seizure is only for a week or a month, the condemnation is complete and the United States must pay compensation for the temporary possession. *United States v. General Motors Corp.*, 323 U.S. 373; *United States v. Pewee Coal Co., supra.*

The power of the Federal Government to condemn property is well established. *Kohl v. United States*, 91 U.S. 367. It can condemn for any public purpose; and I have no doubt but that condemnation of a plant, factory, or industry in order to promote industrial peace would be constitutional. But there is a duty to pay for all property taken by the Government. The command of the Fifth Amendment is that no "private property be taken for public use, without just compensation." That constitutional requirement has an important bearing on the present case.

The President has no power to raise revenues. That power is in the Congress by Article I, Section 8 of the Constitution. The President might seize and the Congress by subsequent action might ratify the seizure. But until and unless Congress acted, no condemnation would be lawful. The branch of government that has the power to pay compensation for a seizure is the only one able to authorize a seizure or make lawful one that the President had effected. . . .

The great office of President is not a weak and powerless one. The President represents the people and is their spokesman in domestic and foreign affairs. The office is respected more than any other in the land. It gives a position of leadership that is unique. The power to formulate policies and mould opinion inheres in the Presidency and conditions our national life. The impact of the man and the philosophy he represents may at times be thwarted by the Congress. Stalemates may occur when emergencies mount and the Nation suffers for lack of harmonious, reciprocal action between the White House and Capitol Hill. That is a risk inherent in our system of separation of powers. The tragedy of such stalemates might be avoided by allowing the President the use of some legislative authority. The Framers with memories of the tyrannies produced by a blending of executive and legislative power rejected that political arrangement. Some future generation may, however, deem it so urgent that the President have legislative authority that the Constitution will be amended. We could not sanction the seizures and condemnations of the steel plants in this case without reading Article II as giving the President not only the power to execute the laws but to make some. Such a step would most assuredly alter the pattern of the Constitution.

We pay a price for our system of checks and balances, for the distribution of power among the three branches of government. It is a price that today may seem exorbitant to many. Today a kindly President uses the seizure power to effect a wage increase and to keep the steel furnaces in production. Yet tomorrow another President might use the same power to prevent a wage increase, to curb trade unionists, to regiment labor as oppressively as industry thinks it has been regimented by this seizure.

MR. JUSTICE JACKSON, concurring in the judgment and opinion of the Court. . . .

A judge, like an executive adviser, may be surprised at the poverty of really useful and unambiguous authority applicable to concrete problems of executive power as they actually present themselves. Just what our forefathers did envision, or would have envisioned had they foreseen modern conditions, must be divined from materials almost as enigmatic as the dreams Joseph was called upon to interpret for Pharaoh. A century and a half of partisan debate and scholarly speculation yields no net result but only supplies more or less apt quotations from respected sources on each side of any question. They largely cancel each other. And court decisions are indecisive because of the judicial practice of dealing with the largest questions in the most narrow way. . . . We may well begin by a somewhat over-simplified grouping of practical situations in which a President may doubt, or others may challenge, his powers, and by distinguishing roughly the legal consequences of this factor of relativity.

1. When the President acts pursuant to an express or implied authorization of Congress, his authority is at its maximum, for it includes all that he possesses in his own right plus all that Congress can delegate. In these circumstances, and in these only, may he be said (for what it may be worth), to personify the federal sovereignty. If his act is held unconstitutional under these circumstances, it usually means that the Federal Government as an undivided whole lacks power. A seizure executed by the President pursuant to an Act of Congress would be supported by the strongest of presumptions and the widest latitude of judicial interpretation, and the burden of persuasion would rest heavily upon any who might attack it.

2. When the President acts in absence of either a congressional grant or denial of authority, he can only rely upon his own independent powers, but there is a zone of twilight in which he and Congress may have concurrent authority, or in which its distribution is uncertain. Therefore, congressional inertia, indifference or quies-

cence may sometimes, at least as a practical matter, enable, if not invite, measures on independent presidential responsibility. In this area, any actual test of power is likely to depend on the imperatives of events and contemporary imponderables rather than on abstract theories of law.

3. When the President takes measures incompatible with the expressed or implied will of Congress, his power is at its lowest ebb, for then he can rely only upon his own constitutional powers minus any constitutional powers of Congress over the matter. Courts can sustain exclusive Presidential control in such a case only by disabling the Congress from acting upon the subject. Presidential claim to a power at once so conclusive and preclusive must be scrutinized with caution, for what is at stake is the equilibrium established by our constitutional system.

Into which of these classifications does this executive seizure of the steel industry fit? It is eliminated from the first by admission, for it is conceded that no congressional authorization exists for this seizure. That takes away also the support of the many precedents and declarations which were made in relation, and must be confined, to this category.

Can it then be defended under flexible tests available to the second category? It seems clearly eliminated from that class because Congress has not left seizure of private property an open field but has covered it by three statutory policies inconsistent with this seizure. In cases where the purpose is to supply needs of the Government itself, two courses are provided: one, seizure of a plant which fails to comply with obligatory orders placed by the Government, another, condemnation of facilities, including temporary use under the power of eminent domain. The third is applicable where it is the general economy of the country that is to be protected rather than exclusive governmental interests. None of these were invoked. In choosing a different and inconsistent way of his own, the President cannot claim that it is necessitated or invited by failure of Congress to legislate upon the occasions, grounds and methods for seizure of industrial properties.

This leaves the current seizure to be justified only by the severe tests under the third grouping, where it can be supported only by any remainder of executive power after subtraction of such powers as Congress may have over the subject. In short, we can sustain the President only by holding that seizure of such strike-bound industries is within his domain and beyond control by Congress. Thus, this Court's first review of such seizures occurs under circumstances which leave Presidential power most vulnerable to attack and in the least favorable of possible constitutional postures. . . .

The Solicitor General seeks the power of seizure in three clauses of the Executive Article, the first reading, "The Executive Power shall be vested in a President of the United States of America." . . . I cannot accept the view that this clause is a grant in bulk of all conceivable executive power but regard it as an allocation to the presidential office of generic powers thereafter stated.

The clause on which the Government next relies is that "The President shall be Commander in Chief of the Army and Navy of the United States. . . ."

. . . Assuming that we are in a war *de facto*, whether it is or is not a war *de jure*, does that empower the Commander-in-Chief to seize industries he thinks necessary to supply our army? The Constitution expressly places in Congress power "to raise and *support* Armies" and "to *provide* and *maintain* a Navy." (Emphasis supplied.) This certainly lays upon Congress primary responsibility for supplying the armed forces. Congress alone controls the raising of revenues and their appropriation and may determine in what manner and by what means they shall be spent for military and naval procurement. . . .

We should not use this occasion to circumscribe, much less to contract, the lawful role of the President as Commander-in-Chief. I should indulge the widest latitude of interpretation to sustain his exclusive function to command the instruments of national force, at least when turned against the outside world for the security of our society. But, when it is turned inward, not because of rebellion but because of a lawful economic struggle between industry and labor, it should have no such indulgence. . . .

The third clause in which the Solicitor General finds seizure powers is that "he shall take Care that the Laws be faithfully executed. . . ." That authority must be matched against words of the Fifth Amendment that "No person shall be . . . deprived of life, liberty or property, without due process of law. . . ." One gives a governmental authority that reaches so far as there is law, the other gives a private right that authority shall go no farther. These signify about all there is of the principle that ours is a government of laws, not of men, and that we submit ourselves to rulers only if under rules.

The Solicitor General lastly grounds support of the seizure upon nebulous, inherent powers never expressly granted but said to have accrued to the office from the customs and claims of preceding administrations. The plea is for a resulting power to deal with a crisis or an emergency according to the necessities of the case, the unarticulated assumption being that necessity knows no law. . . .

The Solicitor General, acknowledging that Congress has never authorized the seizure here, says practice of prior Presidents has authorized it. He seeks color of legality from claimed executive precedents, chief of which is President Roosevelt's seizure on June 9, 1941, of the California plant of the North American Aviation Company. Its superficial similarities with the present case, upon analysis, yield to distinctions so decisive that it cannot be regarded as even a precedent, much less an authority for the present seizure.[1]

---

[1] The North American Aviation Company was under direct and binding contracts to supply defense items to the Government. No such contracts are claimed to exist here. Seizure of plants which refused to comply with Government orders had been expressly authorized by Congress in §9 of the Selective Service Act of 1940, 54 Stat. 885, 892, so that the seizure of the North American plant was entirely consistent with congressional policy. The company might have objected on technical grounds to the seizure, but it was taken over with acquiescence, amounting to all but consent, of the owners who had admitted that the situation was beyond their control. The strike involved in the *North American* case was in violation of the union's collective agreement and the national labor leaders approved the seizure to end the strike. It was described as in the nature of an insurrection, a Communist-led political strike against the Government's lend-lease policy. Here we have only a loyal, lawful, but regrettable economic disagreement between management and labor. The North American plant contained government-owned machinery, material and goods in the process of production to which workmen were forcibly denied access by picketing strikers. Here no Government property is protected by the seizure. . . . [Footnote by the Justice.]

The appeal, however, that we declare the existence of inherent powers *ex necessitate* to meet an emergency asks us to do what many think would be wise, although it is something the forefathers omitted. They knew what emergencies were, knew the pressures they engender for authoritative action, knew, too, how they afford a ready pretext for usurpation. We may also suspect that they suspected that emergency powers would tend to kindle emergencies. . . .

In the practical working of our Government we already have evolved a technique within the framework of the Constitution by which normal executive powers may be considerably expanded to meet an emergency. Congress may and has granted extraordinary authorities which lie dormant in normal times but may be called into play by the Executive in war or upon proclamation of a national emergency. In 1939, upon congressional request, the Attorney General listed ninety-nine such separate statutory grants by Congress of emergency or war-time executive powers. They were invoked from time to time as need appeared. Under this procedure we retain Government by law—special, temporary law, perhaps, but law nonetheless. The public may know the extent and limitations of the powers that can be asserted, and persons affected may be informed from the statute of their rights and duties.

In view of the ease, expedition and safety with which Congress can grant and has granted large emergency powers, certainly ample to embrace this crisis, I am quite unimpressed with the argument that we should affirm possession of them without statute. Such power either has no beginning or it has no end. If it exists, it need submit to no legal restraint. I am not alarmed that it would plunge us straightway into dictatorship, but it is at least a step in that wrong direction.

As to whether there is imperative necessity for such powers, it is relevant to note the gap that exists between the President's paper powers and his real powers. The Constitution does not disclose the measure of the actual controls wielded by the modern presidential office. That instrument must be understood as an Eighteenth-Century sketch of a government hoped for, not as a blueprint of the Government that is. Vast accretions of federal power, eroded from that reserved by the States, have magnified the scope of presidential activity. Subtle shifts take place in the centers of real power that do not show on the face of the Constitution.

Executive power has the advantage of concentration in a single head in whose choice the whole Nation has a part, making him the focus of public hopes and expectations. In drama, magnitude and finality his decisions so far overshadow any others that almost alone he fills the public eye and ear. No other personality in public life can begin to compete with him in access to the public mind through modern methods of communications. By his prestige as head of state and his influence upon public opinion he exerts a leverage upon those who are supposed to check and balance his power which often cancels their effectiveness.

Moreover, rise of the party system has made a significant extra-constitutional supplement to real executive power. No appraisal of his necessities is realistic which overlooks that he heads a political system as well as a legal system. Party loyalties and interests, sometimes more binding than law, extend his effective control into branches of government other than his own and he often may win, as a political leader, what he cannot command under the Constitution. Indeed, Woodrow Wilson, commenting on the President as leader both of his party and of the Nation, observed, "If he rightly interpret the national thought and boldly insist upon it he is irresistible. . . . His office is anything he has the sagacity and force to make it." I cannot be brought to believe that this country will suffer if the Court refuses further to aggrandize the presidential office, already so potent and so relatively immune from judicial review, at the expense of Congress. . . .

MR. JUSTICE BURTON, concurring in both the opinion and judgment of the Court. . . .

The controlling fact here is that Congress, within its constitutionally delegated power, has prescribed for the President specific procedures, exclusive of seizure, for his use in meeting the present type of emergency. Congress has reserved to itself the right to determine where and when to authorize the seizure of property in meeting such an emergency. Under these circumstances, the President's order of April 8 invaded the jurisdiction of Congress. It violated the essence of the principle of the separation of governmental powers. Accordingly, the injunction against its effectiveness should be sustained.

MR. JUSTICE CLARK, concurring in the judgment of the Court. . . .

I conclude that where Congress has laid down specific procedures to deal with the type of crisis confronting the President, he must follow those procedures in meeting the crisis; but that in the absence of such action by Congress, the President's independent power to act depends upon the gravity of the situation confronting the nation. I cannot sustain the seizure in question because here, as in *Little v. Barreme*, Congress had prescribed methods to be followed by the President in meeting the emergency at hand.

Three statutory procedures were available: those provided in the Defense Production Act of 1950, the Labor Management Relations Act, and the Selective Service Act of 1948. In this case the President invoked the first of these procedures; he did not invoke the other two. . . .

These three statutes furnish the guideposts for decision in this case. Prior to seizing the steel mills on April 8 the President had exhausted the mediation procedures of the Defense Production Act through the Wage Stabilization Board. Use of those procedures had failed to avert the impending crisis; however, it had resulted in a 99-day postponement of the strike. The Government argues that this accomplished more than the maximum 80-day waiting period possible under the sanctions of the Taft-Hartley Act, and therefore amounted to compliance with the substance of that Act. Even if one were to accept this somewhat hyperbolic conclusion, the hard fact remains that neither the Defense Production Act nor Taft-Hartley authorized the seizure challenged here, and the Government made no effort to comply with the procedures established by the Selective Service Act of 1948, a statute which expressly authorizes seizures when producers fail to supply necessary defense matériel.

For these reasons I concur in the judgment of the Court. . . .

MR. CHIEF JUSTICE VINSON, with whom MR. JUSTICE REED and MR. JUSTICE MINTON join, dissenting. . . .

I.

In passing upon the question of Presidential powers in this case, we must first consider the context in which those powers were exercised.

Those who suggest that this is a case involving extraordinary powers should be mindful that these are extraordinary times. A world not yet recovered from the devastation of World War II has been forced to face the threat of another and more terrifying global conflict.

Accepting in full measure its responsibility in the world community, the United States was instrumental in securing adoption of the United Nations Charter, approved by the Senate by a vote of 89 to 2. The first purpose of the United Nations is to "maintain international peace and security, and to that end: to take effective collective measures for the prevention and removal of threats to the peace, and for the suppression of acts of aggression or other breaches of the peace, ..." In 1950, when the United Nations called upon member nations "to render every assistance" to repel aggression in Korea, the United States furnished its vigorous support. For almost two full years, our armed forces have been fighting in Korea, suffering casualties of over 108,000 men. Hostilities have not abated. The "determination of the United Nations to continue its action in Korea to meet the aggression" has been reaffirmed. Congressional support of the action in Korea has been manifested by provisions for increased military manpower and equipment and for economic stabilization, as hereinafter described.

Further efforts to protect the free world from aggression are found in the congressional enactments of the Truman Plan for assistance to Greece and Turkey and the Marshall Plan for economic aid needed to build up the strength of our friends in Western Europe. In 1949, the Senate approved the North Atlantic Treaty under which each member nation agrees that an armed attack against one is an armed attack against all. Congress immediately implemented the North Atlantic Treaty by authorizing military assistance to nations dedicated to the principles of mutual security under the United Nations Charter. The concept of mutual security recently has been extended by treaty to friends in the Pacific.

Our treaties represent not merely legal obligations but show congressional recognition that mutual security for the free world is the best security against the threat of aggression on a global scale. The need for mutual security is shown by the very size of the armed forces outside the free world. Defendant's brief informs us that the Soviet Union maintains the largest air force in the world and maintains ground forces much larger than those presently available to the United States and the countries joined with us in mutual security arrangements. Constant international tensions are cited to demonstrate how precarious is the peace. . . . Following the attack in Korea, the President asked for authority to requisition property and to allocate and fix priorities for scarce goods. In the Defense Production Act of 1950, Congress granted the powers requested and, *in addition,* granted power to stabilize prices and wages and to provide for settlement of labor disputes arising in the defense program. The Defense Production Act was extended in 1951, a Senate Committee noting that in the dislocation caused by the programs for purchase of military equipment "lies the seed of an economic disaster that might well destroy the military might we are straining to build." Significantly, the Committee examined the problem "in terms of just one commodity, steel," and found "a graphic picture of the over-all inflationary danger growing out of reduced civilian supplies and rising incomes." Even before Korea, steel production at levels above theoretical 100% capacity was not capable of supplying civilian needs alone. Since Korea, the tremendous military demand for steel has far exceeded the increases in productive capacity. This Committee emphasized that the shortage of steel, even with the mills operating at full capacity, coupled with increased civilian purchasing power, presented grave danger of disastrous inflation. . . . [Here, Chief Justice Vinson sketched the history of the steel dispute, quoted the seizure order and President Truman's messages to Congress, described the lower court proceedings, and stressed the affidavits filed in court by executive officials warning of the danger of a strike to the defense and foreign policies of the nation.]

One is not here called upon even to consider the possibility of executive seizure of a farm, a corner grocery store or even a single industrial plant. Such considerations arise only when one ignores the central fact of this case—that the Nation's entire basic steel production would have shut down completely if there had been no Government seizure. Even ignoring for the moment whatever confidential information the President may possess as "the Nation's organ for foreign affairs," the uncontroverted affidavits in this record amply support the finding that "a work stoppage would immediately jeopardize and imperil our national defense."

Plaintiffs do not remotely suggest any basis for rejecting the President's finding that *any* stoppage of steel production would immediately place the Nation in peril. Moreover, even self-generated doubts that *any* stoppage of steel production constitutes an emergency are of little comfort here. The Union and the plaintiffs bargained for 6 months with over 100 issues in dispute—issues not limited to wage demands but including the union shop and other matters of principle between the parties. At the time of seizure there was not, and there is not now, the slightest evidence to justify the belief that any strike will be of short duration. The Union and the steel companies may well engage in a lengthy struggle. Plaintiff's counsel tells us that "sooner or later" the mills will operate again. That may satisfy the steel companies and, perhaps, the Union. But our soldiers and our allies will hardly be cheered with the assurance that the ammunition upon which their lives depend will be forthcoming— "sooner or later," or, in other words, "too little and too late."

Accordingly, if the President has any power under the Constitution to meet a critical situation in the absence of express statutory authorization, there is no basis whatever for criticizing the exercise of such power in this case. . . .

II. [omitted] . . .

III.

A review of executive action demonstrates that our Presidents have on many occasions exhibited the leadership contemplated by the Framers when they made the President Commander in Chief, and imposed upon him the trust to "take Care that the Laws be faithfully executed." With or without explicit statutory authorization, Presidents have at such times dealt with national emergencies by acting promptly and resolutely to enforce legislative programs, at least to save those programs until Congress could act. Congress and the courts have responded to such executive initiative with consistent approval.

Our first President displayed at once the leadership contemplated by the Framers. When the national revenue laws were openly flouted in some sections of Pennsylvania, President Washington, without waiting for a call from the state government, summoned the militia and took decisive steps to secure the faithful execution of the laws. When international disputes engendered by the French revolution threatened to involve this country in war, and while congressional policy remained uncertain, Washington issued his Proclamation of Neutrality. . . .

President John Adams issued a warrant for the arrest of Jonathan Robbins in order to execute the extradition provisions of a treaty.

This action was challenged in Congress on the ground that no specific statute prescribed the method to be used in executing the treaty. John Marshall, then a member of the House of Representatives, made the following argument in support of the President's action:

"The treaty, which is a law, enjoins the performance of a particular object. The person who is to perform this object is marked out by the Constitution, since the person is named who conducts the foreign intercourse, and is to take care that the laws be faithfully executed. The means by which it is to be performed, the force of the nation, are in the hands of this person. Ought not this person to perform the object, although the particular mode of using the means has not been prescribed? Congress, unquestionably may prescribe the mode, and Congress may devolve on others the whole execution of the contract; but, till this be done, it seems the duty of the Executive department to execute the contract by any means it possesses."

. . . Jefferson's initiative in the Louisiana Purchase, the Monroe Doctrine, and Jackson's removal of Government deposits from the Bank of the United States further serve to demonstrate by deed what the Framers described by word when they vested the whole of the executive power in the President.

Without declaration of war, President Lincoln took energetic action with the outbreak of the Civil War. He summoned troops and paid them out of the Treasury without appropriation therefor. He proclaimed a naval blockade of the Confederacy and seized ships violating that blockade. Congress, far from denying the validity of these acts, gave them express approval. The most striking action of President Lincoln was the Emancipation Proclamation, issued in aid of the successful prosecution of the Civil War, but wholly without statutory authority.

In an action furnishing a most apt precedent for this case, President Lincoln directed the seizure of rail and telegraph lines leading to Washington without statutory authority. Many months later, Congress recognized and confirmed the power of the President to seize railroads and telegraph lines and provided criminal penalties for interference with Government operation. This Act did not confer on the President any additional powers of seizure. Congress plainly rejected the view that the President's acts had been without legal sanction until ratified by the legislature. Sponsors of the bill declared that its purpose was only to confirm the power which the President already possessed. Opponents insisted a statute authorizing seizure was unnecessary and might even be construed as limiting existing Presidential powers.

Other seizures of private property occurred during the Civil War, just as they had occurred during the previous wars. . . .

President Hayes authorized the wide-spread use of federal troops during the Railroad Strike of 1877. President Cleveland also used the troops in the Pullman Strike of 1895 and his action is of special significance. No statute authorized this action. No call for help had issued from the Governor of Illinois; indeed Governor Altgeld disclaimed the need for supplemental forces. But the President's concern was that federal laws relating to the free flow of interstate commerce and the mails be continuously and faithfully executed without interruption. To further this aim his agents sought and obtained the injunction upheld by this Court in *In re Debs*, 158 U.S. 564 (1895). The Court scrutinized each of the steps taken by the President to insure execution of the "mass of legislation" dealing with commerce and the mails and gave his conduct full approval. . . .

President Theodore Roosevelt seriously contemplated seizure of Pennsylvania coal mines if a coal shortage necessitated such action. . . .

In 1909, President Taft was informed that government owned oil lands were being patented by private parties at such a rate that public oil lands would be depleted in a matter of months. Although Congress had explicitly provided that these lands were open to purchase by United States citizens, 29 Stat. 526 (1897), the President nevertheless ordered the lands withdrawn from sale "[i]n aid of proposed legislation." In *United States v. Midwest Oil Co.*, 236 U.S.

459 (1915), the President's action was sustained as consistent with executive practice throughout our history. . . .

During World War I, President Wilson established a War Labor Board without awaiting specific direction by Congress. With William Howard Taft and Frank P. Walsh as co-chairmen, the Board had as its purpose the prevention of strikes and lockouts interfering with the production of goods needed to meet the emergency. Effectiveness of War Labor Board decision was accomplished by Presidential action, including seizure of industrial plants. Seizure of the Nation's railroads was also ordered by President Wilson.

Beginning with the Bank Holiday Proclamation and continuing through World War II, executive leadership and initiative were characteristic of President Franklin D. Roosevelt's administration. In 1939, upon the outbreak of war in Europe, the President proclaimed a limited national emergency for the purpose of strengthening our national defense. By May of 1941, the danger from the Axis belligerents having become clear, the President proclaimed "an unlimited national emergency" calling for mobilization of the Nation's defenses to repel aggression. The President took the initiative in strengthening our defenses by acquiring rights from the British Government to establish air bases in exchange for overage destroyers.

In 1941, President Roosevelt acted to protect Iceland from attack by Axis powers when British forces were withdrawn by sending our forces to occupy Iceland. Congress was informed of this action on the same day that our forces reached Iceland. The occupation of Iceland was but one of "at least 125 incidents" in our history in which Presidents, "without Congressional authorization, and in the absence of a declaration of war, [have] ordered the Armed Forces to take action or maintain positions abroad."

Some six months before Pearl Harbor, a dispute at a single aviation plant at Inglewood, California, interrupted a segment of the production of military aircraft. In spite of the comparative insignificance of this work stoppage to total defense production as contrasted with the complete paralysis now threatened by a shut-down of the entire basic steel industry, and even though our armed forces were not then engaged in combat, President Roosevelt ordered the seizure of the plant "pursuant to the powers vested in [him] by the Constitution and laws of the United States, as President of the United States of America and Commander in Chief of the Army and Navy of the United States." . . .

Meanwhile, and also prior to Pearl Harbor, the President ordered the seizure of a shipbuilding company and an aircraft parts plant. Following the declaration of war, but prior to the Smith-Connally Act of 1943, five additional industrial concerns were seized to avert interruption of needed production. During the same period, the President directed seizure of the Nation's coal mines to remove an obstruction to the effective prosecution of the war.

The procedures adopted by President Roosevelt closely resembled the methods employed by President Wilson. A National War Labor Board, like its predecessor of World War I, was created by Executive Order to deal effectively and fairly with disputes affecting defense production. Seizures were considered necessary, upon disobedience of War Labor Board orders, to assure that the mobilization effort remained a "going concern," and to enforce the economic stabilization program.

At the time of the seizure of the coal mines, Senator Connally's bill to provide a statutory basis for seizures and for the War Labor Board was again before Congress. As stated by its sponsor, the purpose of the bill was not to augment Presidential power, but to "let the country know that the Congress is squarely behind the President." As in the case of the legislative recognition of President Lincoln's power to seize, Congress again recognized that the President already had the necessary power, for there was no intention to "ratify" past actions of doubtful validity. . . .

Following passage of the Smith-Connally Act, seizures to assure continued production on the basis of terms recommended by the War Labor Board were based upon that Act as well as upon the President's power under the Constitution and the laws generally. A question did arise as to whether the statutory language relating to "any plant, mine or facility equipped for the manufacture, production, or mining of any articles or materials" authorized the seizure of properties of Montgomery Ward & Co., a retail department store and mail order concern. The Attorney General (Biddle) issued an opinion that the President possessed the power to seize Montgomery Ward properties to prevent a work stoppage whether or not the terms of the Smith-Connally Act authorized such a seizure. This opinion was in line with the views on Presidential powers maintained by the Attorney General's predecessors (Murphy and Jackson) and his successor (Clark). Accordingly, the President ordered seizure of the Chicago properties of Montgomery Ward in April, 1944, when that company refused to obey a War Labor Board order concerning the bargaining representative of its employees in Chicago. In Congress, a Select Committee to Investigate Seizure of the Property of Montgomery Ward & Co., assuming that the terms of the Smith-Connally Act did not cover this seizure, concluded that the seizure "was not only within the Constitutional power but was the plain duty of the President." Thereafter, an election determined the bargaining representative for the Chicago employees and the properties were returned to Montgomery Ward & Co. In December, 1944, after continued defiance of a series of War Labor Board orders, President Rosevelt ordered the seizure of Montgomery Ward properties throughout the country. The Court of Appeals for the Seventh Circuit upheld this seizure on statutory grounds and also indicated its disapproval of the lower court's denial of seizure power apart from express statute. . . .

This is but a cursory summary of executive leadership. But it amply demonstrates that Presidents have taken prompt action to enforce the laws and protect the country whether or not Congress happened to provide in advance for the particular method of execution. At the minimum, the executive actions reviewed herein sustain the action of the President in this case. And many of the cited examples of Presidential practice go far beyond the extent of power necessary to sustain the President's order to seize the steel mills. The fact that temporary executive seizures of industrial plants to meet an emergency have not been directly tested in this Court furnishes not the slightest suggestion that such actions have been illegal. Rather, the fact that Congress and the courts have consistently recognized and given their support to such executive action indicates that such a power of seizure has been accepted throughout our history. . . .

IV.

. . . Much of the argument in this case has been directed at straw men. We do not now have before us the case of a President acting solely on the basis of his own notions of the public welfare. Nor is there any question of unlimited executive power in this case. The President himself closed the door to any such claim when he sent his Message to Congress stating his purpose to abide by any action of Congress, whether approving or disapproving his seizure action. Here, the President immediately made sure that Congress was fully informed of the temporary action he had taken only to preserve the legislative programs from destruction until Congress could act.

The absence of a specific statute authorizing seizure of the steel mills as a mode of executing the laws—both the military procurement program and the anti-inflation program—has not until today been thought to prevent the President from executing the laws. Unlike an administrative commission confined to the enforcement of the statute under which it was created, or the head of a department when administering a particular statute, the President is a constitutional officer charged with taking care that a "mass of legislation" be executed. Flexibility as to mode of execution to meet critical situations is a matter of practical necessity. This practical construction of the "Take Care" clause, advocated by John Marshall, was adopted by this Court in *In re Neagle, In re Debs* and other cases cited *supra*. See also *Ex parte Quirin*, 317 U.S. 1, 26 (1942).

. . . In *United States v. Midwest Oil Co., supra*, this Court approved executive action where, as here, the President acted to preserve an important matter until Congress could act—even though his action in that case was contrary to an express statute. . . .

V.

Plaintiffs place their primary emphasis on the Labor Management Relations Act of 1947, hereinafter referred to as the Taft-Hartley Act, but do not contend that that Act contains any provision prohibiting seizure. . . . Plaintiffs admit that the emergency procedures of Taft-Hartley are not mandatory. Nevertheless, plaintiffs apparently argue that, since Congress did provide the 80-day injunction method for dealing with emergency strikes, the President cannot claim that an emergency exists until the procedures of Taft-Hartley have been exhausted. This argument was not the basis of the District Court's opinion and, whatever merit the argument might have had following the enactment of Taft-Hartley, it loses all force when viewed in light of the statutory pattern confronting the President in this case.

In Title V of the Defense Production Act of 1950, Congress stated:

> "It is the intent of Congress, in order to provide for effective price and wage stabilization pursuant to title IV of this Act and to maintain uninterrupted production, that there be effective procedures for the settlement of labor disputes affecting national defense." (§501).

Title V authorized the President to initiate labor-management conferences and to take action appropriate to carrying out the recommendations of such conferences and the provisions of Title V. (§502). Due regard is to be given to collective bargaining practice and stabilization policies and no action taken is to be inconsistent with Taft-Hartley and other laws. (§503.) The purpose of these provisions was to authorize the President "to establish a board, commission or other agency, similar to the War Labor Board of World War II, to carry out the title."

The President authorized the Wage Stabilization Board (WSB), which administers the wage stabilization functions of Title IV of the Defense Production Act, also to deal with labor disputes affecting the defense program. When extension of the Defense Production Act was before Congress in 1951, the Chairman of the Wage Stabilization Board described in detail the relationship between the Taft-Hartley procedures applicable to labor disputes imperiling the national health and safety and the new WSB dispute procedures especially devised for settlement of labor disputes growing out of the needs of the defense program. Aware that a technique separate from Taft-Hartley had been devised, members of Congress attempted to divest the WSB of its disputes powers. These attempts were defeated in the House, were not brought to a vote in the Senate and the Defense Production Act was extended through June 30, 1952, without change in the disputes powers of the WSB. Certainly this legislative creation of a new procedure for dealing with defense disputes negatives any notion that Congress intended the earlier and discretionary Taft-Hartley procedure to be an exclusive procedure.

Accordingly, as of December 22, 1951, the President had a choice between alternate procedures for settling the threatened strike in the steel mills: one route created to deal with peacetime disputes; the other route specially created to deal with disputes growing out of the defense and stabilization program. . . .

VI.

The diversity of views expressed in the six opinions of the majority, the lack of reference to authoritative precedent, the repeated reliance upon prior dissenting opinions, the complete disregard of the uncontroverted facts showing the gravity of the emergency and the temporary nature of the taking all serve to demonstrate how far afield one must go to affirm the order of the District Court.

The broad executive power granted by Article II to an officer on duty 365 days a year cannot, it is said, be invoked to avert disaster. Instead, the President must confine himself to sending a message to Congress recommending action. Under this messenger-boy concept of the Office, the President cannot even act to preserve legislative programs from destruction so that Congress will have something left to act upon. There is no judicial finding that the executive action was unwarranted because there was in fact no basis for the President's finding of the existence of an emergency for, under this view, the gravity of the emergency and the immediacy of the threatened disaster are considered irrelevant as a matter of law.

Seizure of plaintiffs' property is not a pleasant undertaking. Similarly unpleasant to a free country are the draft which disrupts the home and military procurement which causes economic dislocation and compels adoption of price controls, wage stabilization and allocation of materials. The President informed Congress that even a temporary Government operation of plaintiffs' properties was "thoroughly distasteful" to him, but was necessary to prevent immediate paralysis of the mobilization program. Presidents have been in the past, and any man worthy of the Office should be in the future, free to take at least interim action necessary to execute legislative programs essential to survival of the Nation. A sturdy judiciary should not be swayed by the unpleasantness or unpopularity of necessary executive action, but must independently determine for itself whether the President was acting, as required by the Constitution, "to take Care that the Laws be faithfully executed."

As the District Judge stated, this is no time for "timorous" judicial action. But neither is this a time for timorous executive action. Faced with the duty of executing the defense programs which Congress had enacted and the disastrous effects that any stoppage in steel production would have on those programs, the President acted to preserve those programs by seizing the steel mills. There is no question that the possession was other than temporary in character and subject to congressional direction—either approving, disapproving or regulating the manner in which the mills were to be administered and returned to the owners. The President immediately informed Congress of his action and clearly stated his intention to abide by the legislative will. No basis for claims of arbitrary action, unlimited powers or dictatorial usurpation of congressional power appears from the facts of this case. On the contrary, judicial, legislative and executive precedents throughout our history demonstrate that in this case the President acted in full conformity with his duties under the Constitution. Accordingly, we would reverse the order of the District Court.

Steel Strike Calendar, June 2 to July 24

June 2   Following the Supreme Court's opinion, Secretary Sawyer signs order returning the steel companies to private management, the United Steel Workers of America go out on strike, and all steel production ceases.

June 4   The House Judiciary Committee postpones indefinitely consideration of bills seeking to impeach the President or to define more specifically what presidential powers are under the Constitution.

June 5   Debate on the Defense Production Act begins in the Senate. Senator Harry Byrd (Dem.–Va.) proposes an amendment requesting the President to use the Taft-Hartley Act against the Steel Workers. After heated debate on this and several alternative proposals, action is put over until June 10.

June 9   Sources close to the steel parties report that labor-management talks have collapsed and no agreement can be expected.

June 10   President Truman addresses a Joint Session of Congress asking that he be given statutory permission to seize the steel industry and restore production, stating his belief that it would be unwise and unfair to invoke the Taft-Hartley Act.

June 10   On the same day as his address, the Senate rejects the President's request and adopts, 49–30, the Byrd amendment requesting the President to get a Taft-Hartley injunction. Steel strike continues.

170

June 11   A series of amendments by Senate Democrats and Senator Morse to give the President seizure power are all rejected.

June 25   In House debate on the Defense Production Act, an amendment is adopted which requests the President to use the Taft-Hartley Act.

June 26   The House, 228–114, confirms passage of an amendment requesting use of the Taft-Hartley Act.

June 27   Pittsburgh Steel Company and the United Steel Workers reach an agreement, 12½ cents hourly wage increase and modified union shop.

June 28   Congress accepts the conference version of the Defense Production Act, including provisions stripping the Wage Stabilization Board of its power in labor disputes and calling upon the President to use the Taft-Hartley Act.

July 3   President Truman refuses to invoke Taft-Hartley Act, charges a company conspiracy against the public interest, and praises the union. The Senate passes a resolution, introduced by liberal Democrats, calling on the Steel Workers and steel companies to resume bargaining, agree on interim terms upon which to restore work, and move on to iron out their differences

July 10   Bargaining talks resume.

July 12   Three steel company executives called to the White House for conferences on the steel situation. No results.

July 14   Chrysler Corporation shuts down all its auto and truck assembly lines in Michigan.

July 18   The President warns that unless an agreement is reached soon, he will seize certain plants under authority given him by the Selective Service Act; about 10% of the steel industry estimated to be affected.

July 22   Steel shortages force the Army to shut down the nation's largest shell making plant, at St. Louis, Missouri.

July 23   President Truman calls Benjamin Fairless and Philip Murray to the White House for conferences.

July 24   President Truman announces settlement of the steel strike and an immediate return to work. Terms of the agreement are a 16-cent hourly wage rise and fringe benefits of 5.4 cents per hour, with the companies obtaining a $5.20 a ton price rise from Government.

Mr. Justice Truman, Dissenting

Harry S. Truman, Memoirs[1]

It seems to me that there have been few instances in history where the press was more sensational or partisan than in its handling of the steel seizure. What was more disturbing was what amounted to editorial intervention by the press of America in a case pending before the Supreme Court of the United States. News stories and editorials decrying seizure and inflaming public opinion were prejudging and deciding the case at the very time the Court itself was hearing arguments for both sides. The steel companies bought full-page advertisements and ran them in newspapers throughout the country to denounce the President of the United States. Large sums of money were spent to influence public opinion against the government. . . . The public relations experts for the companies skillfully shifted public attention from the price demands of the industry to the supposedly abnormal and unprecedented act of the President.

A little reading of history would have shown that there was nothing unusual about this action—that strike-threatened plants had been seized before by the government, even before the nation was engaged in any shooting conflict. But these matters received no mention or, if they were mentioned, were glossed over quickly, as if they had no meaning for the present.

[1] Harry S. Truman, *Memoirs: Years of Trial and Hope*, II, pp. 475–478. Doubleday and Co., N.Y., 1956. Used with permission of the copyright holder, *Time, Inc.*

I would, of course, never conceal the fact that the Supreme Court's decision, announced on June 2, was a deep disappointment to me. I think Chief Justice Vinson's dissenting opinion hit the nail right on the head, and I am sure that someday his view will come to be recognized as the correct one.

I am not a lawyer, and I leave the legal arguments to others. But as a layman, as an official of the government, and as a citizen, I have always found it difficult to understand how the Court could take the affidavits of men like Lovett, Chapman, and many others, all of whom testified in great detail to the grave dangers that a steel shutdown would bring to the nation—affidavits that were neither contradicted nor even contested by the companies—and ignore them entirely.

I could not help but wonder what the decision might have been had there been on the Court a Holmes, a Hughes, a Brandeis, a Stone.

Word of the Court's decision reached me in my office in the early afternoon of June 2, and before three o'clock I had issued an order to Secretary of Commerce Sawyer to comply with the decision and return the plants to the steel industry. At four-thirty a hurriedly called meeting convened in my office. Defense Secretary Lovett was present, along with Secretary of Commerce Sawyer. The new Attorney General, James P. McGranery, was also there, together with Solicitor General Perlman, Secretary of Labor Tobin, and several members of the White House staff. I wanted to know what course these advisers would recommend in the light of the Court's decision. Should we now resort to the Taft-Hartley Act's injunction? And, if not, what else was there to do? Going around the table, I asked each of those present to state his opinion. Only one or two thought that I should start proceedings under the Taft-Hartley Act. Most took the position that, having used the Wage Stabilization Board, this route was no longer open to me. There was also some feeling that the Supreme Court opinion had strengthened the bargaining position of the industry to such an extent that it would be even more difficult than before to mediate any sort of settlement.

On June 10 I made one further effort, by an appeal for legislation to permit me to seize the strikebound plants. But the Congress refused to grant this authority. Throughout the nation the steel mills lay idle.

The strike lasted fifty-three days and ended only when an agreement was finally reached between management and labor. This came only after an increase had been granted in the price of steel. To settle the strike, the companies were allowed to add as much as $5.65 per ton.

I approved this price increase with a reluctant heart, for I was convinced that it was wrong—as wrong as it had been in March and April when I had refused to consider approving that much. But now the Supreme Court had denied the power to bring the plants under government operation, and Congress had turned down my appeal for authority to seize. The companies therefore now held all the advantages. If we wanted [steel] very badly—it would have to be on the industry's terms.

The strike ended on July 24. Six hundred thousand steel workers had been idle for over seven weeks. Twenty-five thousand iron-ore workers had been on a sympathy strike for a part of that time, and lack of steel had caused the layoff of three hundred thousand workers in the automobile industry. The daily loss in wages and production during this period was estimated at forty million dollars. The total loss was estimated in excess of two billion dollars! Nor does this take into consideration the higher price the nation paid after the settlement for the steel and steel products needed for the defense effort.

When General Van Fleet came back from Korea in March 1953, he complained that his troops had been short of certain types of ammunition in the summer and early fall of 1952. This was a fact that should have been no surprise to the American public. The affidavits of Secretary Lovett and National Production Administrator Fowler in the steel case had stated that a stoppage of steel production would affect our ability to ship sufficient munitions to the front in Korea!

I think that we were fortunate that nothing more serious happened in Korea as a result of the steel shutdown. The actions of the administration succeeded in keeping production going from December 31, when the strike was first set to begin, until June 2— fully five months. This was valuable time gained. But the seven weeks that were lost could never be replaced, no matter how the lawyers argue.

Whatever the six justices of the Supreme Court meant by their differing opinions about the constitutional powers of the President, he must always act in a national emergency. It is not very realistic for the justices to say that comprehensive powers shall be available to the President only when a war has been declared or when the country has been invaded. We live in an age when hostilities begin without polite exchanges of diplomatic notes. There are no longer sharp distinctions between combatants and noncombatants, between military targets and the sanctuary of civilian areas. Nor can we separate the economic facts from the problems of defense and security.

In this day and age the defense of the nation means more than building an army, navy, and air force. It is a job for the entire resources of the nation. The President, who is Commander in Chief and who represents the interest of all the people, must be able to act at all times to meet any sudden threat to the nation's security. A wise President will always work with Congress, but when Congress fails to act or is unable to act in a crisis, the President, under the Constitution, must use his powers to safeguard the nation.

Editor's Comments

While the anatomical structure of the *Youngstown* case is typical of the species, there are some special characteristics of this decision which should be noted. First, the case was conducted from start to finish in a blaze of public attention, with heavy political overtones, and with a maximum sense of urgency in the various courtrooms where the lawyers contended. This is not unique with *Youngstown*, of course. There have been cases which breathed politics and were closely followed in the newspapers from the days of *Dred Scott* to the Income Tax decision of 1895 down to the *Segregation Cases* of 1954. What it does signify is that *Youngstown* is an example of the political *cause celebre* in constitutional law, an exception to the detached atmosphere and sense of isolation from public strife in which most cases—even many which decide the largest principles of constitutional law—are normally adjudicated.

Second, the steel case portrays that type of constitutional litigation in which private parties are on one side and the government is on the other. While this would strike the fresh observer as the normal way in which matters of state are decided, along with cases between two government authorities, it is a special characteristic of the American judicial process that the same sort of issues can be raised in suits between two private parties disputing over lemons, insurance, or corporation policy. Recognizing the danger that such private litigation could result in limitations on powers of Congress which government lawyers might never have a chance to challenge in court, the Federal Judiciary Act of 1937 gave the United States the right to intervene in private suits when the constitutionality of a federal statute was drawn into question. This did not extend to cases where the validity of presidential action was involved or where two citizens were contesting in a manner which involved the powers of the states.

Again, the steel case reached the Supreme Court through the "federal channel." Many cases arrive after being tried and heard on appeal by state courts. When the Supreme Court hears such cases, it may be called upon to umpire a dispute between the states and the federal government over power to regulate a business activity, or to see whether a state police practice violates the 14th Amendment, or to decide "private law" issues relating to automobile accidents, divorces, and contracts. In such cases, different standards of review are often employed than those utilized when the Court is passing on the powers of coordinate agencies of the federal government or revising the rulings of lower federal judges.

Another somewhat distinctive feature of the steel case was that only two months elapsed between the date of the President's seizure and the Supreme Court's ruling. The average case takes from two to five years to make its way to the Courtroom in Washington. Here too, though, the *Youngstown* decision was not unique. Matters of vital importance to government operations and the national economy have occasionally been speeded along the judicial runway, notably the consideration of the Gold Clause legislation and the Social Security Act during the 1930's, the Nazi saboteurs case in 1943, and the contempt of court trial of the United Mine Workers in 1946.

A final feature to mark is that the *Youngstown* ruling, unlike some decisions of the Court, produced immediate compliance by the "offending" party. There are important situations in which the judicial thunderclap does not command such obedience as President Truman displayed. As in Southern officialdom's reaction to the *Segregation Cases*, the Court's rulings can be openly flouted. As with F.B.I. wire tapping practices and the search policies of some state police forces, Supreme Court mandates can be viewed as momentary handslaps in a game of constitutional tag, and the condemned actions may be performed again and again. In these situations, the Justices face the task of enforcing their rulings or in applying them to new actions testing the limits of the Court's rule. Studies of such cases would be incomplete without consideration of what happened after the Court's initial pronouncement— both in terms of acceptance by the parties and application of the Court's doctrine.

A word might also be added about the perspective in which this study has been written. An attempt has been made to recreate, as far as possible, the factual and emotional setting of 1952. The reader has been given approximately the same facts and rumors which were available to the judges when the steel crisis was unfolding. (An ideal reconstruction is impossible, of course, because the student knows that the Korean War was not extended, that East Germany did not invade the Western Sectors of Berlin, and that the strike was settled in a comparatively short time.) If the contemporary focus helps students to appreciate the uncertainty as to critical facts and the painful speculation about the possible results of decisions which judges must face in the constitutional process, the technique will have served its purpose.

Although contemporary insight, rather than hindsight, is the measuring rod for judicial statesmanship, students should not turn their backs on later disclosures and historical reconstructions. In the case of the steel dispute, an excellent study of the seizure, drawn from sources inside the White House, is Grant McConnell's, *The Steel Seizure of 1952*, Inter-University Case Program, N.Y., 1958. For such matters as the background of President Truman's decision to seize, the relation of the White House to the seizure litigation, the limits upon the Administration's freedom of action imposed by its tie with the Steel Workers Union, and the failure of the Administration to dramatize its case effectively to the nation, McConnell's study is warmly recommended.

Questions and Judgments for Analysis

Analyses of constitutional law decisions usually include inquiries into the wisdom of the law expounded on this particular subject, the standard of judicial review employed by the Court, and the relation of each opinion to the general position of that individual Justice. The following are a sample of queries for the *Youngstown* case.

1. One analysis of the steel case has stressed the improvisation, sense of unconcern for regular procedures, and inability to frame a clear line of constitutional argument which marked the Executive's handling of the situation. According to this view, the Supreme Court, and particularly Justices Frankfurter and Jackson, with their especially strong allegiance to constitutional regularity, simply could not choke down the seizure as self-respecting judges.

Another view has depicted Truman as a responsible Chief Executive balked by a politically-hostile Congress which ducked its responsibilities in the steel crisis and left the President to take the abuse. According to this reasoning, the Supreme Court, heeding a strong but far from rational public opinion, forgot its own place in the constitutional scheme and entered the "political arena," producing a theoretical limit on emergency power which is highly unrealistic.

With which of these general positions are you most in agreement?

2. The Government argued repeatedly that the case of Hurley v. Kincaid (1932) was "directly controlling." There, the Federal Government had taken a large amount of land by condemnation proceedings in order to construct a flood-control project along the Mississippi River. Kincaid, the owner of a 160 acre farm, had *not* had his land taken nor paid for and he protested, since he claimed that the presence of the

project would flood his land by the overflow at high water time. The Government did not believe that its project would have this effect on Kincaid's land and thus had not taken the Kincaid farm under the applicable Congressional act which authorized condemnation proceedings. Kincaid sued in Federal District Court for an injunction against the Secretary of War and the Mississippi River Project Commissioners to prevent them from going ahead with the project.

The Supreme Court dismissed Kincaid's suit, stating that there was a sufficient statutory basis for the Government's project to raise the obligation of the Government to pay Kincaid just compensation if he could show damage. Kincaid's proper remedy, said the Court, was an action in the Court of Claims.

Not a single Justice in the *Youngstown* case mentioned the *Hurley* case. Do you think it is in point? If not, how do you distinguish the Truman seizure situation?

3. A political scientist made the following comment:[1]

The legal arguments between the two divisions of the Court were . . . of little significance; the vital disagreement was over premises. Granted the assumption that no emergency existed, the majority view fell into the tradition of limitation [of the Executive]. Granted the assumption that an emergency existed, the minority opinion fell into an equally well-defined tradition of judicial restraint. It is submitted that this argument over premises is not one that can be solved by the process of legal ratiocination, but rather it must be determined through judicial insight into the attitudes and opinions of the American community—particularly as reflected in the views of Congressmen. It is essentially a problem in social psychology, not in law.

What is the competence of the Supreme Court Justice for public opinion analysis and social psychology? Would a legal doctrine that the political branches of the Federal Government define the nature of the emergency and that the Court could not make an independent judgment produce more or less crystallization of the majority will on an issue such as the steel seizure? What should be the Court's guide when one political branch of the Federal Government considers this to be an emergency and the other disagrees?

[1] John P. Roche, "Executive Power and Domestic Emergency: The Quest for Prerogative," 4 *Western Pol. Quar.*, 592, 617 (1952).

4. Suppose President Truman had obtained an 80-day Taft-Hartley injunction. After the time had run, suppose a strike had been called and the President had seized the mills, reciting his inherent powers. Do you think this action would have been upheld by the Supreme Court?

5. If you make a list of the individual Justices who stated that the President does possess inherent powers under Article II, how many do you have? Consider this problem in light of the comment that the *Youngstown* decision means very little as a definition of inherent powers and as a precedent for the future, except that the President *has* temporary emergency powers.

6. It was rumored that the companies had made a decision to settle the strike by negotiation if the legal suit was not allowed to by-pass the Court of Appeals and go right to the Supreme Court. Does this possibility add weight, in your mind, to the argument of Justices Burton and Frankfurter that certiorari should have been denied at this stage of the proceedings?

7. In evaluating the effect of judicial review on the conduct of American government, what do you think of the statement that it was the availability of Supreme Court review which encouraged Congress to take no action on the seizure, either legislating to authorize it or stating that it was improper? Note in this regard that the House of Representatives never added a rider to the Supplemental Appropriations Bill, denying funds for the seizure, so that the Senate's action cannot be properly regarded as an official action of Congress.

8. One of the basic rules of constitutional decision is that cases should not be decided before they are "ripe." In this regard, it has been suggested that the Supreme Court should have returned the case to the District Court for a factual hearing on whether the companies would suffer damage if wage increases were given and the price increase available to the companies were accepted. Another suggestion was that the injunction suit should not have been decided until a test had been made in the Court of Claims to see whether compensation from the Government was available.[1] What do you think of these ideas? If ripening cases means continued action under an "unconstitutional" measure, what is the counter-balancing advantage to be had by delay?

9. A leading authority on the Presidency has written:[2]

[1] See Paul A. Freund, "The Year of the Steel Case," 66 Harv. L. Rev. 89 (1952).

[2] Edward S. Corwin, *The President: Office and Powers*, 1787–1957, p. 155, N.Y. Univ. Press, N.Y., 1957.

able to determine what compensation, if any, the companies could re
cover?[1]

10. A leading authority on the Presidency has written:[2]

The pivotal position of "the opinion of the Court," so-called, by
Justice Black is that, inasmuch as Congress could have ordered the
seizure of the mills, the President lacked power to seize them without its authorization. In support of this position, which purported
to have the endorsement of four other members of the Court, Justice
Black invoked the principle of the Separation of Powers, but otherwise adduced no proof from previous decisions or from governmental practice. In the circumstances of the case this course of
reasoning was self-refuting. If the principle of the Separation of
Powers prevents the President from doing anything that Congress
may do, then by the same token it bars the Supreme Court from
doing anything that Congress may do. Yet everybody conceded that
Congress could have ended the seizure of the steel mills at any
time—precisely what the Supreme Court undertook to do in this
case!

Another authority has challenged the idea that Congress' position was
(or should be considered to be) as strong as suggested above.[3]

The burden should not be placed on Congress to negate an over-
reaching in the assertion of executive authority. Positive disaffirmance
of the President's action is not as easy as the dissenting opinion
would make it appear to be. The President by vetoing such overriding legislation could frustrate the majority action of Congress in
order to maintain his prerogative. Even more serious are the political
difficulties in such a situation. A legislative proposal to disaffirm
executive action could readily be stigmatized as a censure carrying
political overtones and inviting partisan controversy which could

[1] See Paul A. Freund, "The Year of the Steel Case," 66 Harv. L. Rev. 89
(1952).

[2] Edward S. Corwin, *The President: Office and Powers*, 1787–1957, p. 155,
N.Y. Univ. Press, N.Y., 1957.

[3] Paul G. Kauper, "The Steel Seizure Case: Congress, the President and the
Supreme Court," 51 *Mich. L. Rev.* 141, 181–182 (1952).

10. In what way could one conclude that Justices Black and Douglas were more closely alligned with the minority Justices, on the question of the role of the Supreme Court toward presidential powers, than with their colleagues in the majority?

11. Among the criticisms of the majority decision was the following:[1]

For a judicial tribunal to speak with certainty in deciding an important case, it is essential that it speak with a single voice. But this is precisely what was not done. . . . The diversity in opinion expressed among the Justices tends to destroy much of the force of their holding that the President's order was invalid.

Is the need for a "single voice" more important than what Justice Frankfurter described as the importance of stating differences in "emphasis and nuance"? Would it have been possible to frame one opinion for all the Justices in the majority?[2]

[1] Bernard Schwartz, *The Supreme Court: Constitutional Revolution in Retrospect*, p. 71, Ronald Press, N.Y., 1957.

[2] For other valuable discussions of the steel case, see Edward S. Corwin, "The Steel Seizure Case: A Judicial Brick without Straw," 53 *Col. L. Rev.* 1 (1953); John P. *Frank*, "The Future of Presidential Seizure," *Fortune*, July, 1952; Joseph Tanenhaus, "The Supreme Court and Presidential Power," *The Annals*, Vol. 307, September, 1956; Donald Richberg, "The Steel Seizure Cases," 38 *Va. L. Rev.* 714 (1952); Robert F. Banks, "Steel, Sawyer, and the Executive Power," 14 *Pitts. L. Rev.* 467 (1953).

Postscript to the Morningside Edition:
The Steel Seizure Case: Four Decades Later

Introduction

For this new section viewing the Steel Seizure case from 1990, I have chosen to present commentary and materials that deal with three main themes:

1. What we now know more fully about the processes of presidential thinking and Administration decision-making relating to seizure of the steel mills and efforts to produce a settlement between the parties during various stages of the litigation;

2. What we now know somewhat more fully about the processes by which the Supreme Court Justices deliberated on the case and reached their majority and minority positions;

3. How the *Youngstown* ruling and the various individual opinions written as concurrences have been used by the courts since 1952, especially the Supreme Court itself.

As these sections unfold, it will become apparent that controversies of fact and of interpretation still persist over the motives, perceptions, and actions of various key participants in the Steel Seizure case. The best single source of historical recreation that current readers can consult is Dr. Maeva Marcus's excellent study, *Truman and the Steel Seizure: The Limits of Presidential Power*, published in 1977 by Columbia University Press. Two treatments of the case also of primary value are the classic volume by Richard Neustadt, a White House aide during this period,

Presidential Power: The Politics of Leadership (1960) and Grant Mc-
Connell, *The Steel Seizure of 1952*, an Inter-University Case Program
monograph also published in 1960. Other revealing memoirs, histories,
and analyses will be referenced in the sections that follow, and full
citations will be found in the Selected Bibliography.

It should be noted that for sections 1 and 2 above, I will be adding what
might be called supplementary material to the full-dress, contemporary
accounts that appeared earlier in this volume. The style is therefore
additive rather than being a fresh presentation.

Section 3 is obviously a new topic. It treats the way that the *Youngstown*
case—the Court's ruling and also the various concurring opinions—has
been used as a precedent by the Supreme Court from 1953 to the present.
This section explores both the constitutional and the political impacts of
the *Youngstown* case as the American nation moved from the Vinson
Court into the liberal activist era of the Warren Court, and then into the
increasingly moderate to conservative orientations of the Burger and
Rehnquist Courts.

1. INSIDE THE TRUMAN ADMINISTRATION

How Truman Viewed His Power to Seize

In considering whether President Truman felt he had a sound
legal basis for the seizure option and, if the case went to the
Supreme Court, whether he believed he would prevail there, Truman biographer Robert J. Donovan (1982) relates "two fascinating
developments" that exerted major effects on White House thinking.

First, Truman and his advisors "placed heavy reliance on a
memorandum that Associate Justice Tom Clark had submitted on
inherent presidential powers while Clark was still Attorney General.
It had been sent to the White House in February 1949, when
Truman was seeking repeal of the Taft-Hartley Act. The substitute
bill that Truman wanted Congress to pass did not specify the use of
injunctions to halt strikes threatening to cause a national emergency . . . Attorney General Clark had informed him that he had
authority to deal with the crisis under 'implied' constitutional pow-

ers. The memorandum supplied by Clark said, 'If crises arising from labor disputes in peacetime necessitate unusual steps, such as seizure, to prevent paralysis of the National economy, other inherent powers of the President may be expected to be found equal to the occasion.' " Donovan says that the White House interpreted the 1949 Clark memo as justifying the seizure option in 1952. It was also seen as predicting Clark's support for seizure if the case ever got to the Supreme Court (Donovan, 386).

The second and "more unusual development" Donovan disclosed "was that Fred Vinson, in a most questionable act for a chief justice who might later have to weigh a case in court, privately advised the president to go ahead with seizure, basing the recommendation on legal grounds." Donovan relates that when Secretary of the Treasury Snyder argued forcefully to Truman that he should not seize the mills, and might not be able to demonstrate that a strike would cause steel shortages dangerous to the nation, Truman "replied that the chief justice himself had assured him that the way was clear for the president legally to seize the steel industry. Truman said that Vinson had advised him that such an act would be constitutional" (Donovan, 386).

Knowledge of the Clark memo and Vinson's direct advice, Donovan concluded, coupled with the facts that four of the Justices were Truman's appointees and close personal friends and the other five were FDR's New Deal appointees, encouraged Truman that "a decision by him to seize the steel plants would be sustained by the Supreme Court" (Donovan, 387).

How Truman Planned To Achieve a Settlement and Make Litigation Moot

In his famous book on presidential power, political scientist Richard Neustadt, an aide to Presidential Counsel Charles Murphy, used the Steel Seizure as one of his three central case studies. After relating the challenges and "misadventures" that led up to the Seizure decision, Neustadt describes the key strategy by which the

White House expected to compel a resolution of the dispute within a few days or weeks, and thereby assure that the federal courts would dismiss legal challenges to the President's authority as moot.

Neustadt says that "the White House wanted to get rid of [the mills] as fast as possible—which meant as fast as it could gain assurance that production would continue once they were returned to private hands." To make continued government administration "so unattractive in the eyes of both disputants that they would prefer [reaching] agreement with each other," the White House set out to have Secretary Sawyer put into effect that portion of the steelworkers' wage increase that could be instituted under the "cost of living" adjustment allowed under wage-control policy but going no higher. At the same time, Sawyer would give the steel companies a limited price increase that could be instituted under the "pass-through" adjustments of existing price-control rules. Secretary Sawyer would then declare that these actions were all that the government was prepared to do, and that it was now up to the parties to reach a negotiated settlement. By satisfying minimum demands of each party and "foreclosing" better terms for eith-erf]during the government's seizure, the White House hoped to convince both sides that "more was to be gained from settlement than from continued government direction."

In pursuit of this strategy, Neustadt relates, Truman clearly and without ambiguity "asked that Sawyer act at once." But, "Sawyer did not act." As a businessman in the Truman Administration, and as someone who "officially and personally . . . had no liking for the seizure," Sawyer was "unhappy at the prospect of his signature on wage orders and price requests committing the steel industry. Although he did not refuse to act, he managed to immerse himself in preparations." The result was that the Truman Administration lost the ability to apply the bargaining pressure of a partial settlement to both sides at two critical points in the developing stages of the case in the courts: first, while it was pending before Judge Pine but before he ruled against the President's authority to seize and second in the period when the Court of Appeals restored the President's power to hold the mills while the appeal went to the Supreme Court, but without stipulating that there be no change in conditions. Had Sawyer acted in either of those time periods, Neustadt writes, a settlement between the parties might have been induced.

In his autobiography, *Concerns of a Conservative Democrat*, Secretary of Commerce Charles Sawyer disputes Neustadt's account as "pure fiction," and contends in both the text and long documentary footnotes that others and not he were responsible for the failure to order a wage increase. (Sawyer, 1968, 274–276 and 379–381). However, in her authoritative reconstruction of this debate, Maeva Marcus finds Sawyer's account flawed and leaves the basic Neustadt rendition intact (Marcus, 1977, 306–309).

2. The Steel Seizure Case Inside the Supreme Court

Justice Tom Clark's Path to Decision

Until the Steel Seizure decision in June of 1952, Justice Tom Clark had invariably voted with his close friend and Truman Administration colleague, Chief Justice Fred Vinson. A law clerk to the Chief Justice in 1952 told me (interview in 1990) that the Chief Justice believed passionately that Truman had the constitutional power to seize the mills as he had done in April of 1952 and that Vinson had "lobbied Clark hard" in an effort to convince him of that position.

However, Clark was deeply troubled by the seizure. He felt loyal to Truman as the president who had appointed him, and felt that Truman had acted in a highly responsible fashion in trying to resolve the strike problem, a task on which he had received no help from Congress. Clark also felt, as his 1949 memo to Truman had laid out, that there was a residual executive power on which the President could draw to deal with substantial domestic emergencies such as the steel strike. On the other hand, the presence of the

Taft-Hartley Act and Truman's refusal to invoke it, though understandable politically, made the 1952 situation different for Clark than what he had set forth as a general principle in his 1949 memo. Clark was worried that allowing Truman to sidestep an available Congressional procedure was a dangerous precedent to set.

Torn by these competing considerations, Clark had a private meeting with Chief Justice Vinson. He said that if the Chief Justice could get three other Justices to join him, Clark would vote with them to make up a five-Justice majority. He felt that "he owed that to the President, and also to the Chief." However, if four Justices were not ready to vote to uphold the seizure, Clark said, he would prefer—and would—join the majority and explain why he felt Truman's actions were not lawful under the circumstances of this case. (This account was related to the author in 1959 by Justice Felix Frankfurter. Conversations with clerks to Justice Clark and Chief Justice Vinson resulted in judgments that the story was quite plausible, given what the clerks knew of their judge's views, but that they did not have direct knowledge of such a conversation.)

However, at the Conference discussion, it became clear that only the Chief Justice and Justices Reed and Minton would vote to uphold the seizure. If only one other Justice had joined them, Clark's pledge to the Chief would have swung the ruling the other way, and the Steel Seizure case would have produced a carefully written opinion by the Chief Justice supporting the President's action. Thus it was especially ironic that Justice Frankfurter, normally a staunch advocate of judicial self-restraint, decided that he would reach the merits of the case despite his concern over the accelerated consideration of the appeal by the Supreme Court. Frankfurter might also have declined to overturn the seizure on the basis that Congress could have asserted its own authority to check the President in this dispute and that the judiciary ought not to enter what could be considered an essentially "political thicket." Had Frankfurter adopted either of those views, Clark's readiness to "provide the fifth vote" might have changed history.

How Harry Truman Reacted to the Clark Vote

For Truman, the 6–3 majority holding his seizure action unconstitutional was both a blow to his conception of the responsible
presidency and a personal disappointment. Clark's vote with the
majority—in the context of his 1949 memorandum and his heretofore solid stance in major decisions alongside the Chief Justice,
had for the wounded Truman an "et tu, Brutus" quality. As Dennis
Dorin put it, Truman felt betrayed in 1952; by 1961–62, Truman's
dismay with several of Clark's actions led him to remark that
appointing Clark to the Court was the "worst mistake of his presidency" (Dorin, 1986).

How Some Majority Justices Tried to Heal the Wound

Several of the liberal Justices, aware that Truman was embittered
by the decision, made efforts to assuage the President. Dorin tells
the story as follows:

"The Justices could imagine Truman's anguish. Douglas recalled that the President was 'so upset that Hugo Black gave him a
party.' All of the Court's members attended a stag dinner for Truman in Black's Alexandria garden. There were a number of good-
natured barbs about the ruling, as 'the Court' poured 'a lot of
bourbon down Harry Truman.' Although this hardly changed the
President's mind, Douglas rememberd, 'he felt a little better, at
least for a few hours.'

"But Truman's demeanor may have masked the full extent of his
anger. A letter he initially planned to send to Douglas, but con-
signed, instead, to his 'strictly personal and confidential' file, no
doubt more accurately captured it. Truman had stated that he was
sorry that he had not been able to discuss precedents with Douglas
before Douglas' vote and opinion in 'that crazy decision that has
tied up the country.' 'I am writing a monograph on just what makes
Justices . . . tick,' the furious President had continued. . . . 'I don't
see how a Court made up of so-called 'liberals' could do what that
Court did to me,' he concluded . . ." (Dorin, 345–346). Later,

Truman was to compare the Steel Seizure decision to the infamous *Dred Scott* case (Dorin, 353).

How The Court Accepted the Case and Then Decided It

In her biography of Justice Harold Burton, Mary Frances Berry provides, from the Justice's notes, a detailed account of how the Justices took up and then decided the seizure case. Justice Burton prepared himself by reading Edward Corwin's classic study on *The President: Office and Powers*, and the *Curtiss-Wright* decision on presidential inherent powers. When the issue of expedited hearing of the case was discussed in conference, Burton (who voted to deny accelerated hearing) noted that Chief Justice Vinson stated that, while he did not like to bypass the circuit court, he felt the Court had to do so in this case, and cited his experiences with emergency actions in the executive branch during World War II. Black and Reed agreed that the cases should be argued as soon as possible. Frankfurter presented the counterargument. He opposed the "eagerness to settle" and for the Court "to seize a big abstract issue." Minton commented only that he felt "we have to grant certiorari."

Once the case was taken but before the conference vote, Burton noted that he "feared I might be the only one to reject seizure . . ." Berry explains that Burton "received the impression from the sympathetic comments expressed by Vinson, Black, Reed, Clark, and Minton, that he would be 'largely alone in holding [that] the President was without power to seize the steel plants in the face of the Taft-Hartley Act providing a different procedure."

Once the case got to conference, Justice Burton's notes were used by Berry to provide the following account of discussion among the Justices:

> After the oral argument was heard, Vinson uncharacteristically embarked on a long discussion of the case, explaining that no one was arguing that the President was exercising unlimited power; Truman had asked the Congress to act, but "Congress has done nothing." The President "would have been derelict

had he gone the Taft-Hartley route"; and if he had not seized the mills, "the howls would have been greater." Black retorted that "most of what Vinson said is irrelevant." Also, in his opinion, the case was not simply one of which statute to use; the seizure was wrong, but an "injunction is a serious thing for this court to do with no army. It is a serious thing to order the President." He thought the Court could find a solution which did not involve a direct order to give up the mills. Reed elaborated on the necessity for the Court to proceed slowly. He supported the President's power, but he hoped Congress or the President would act so that the Court would not be solely responsible for the resolution of the problem. He would like to "put off the decision . . . [and] simply leave [it] with the President temporarily."

Frankfurter was deeply concerned with the crisis-ridden posture of the case. Even though he was opposed to the seizure, he was more interested in the role demanded of the Court. He hoped "nine opinions . . . [would] be written"; he could not "escape it." He then read aloud an article he had written on the subject of presidential powers some twenty-five years before and outlined the history of government seizures, citing statutes, cases, and other relevant materials. In conclusion, he found that "no cases sustained inherent power in the President." After Frankfurter's lecture, Douglas merely commented that he agreed with Black. Jackson stated that he knew the difficulties a president must have in such crises but that there "were no inherent powers in the executive branch to commit such acts as these." Burton and Clark voted to affirm without comment. After an interval of near silence, Minton, speaking last, discussed the case in terms of his view of the political and economic crisis facing the President: "We have an acute emergency hanging over the world." On presidential powers, he asserted that "if Congress has not prohibited it and the Constitution has not, he need not stand by—he has implied power to act." When the votes were counted, it was 6–3 to invalidate the seizure, with Vinson, Reed, and Minton dissenting. . . . (Berry, 1978, 130–131.)

A recent biography of Justice Black provides us with additional useful material as to what Black said in the conference: "In conference [Black] had recalled his Senate opposition to the National Recovery Act and its delegation of lawmaking authority to the executive ·and private industries. He had also insisted that the president was not a legislator and that there was no congressional authorization for the seizure. Alluding no doubt to recent decisions upholding sanctions against Communists, he apparently rejected, too, the president's assessment of the dangers the threatened work stoppages posed; the Court's decisions of the past two years, he pointedly observed, had constituted a greater threat to liberty than any threatened strike" (Yarbrough, 1988, 40).

Chief Justice Rehnquist Views the Steel Seizure Case

Chief Justice William Rehnquist was a law clerk to Justice Robert Jackson during the term that the Steel Seizure case was decided. In 1986, he provided a detailed account of his recollections and interpretation of the case in a lecture delivered at Suffolk University Law School (Rehnquist, 1986), and then expanded on this narrative in his 1987 memoir, *The Supreme Court: How It Was, How It Is* (Rehnquist, 1987).

Rehnquist recalls that "the consensus among the law clerks, and perhaps of other people trained as lawyers with whom I spoke at the time, was that the courts would probably never reach the constitutional issue of the President's authority to seize the steel mills under these circumstances . . . based on the same set of reasons that seem to have moved Judge Holtzoff . . ." (Rehnquist, 1987, 48). However, Rehnquist describes what he sees as the "dramatic transfiguration" that the case underwent as it moved into Judge Pine's courtroom, and then as it moved each new step forward in the public and judicial processes.

This is the way Chief Justice Rehnquist explains what he saw happen, and why the Supreme Court decided the case as it did:

I had been quite surprised when Justice Jackson told us, "Boys, the President got licked." I thought about the outcome of the Steel Seizure Case some at the time, and I have thought about it a good deal more while writing this book. The law on the equitable issues was clearly in favor of the government, and while the law on the constitutional question was more or less up for grabs, the whole trend of the Court's decisions in the preceding fifteen years leaned toward the government. Why, then, did six members of the Court vote against the government in this case? I think that this is one of those celebrated constitutional cases where what might be called the tide of public opinion suddenly began to run against the government, for a number of reasons, and that this tide of public opinion had a considerable influence on the Court.

This was a case that unfurled in the newspapers before the very eyes of the justices long before any papers were filed in the Supreme Court. The members of the Court began learning about it the morning after President Truman's announcement of his seizure of the mills, when the press reported that the steel companies' attorneys had gone to Judge Bastian's home late in the evening to attempt to secure a temporary restraining order against the government. From beginning to end, the facts of the case and its progress through the courts were very much of a local event in Washington, heavily covered by the Washington newspapers. At that time, neither *The Washington Post*, *The Washington Evening Star*, nor *The Washington Times Herald* had the sort of national coverage *The Washington Post* has today, and if the lawsuit had been brought in Chicago, New York, or San Francisco, only those justices who regularly read *The New York Times* would have known about its course in such great detail.

The manner in which the case proceeded in the district court before Judge Pine had a considerable influence on public opinion. The government's original arguments in the district court, to the effect that the president's power was plenary unless some provision of the Constitution expressly denied authority to him, was rightly regarded as an extraordinary argument. The newspapers and commentators denounced it, and it obviously played a part in Judge Pine's decision in favor of the steel companies. The government quickly sensed that it had made a mistake in making these arguments, and recanted them almost immediately; by the time the case was argued in the Supreme Court, the arguments made by Holmes Baldridge in the district court had been entirely abandoned, but speaking as one who was on the scene at the time, I don't think they could be erased from anyone's mind. The government's litigation strategy in the district court, reported blow by blow in the Washington newspapers, undoubtedly had an effect on how the case was finally decided by the Supreme Court.

But I also think another, more deep-seated factor played a part in the tides of public opinion that were running at this time. There was a profound ambivalence on the part of much of the public about the Korean War, which was the principal basis upon which President Truman justified his seizure of the steel mills. When North Korea invaded South Korea, President Truman and his top advisers deliberately refrained from asking Congress for a declaration of war, and the United States continued to refer to the Korean conflict as a "police action" under the aegis of the United Nations rather than as a war. But in fact it seemed indistinguishable to most people from a war, in which the fortunes of the United States contrasted rather sharply with the success of that country and its Allies in the Second World War. In the latter conflict the United States had been attacked by the Japanese at Pearl Harbor, the President had asked Congress to declare war, and the country had mobilized for what rightly was seen to be a long, hard battle against the

Axis powers. Things looked very dark for the Allied powers at the time the United States first entered the war, but beginning with the Casablanca invasion in the European theater and the Guadalcanal landings in the Pacific theater, the Allies had gradually pushed back their enemies on both fronts in a series of hard-fought victories.

The Korean conflict was quite different. The initial momentum of the North Koreans carried them far into South Korean territory, but then General MacArthur's landing at Inchon had regained the initiative for the allies and they victoriously crossed back over the thirty-eighth parallel boundary. But then the Chinese entered the war, and the allies were forced back from their earlier gains at great cost in men and matériel. In the spring of 1952, the Korean conflict appeared to be pretty much of a stalemate; the result was an erosion of public willingness to sacrifice. We had a draft, we had price controls, we had rent controls, we had production controls, but these measures, which had been borne resolutely during the Second World War, were borne less resolutely and with considerably more grumbling during the Korean conflict. After President Truman forbade General MacArthur to authorize air strikes beyond the Yalu River, which separated North Korea from China, it seemed very difficult to figure out how the United States could "win" in Korea, and sacrifices that will be cheerfully borne when related to a clearly defined objective will not be so cheerfully borne when the objective seems confused and uncertain. I think that if the steel seizure had taken place during the Second World War, the government probably would have won the case under the constitutional grant to the president of the war power, but I also have the distinct feeling that if the American objectives and strategy in Korea had been less uncertain, the government probably would have fared better in the Supreme Court even without being able to resort to the president's war power.

Finally, although President Truman has today been accorded at least his just deserts by historians who have written since he left office, his standing in public opinion at the time of the Steel Seizure Case was at its nadir. When Truman first succeeded Roosevelt in 1945, Roosevelt loyalists were wont to say that the mistakes of the new administration never would have happened if Roosevelt were alive. Now political wags said that the Korean War would never have happened if Truman were alive; others coined the phrase "To err is Truman." The President himself had something of a tendency to put his foot in his mouth, with the result that his press secretary would be required to issue "clarification" of the President's public statements. His administration during the latter part of his second term was beset by influence-peddling scandals; none of them touched the President, but they nonetheless created an atmosphere referred to by his political opponents as "the mess in Washington." Though all but one of the justices of the Supreme Court had been allied with the Democratic party before their appointments, Democrats were often as critical of Truman as Republicans were; the former compared him frequently to Franklin Roosevelt, and all but invariably found him wanting.

These are the factors that I think played a considerable part in the way the Steel Seizure Case was decided. I was recently asked at a meeting with some people in Washington, who were spending a year studying various aspects of the government, whether the justices were able to isolate themselves from the tides of public opinion. My answer was that we are not able to do so, and it would probably be unwise to try. We read newspapers and magazines, we watch news on television, we talk to our friends about current events. No judge worthy of his salt would ever cast his vote in a particular case simply because he thought the majority of the public wanted him to vote that way, but that is quite a different thing from saying that no judge is ever influenced by the great tides of public opinion that run in a country such as ours. Judges are influenced by them, and I think that such influence played an appreciable part in causing the Steel Seizure Case to be decided the way it was. (Rehnquist, 1987, 94–97.)

3. The Constitutional and Political Impact of the Steel Seizure Decision and Opinions

The *Youngstown* case has had major significance as both a Supreme Court precedent and a framework for political discourse. We will describe and analyze these uses in two presentations.

When she published her study of the Steel Case in 1977, Maeva Marcus wrote a fine chapter on "The Constitutional Significance of the Youngstown Decision" (Marcus, 1977). It seems appropriate as the first presentation in this section to use an edited version of that chapter to relate the story of *Youngstown* as a precedent down to 1976. In the second presentation, I will provide an overall account of how the decision and concurring opinions from it have been used down to 1990.

Youngstown *in Supreme Court Decision-Making,* 1952–1976 *

The *Steel Seizure* case is one of the "great" constitutional law cases. It is one of the few which discuss at length the powers of the President. Thus, it would not be unreasonable to expect that *Youngstown* has had a significant influence on the development of constitutional law. Its impact, however, cannot be measured by the number of times it has been cited as a legal precedent. The paramount importance of the *Steel Seizure* decision lies in the fact that it was made. The Supreme Court, by invalidating an act of the President, helped redress the balance of power among the three branches of government and

---

* From Marcus, 1977, pages 228–248, footnote numbers and footnotes omitted.

breathed new life into the proposition that the President, like
every other citizen, is "under the law." By its ruling in the
Steel case, the Court created a precedent that future courts and
future Presidents could not ignore.

The *Youngstown* decision served as a prelude to a more
activist period for the Supreme Court. Traditionally reluctant
to deal with constitutional issues if cases could be disposed of
on other grounds, the Court rejected its customary stance in
the *Steel Seizure* case and in subsequent cases as well. New
personnel undoubtedly spurred this change in the Court's attitude. *Brown* v. *Board of Education of Topeka* and the other
School Segregation cases decided in 1954 were only the most
spectacular example of the Court's new willingness to face basic
constitutional questions. But the Court did not wholly abandon
its tradition—one need only read Justice Black's concurrence
in *Peters* v. *Hobby* to confirm this—it merely became less rigid
in adhering to it.

In the 1960s, however, the impact of *Youngstown* became
more evident. Perhaps the most important constitutional initiative in this decade was in legislative apportionment, an area
traditionally regarded as off-limits to the courts. Reapportionment had been considered a political question, although the
criteria for identifying it as such were unclear. Justice Frankfurter's opinion in *Colegrove* v. *Green*, the leading case on the
subject, reflected the widely held view that questions of legislative representation were very complex, involving many considerations, mainly political, which courts were not fit to deal
with. In *Colegrove*, a group of Illinois voters had brought suit
because, they contended, the divisions of Illinois into congressional districts with unequal population constituted a denial of
equal protection of the laws. Voters living in the more popu-
lous districts, usually containing the large urban centers, claimed
that their votes were worth less than the votes of their fellow
citizens who lived in sparsely populated districts. The Supreme

Court denied relief. According to Justice Frankfurter, the apportionment issue was "of a peculiarly political nature and therefore not meet for judicial determination." Questions concerning the proper guidelines for apportionment "bring courts into immediate and active relations with party contests. From the determination of such issues this Court has traditionally held aloof." And, Frankfurter warned, "Courts ought not to enter this political thicket. The remedy for unfairness in districting is to secure state legislatures that will apportion properly, or to invoke the ample powers of Congress."

Hence, when the Court considered a challenge to the apportionment of the Tennessee legislature in 1962, in *Baker* v. *Carr*, it had to demonstrate why apportionment was now susceptible of judicial resolution, and *Youngstown* helped it to do so. In *Baker* the Court reexamined the political question doctrine and fashioned the following criteria:

It is apparent that several formulations which vary slightly according to the settings in which the questions arise may describe a political question, although each has one or more elements which identifies it as essentially a function of the separation of powers. Prominent on the surface of any case held to involve a political question is found a textually demonstrable constitutional commitment of the issue to a coordinate political department; or a lack of judicially discoverable and manageable standards for resolving it; or the impossibility of deciding without an initial policy determination of a kind clearly for nonjudicial discretion; or the impossibility of a court's undertaking independent resolution without expressing lack of the respect due coordinate branches of government; or an unusual need for unquestioning adherence to a political decision already made; or the potentiality of embarrassment from multifarious pronouncements by various departments on one question.

The Court concluded that the reapportionment of the Tennessee legislature presented a justiciable cause of action, in that the issue was one of "the consistency of state action with the Federal Constitution" and none of the common characteristics of a political question applied. Justice Douglas, in a concurring opinion, noted that many of the cases which had been dismissed by the Court because they involved a political question had been "wrongly decided." A number of other cases in which the Court had ruled on the merits contained questions equally or more "political" than those the Court had refused to consider, Douglas asserted, and he mentioned *Youngstown* as one of them. Thus, the mere fact that the Court had made a decision on the merits in the *Steel* case influenced the Justices' reappraisal of the political question doctrine in *Baker* v. *Carr*.

Five years later, the Court's adjudiciation of the issue presented in *Powell* v. *McCormack* again demonstrated the importance of the Court's action in the *Steel Seizure* case. Adam Clayton Powell, Jr., the flamboyant congressman from Harlem, claimed that the House of Representatives had unlawfully excluded him from the 90th Congress. The House had refused to seat Powell in March 1967 because its Select Committee had found that Powell had wrongfully asserted a privilege and immunity from the processes of the New York courts, that he had used House funds illegally, and that he had made false reports on expenditures to the Committee on House Administration. Powell maintained that he could not be excluded, since he met the requirements stated in the Constitution for holding congressional office, and he and some of his constituents brought suit against the Speaker of the House and various congressmen and congressional employees. The House of Representatives insisted that it held discretionary power to decide on the pertinent qualifications of its members and urged that the Court dismiss the suit on the ground that it was a political question whose resolution might lead to an embarrassing disagreement between coordinate branches of the government. The district court agreed with the House and held that the court did not have jurisdiction because the issue raised a political question. Consideration of the merits of the dispute and the granting of relief would violate the separation-of-powers doctrine, Judge Hart stated.

The Supreme Court thought differently. A "determination of petitioner Powell's right to sit would require no more than an interpretation of the Constitution," Chief Justice Warren declared for the Court. This was the traditional function of the judicial branch. And the Court had on occasion interpreted the Constitution in a manner at odds with another branch. "The alleged conflict that such an adjudication may cause cannot justify the courts' avoiding their constitutional responsibility," the Chief Justice stated. The *Youngstown* decision was the prime example of such an occasion, Warren wrote. Hence, it was not the holding in *Youngstown*, that the President could not exercise legislative power, so much as the act of ruling against a coordinate branch of the government that had a marked effect on the constitutional doctrine of separation of powers.

Indeed, while the Court has been increasingly unsympathetic to the claim that each branch is the judge of its own constitutional prerogatives, it has been reluctant to apply another aspect of the doctrine of separation of powers, that the Executive cannot exercise legislative power. Whereas the Court seemed to be adhering to that doctrine in *Kent* v. *Dulles*, it drew back in *Zemel* v. *Rusk*, both of them cases which involved a citizen's right to a passport. In *Kent* the issue was whether the Secretary of State could deny a passport to a citizen who, it was alleged, held Communist beliefs and who declined to file affidavits concerning his present or past membership in the Communist party. Justice Douglas held for the Court in 1958 that he could not. Congress had authorized only two grounds for denial of a passport, lack of citizenship or criminal or unlawful conduct. The Secretary of State did not have "unbridled" discretion to set up restrictive regulations but was limited to these two. But in 1965 in *Zemel*, where the Secretary of State's refusal to issue passports for travel to Cuba was examined, the Court declared that the Secretary had the right to impose area restrictions and distinguished the case from *Kent* by pointing out that area restrictions resulted from foreign policy considerations, a field in which the Executive's discretion was unquestioned, and that the proscription on travel to Cuba was not discriminatory since it touched all citizens. Justice Black dissented. All legislative power was lodged in Congress, he noted.

I cannot accept the Government's argument that the President has "inherent" power to make regulations governing the issuance and use of passports. . . . We emphatically and I think properly rejected a similar argument advanced to support a seizure of the Nation's steel companies by the President. . . . And regulation of passports, just like regulation of steel companies, is a law-making—not an executive, law-enforcing—function.

Justice Goldberg also wrote a dissenting opinion in which he stated, "passport restrictions may be imposed only when Congress makes provision therefor in explicit terms," and he cited *Youngstown* as precedent. "I would hold expressly that the Executive had no inherent authority to impose area restrictions in time of peace," Goldberg concluded.

A notable failure of the Supreme Court to follow what some thought were the logical implications of its action in the *Steel Seizure* case occurred in the many attempts to have the constitutionality of the Vietnam War passed on by the Court. The first indication of the Court's attitude came when it considered a request from the state of Massachusetts, whose legislature had passed a law which excused its citizens from fighting in an undeclared war, for leave to file a complaint challenging the constitutionality of United States participation in the Indochina War. Without stating any reasons, the Court denied the motion. Justices Harlan, Stewart, and Douglas dissented. Harlan and Stewart would have set the motion for argument on the issues of standing and justiciability. Justice Douglas would have granted leave to file a complaint and, at the very least, wanted the motion to be argued. In a dissenting opinion, he explained why.

Douglas believed that Massachusetts had standing and that

the controversy was justiciable. It was on the question of justiciability that Douglas invoked *Youngstown* as well as *Baker* v.
Carr. Douglas reviewed the six standards promulgated in *Baker*
v. *Carr* for finding that a case involved a political question and
concluded that none applied to the question of whether the
Vietnam War was constitutional. One of the criteria was "the
impossibility of a court's undertaking independent resolution
without expressing lack of respect due coordinate branches of
government." The solicitor general urged, Douglas wrote, that
to examine the authority of the chief executive to act in Indochina would be to show disrespect. That had not stopped the
Court in the *Steel Seizure* case, Douglas noted. There the
Court found that its duty was to interpret the Constitution and
to decide if the President had the authority to seize the mills.
Douglas quoted Frankfurter on the necessity for the Court to
exercise its power despite its distaste for inquiry into the powers
of the President and Congress. "It is far more important,"
Douglas concluded in *Massachusetts* v. *Laird*, "to be respectful
to the Constitution than to a coordinate branch of government."

The power of the Commander in Chief was controlled by
constitutional limitations, Douglas continued. That was the
crucial point in the *Youngstown* ruling, he noted. As Justice
Clark had stated, the President must follow the specific procedures laid down by Congress for dealing with the type of emergency in which the President had acted. "If the President must
follow procedures prescribed by Congress," Douglas contended, "it follows *a fortiori* that he must follow procedures
prescribed by the Constitution." The members of the Supreme
Court had not been afraid to reach the merits of the steel
seizure, Douglas declared, and their decision should be "in-
structive."

Douglas drew one more lesson from the *Steel Seizure* case,
and he was to repeat it many times in the next few years, as the
Court consistently refused to consider the constitutionality of

the war in Indochina. In *Youngstown*, private individuals (the steel companies) had asserted that their property had been taken by the Executive without proper authority. In the Massachusetts case, private citizens were claiming that their lives and liberties were being taken without proper authority. The Constitution does not protect property more than life and liberty, Douglas maintained, and it had always been the Court's duty to determine the legality of the taking of any of them. "If Truman could not seize the steel mills," Douglas once rhetorically asked a group of students, "how can they seize you?"

Several cases disputing the constitutionality of the Indochina War were adjudicated by lower courts, however. Some judges dismissed the cases because a political question was involved, others thought the issue justiciable and found that although Congress had not declared war it had ratified American participation in the conflict by its legislative acts to support the war. *Youngstown* was prominently discussed in many of the cases. In *Berk* v. *Laird*, District Judge Judd held that Congress had authorized hostilities in Vietnam in a manner sufficient to meet the constitutional requirements. "This is not a case where the President relied on his own power without any supporting action from Congress, as in the Steel Seizure. . . . In that case it was conceded that there was no Congressional authorization for the seizure. . . . The President had reported his action to Congress, and Congress took no action." District Judge Wyzanski construed *Youngstown* in a similar way when he considered *Massachusetts* v. *Laird*. In a class action suit testing the constitutionality of the war, a three-judge district court divided 2 to 1 over whether the question was political. The majority found it was and distinguished between cases dealing with internal matters as opposed to cases concerned with foreign affairs. According to the court,

The *Steel Seizure Cases*, because of their supposed relevance to this country's participation in the Korean conflict, perhaps went farthest in adjudicat-

ing an issue having potential repercussions beyond the normal judicial sphere.
. . . Even though the nationalization and the Court's injunction of the
President's action might have had some, although indirect, effect on the
foreign relations of this country, such import, if any, would have been clearly
minimal compared to the drastic change which nationalization by the President would otherwise have brought about in the free enterprise system.

The dissenting judge, to the contrary, thought *Youngstown*
more relevant to the Vietnam War issue, since, in *Youngstown*, steel had been a means of maintaining the troops in
Korea and the Court's decision definitely affected the conduct
of foreign affairs.

When these cases came to the Supreme Court on petitions
for certiorari, the Court refused to consider them. The Court's
continued resistance to adjudicating the constitutionality of the
war in Indochina evoked anguished cries from Justice Douglas:

Once again, this Court is confronted with a challenge to the constitutionality of the Presidential war which has raged in Southeast Asia for nearly a
decade. Once again, it denies certiorari. Once again, I dissent.

This Court, of course, should give deference to the coordinate branches of
the Government. But we did not defer in the *Prize Cases* . . . when the issue
was presidential power as Commander in Chief to order a blockade. We did
not defer in the *Steel Seizure Case*, when the issue was presidential power, in
time of armed international conflict, to order the seizure of domestic steel
mills. Nor should we defer here, when the issue is presidential power to
seize, not steel, but people.

Youngstown Sheet & Tube Co. v. *Sawyer* notwithstanding, the
Supreme Court exercised restraint.

But when, in the presidency of Richard M. Nixon, the
Supreme Court was faced with many questions of presidential
power in domestic affairs, its reluctance to act disappeared. The
Steel Seizure case became a useful precedent, both because the
opinion of the Court denied inherent power in the President
and because the ruling struck down a President's order. The
first of these important cases was the attempt of the government
to enjoin the publication of the so-called Pentagon Papers, a

history of American involvement in the Vietnam War, which had been surreptitiously copied by Daniel Ellsberg and given to the *New York Times* to print. The government sought an injunction against publication on the ground that the President had inherent power to protect national security. In a per curiam opinion, the Court held that no injunction could be issued against publication because the government had not met the burden of showing justification for prior restraint. For three Justices—Black, Douglas, and Brennan—the command of the First Amendment was conclusive: "Congress shall make no law . . . abridging the freedom of . . . the press." Prior retraints of publication could never be legal, and the Court could not do what Congress was prohibited from doing. For another three Justices—Stewart, White, and Marshall—however, the holding in the *Steel Seizure* case was decisive. Where Congress had legislated in a particular field, as it had in the Espionage Act of 1917—which dealt in part with the communication of government secrets—and had refused to authorize the remedy the government now sought in the Supreme Court, "It would . . . be utterly inconsistent with the concept of separation of powers for this Court to use its power . . . to prevent behavior that Congress has specifically declined to prohibit." When Congress had enacted legislation concerning a certain subject, the President could not go beyond the specific stipulations of the law. He was precluded from an exercise of inherent power.

A similar question arose when the Nixon administration claimed it had the inherent power to order wiretaps in internal security matters without judicial authorization. Title III of the Omnibus Crime Control and Safe Streets Act of 1968 had empowered the Attorney General to tap telephones in certain types of crimes after he had obtained the approval of a court. The government admitted, however, in a case involving the dynamite bombing of a Central Intelligence Agency office in Michigan which came before Judge Damon Keith of the United States District Court for the Eastern District of Michigan, that it had gotten information about the defendant through a wire-tap ordered solely on the authority of the Attorney General. The district court decided that the electronic surveillance violated the Fourth Amendment and ordered the government to disclose all conversations overheard on the taps. The government challenged this order in the Court of Appeals for the Sixth Circuit. Judge Edwards, for the court, upheld the district court and took issue with the Attorney General's contention that the President possesses inherent power to protect the national security. In dealing with the threat of domestic subversion, every official of the executive branch of the government was subject to the limitations of the Fourth Amendment. The Fourth Amendment was adopted, Judge Edwards pointed out, in response to the colonists' experience under an assertion of inherent power in King George III to authorize uncontrolled searches and seizures. The framers of the United States Constitution had deliberately provided checks on this sovereign power; thus, Judge Edwards denied that the President had any inherent power in domestic subversion cases to dispense with the appropriate procedures to gain authorization for a wiretap. Edwards noted that the Supreme Court had "squarely rejected" the inherent power doctrine in *Steel Seizure* case. Although *Youngstown* did not concern electronic surveillance, the Judge indicated that it was "the authoritative case dealing with the inherent powers of the Presidency—a doctrine which is strongly relied upon by the government in this case."

The Supreme Court emphatically affirmed the court of appeals. Justice Powell, for the Court, observed that if the President had the power to order wiretaps without prior judicial approval, the source of that power had to be in the Constitution. He rejected the government's claim that the wiretap was legal because a section of the Crime Control Act of 1968 stated:

> Nor shall anything contained in this chapter be deemed to limit the constitutional power of the President to take such measures as he deems necessary to protect the United States against the overthrow of the Government by force

or other unlawful means, or against any other clear and present danger to the structure or existence of the Government.

The Court interpreted this section as merely a disclaimer of any congressional intent to define the President's power in this sphere, rather than as a grant of power to the Chief Executive. Therefore, in cases of subversion, the President retained whatever constitutional power he had before the Crime Control Act was enacted, but no more. Hence, the Court had to define the constitutional limits of the Executive's wiretapping authority in national security cases.

Implicit in the Fourth Amendment directive that a warrant shall be obtained is review by a disinterested magistrate of the request of the investigating officers so as to determine the necessity for the search or seizure. For the executive branch to be its own judge of when electronic surveillance should be used would subvert our basic constitutional system. "Individual freedoms will best be preserved through a separation of powers and division of functions among the different branches and levels of Government," Powell asserted. The requirements of prior judicial review, the Court believed, would in no way obstruct the President in carrying out his constitutional duties to protect domestic security.

The *Youngstown* decision served as a useful precedent in challenges to another practice of the Nixon administration: presidential impoundment of congressionally appropriated funds. Cases testing the impoundment authority raised the question of the proper division of power between the executive and Congress. Nixon grounded his impoundment authority on a sweeping claim to constitutional power stemming from the vesting of the executive power in the President. Nixon asserted this claim on his own, for his Justice Department had advised: "With respect to the suggestion that the President had a *constitutional* power to decline to spend appropriated funds, we must conclude that the existence of such a broad power is supported by neither reason nor precedent." Unhindered by the Justice Department's opinion, President Nixon, maintaining that he was acting in the interest of sound fiscal management, proceeded to impound funds from a variety of congressionally approved and funded programs solely on the basis of his own judgment that the expenditure of those monies for those purposes would be harmful to the nation. A host of suits were filed to test the legality of Nixon's impoundment policy. Those decided before Nixon resigned, *Sioux Valley Empire Electric Association, Inc.* v. *Butz*, for example, stressed the point that the appropriation power was the "essence of legislative power" and the President could not "nullify the mandates of Congress." Conceding to the President the authority to impound funds which had been appropriated by Congress in support of programs it had approved, the court declared in the *Sioux Valley* case, would "emasculate" our constitutional system of government.

An even more flagrant abuse of power occurred when the Nixon administration tried to dismantle the Office of Economic Opportunity, which Congress had voted to continue and for whose programs Congress had appropriated funds. Nixon merely neglected to include funds for the OEO programs in his budget message for 1974, and a specially appointed acting director of OEO proceeded to use what funds remained from the previous year to phase out the program. When the employees of OEO brought an action in the United States District Court for the District of Columbia challenging the President's authority to destroy OEO, the government argued that the President's budget message superseded the law enacted by Congress.

Guided by the *Youngstown* precedent, Judge William Jones ruled against the President. Jones held that programs under OEO cannot be terminated before their authorization expires, unless Congress orders such termination either by failing to supply funds or by expressly forbidding the further use of funds for the specific programs. Recalling the *Steel Seizure* case, which he labeled the "leading case on the constitutional division of power between the President and the Congress," Jones declared that the President cannot make law; therefore, the "budget message cannot have the effect of law." The President must carry out laws passed by Congress.

Thus, *Youngstown Sheet & Tube Co. v. Sawyer* proved a valuable precedent for courts faced with deciding a variety of cases challenging assertions of executive power. The separation of powers implicit in the Constitution, which *Youngstown* reaffirmed, was vital to many of these decisions. Ironically, in an attempt to escape the mandates of the courts in his Watergate difficulties, President Nixon sought refuge in the separation-of-powers doctrine. He used it, however, in a very different sense. To Nixon, separation of powers meant not only that the Presidency was an independent branch of the government with its own powers and duties but that the President was not subject to judicial review. In declaring Nixon's theory invalid, the courts found the *Steel Seizure* decision crucial to their determination. The first of the Watergate Tapes cases, *In re Grand Jury Subpoena Duces Tecum Issued to Richard M. Nixon*, and, on appeal, *Nixon v. Sirica*, demonstrated *Youngstown's* importance. . . .

It remained for the Supreme Court to put its imprimatur on this new departure in constitutional law, and it did so in *United States v. Nixon*. This case dealt with many of the same issues present in *Nixon v. Sirica*. But *Nixon v. Sirica* had never been appealed to the Supreme Court. Instead, in an effort to escape compliance with the district court's order, President Nixon on October 20, 1973, fired Watergate Special Prosecutor Archibald Cox, who had refused to agree to any compromise of Sirica's order. The discharge of Cox aroused a storm of protest, however, and under pressure from Congress and the public Nixon announced that he would comply with the subpoena. To avoid congressional legislation establishing an independent Watergate special prosecutor, the President on November 12, 1973, appointed a new special prosecutor, Leon Jaworski, who was given the same powers as Cox had had and who was specifically authorized to resort to judicial process to contest an assertion of executive privilege as to any evidence needed by the prosecution. On April 16, 1974, Jaworski moved for the issuance of a subpoena *duces tecum* to produce tapes and documents relating to sixty-four presidential conversations which the special prosecutor believed necessary in the trial of seven associates of the President indicted by the grand jury in the Watergate matter for conspiracy to defraud the United States and to obstruct justice. The litigation resulting from Jaworski's motion culminated in *United States v. Nixon*.

The district court, by Judge Sirica, ordered the subpoena to issue on April 18, 1974. Counsel for the President filed a formal claim of privilege and a motion to quash. Sirica, after argument, denied the motion, relying on the holding in *Nixon v. Sirica*. Moreover, he rejectd a new contention put forth by the President that the court lacked jurisdiction because the litigation over the tapes was an intra-executive dispute. The court found that the special prosecutor, representing in this case the sovereign, the United States, had sufficient independence and adverse interests from the President as to provide the court with a concrete legal controversy over which the court had jurisdiction under Article III of the Constitution. The President sought review in the court of appeals, but the special prosecutor decided to go directly to the Supreme Court because he needed the subpoenaed evidence quickly. He filed a petition for certiorari before judgment and the Supreme Court granted that petition. In Chief Justice Burger's subsequent opinion, he cited *Youngstown* as a precedent for the granting of certiorari before judgment in the court of appeals when a prompt resolution of important public questions was necessary.

In a unanimous decision, the Supreme Court affirmed the district court's ruling and in effect ratified the holdings in *In re Grand Jury Subpoena* and *Nixon v. Sirica*. *Youngstown* influenced the result in *United States v. Nixon*, as it had in the previous tapes case; it provided a recent and dramatic example of the Court's authority to rule against the President. The most substantial part of Chief Justice Burger's opinion dealt with the President's claim of privilege. The President's major argument, Burger wrote, had been that the separation-of-powers doctrine "precludes judicial review of a President's claim of privilege." But ever since *Marbury v. Madison*, Burger declared, it had been the duty of the courts to state what the law is. Though the Supreme Court had never before ruled specifically on the scope of the judicial power to enforce a subpoena for confidential presidential conversations for use in a criminal prosecution, it had certainly held other exercises of executive authority unconstitutional, and he cited *Youngstown* as precedent. In *Baker v. Carr*, the Court had asserted that it was the final interpreter of the Constitution; therefore, it fell to the Supreme Court to decide if a particular matter had been committed by the Constitution to another department of government or if the action of that department was beyond the authority given to it. Although each branch of government had to respect the others, Burger wrote, federal courts must occasionally interpret the Constitution in a different way from another branch. The Court could not share the judicial power of the United States, assigned to the federal courts by Article III, section 1, of the Constitution, with the executive branch. It was exclusively the function of the courts to state what the law is; therefore to permit the President to be his own judge of executive privilege would be contrary to the doctrine of separation of powers, Burger concluded.

As neither the separation-of-powers doctrine or the need for confidentiality was enough to sustain the Chief Executive's position that he was immune from judicial process, to accede to the President's claim of an absolute privilege, Burger wrote, "would plainly conflict with the function of the courts under Art. III." Burger pointed out that in the American system of government, powers were divided among three branches; but the framers intended these branches to interact, and none was given unqualified independence. Here Burger quoted Justice Jackson's concurring opinion in *Youngstown* for its statement on the interdependence of the branches, just as Judge Sirica had in *In re Grand Jury Subpoena.* The *Youngstown* precedent led Burger to conclude that

To read the Art. II powers of the President as providing an absolute privilege as against a subpoena essential to enforcement of criminal statutes on no more than a generalized claim of the public interest in confidentiality of nonmilitary and nondiplomatic discussions would upset the constitutional balance of "a workable government" and gravely impair the role of the courts under Art. III.

The President's claimed privilege, the Court ruled, "must yield to the demonstrated, specific need for evidence in a pending criminal trial." Hence, the district court had been correct when it ordered the President to comply with the subpoena by submitting the materials for *in camera* inspection.

The decision in *United States* v. *Nixon* endorsed the principle that the President is subject to judicial review, not only by legal challenge to the actions of his subordinates but, if necessary, by suits against the President himself. The *Steel Seizure* case had a critical role in making this decision possible. *Youngstown Sheet & Tube Co.* v. *Sawyer* thus has had a twofold effect on the doctrine of separation of powers. It defined more precisely the division of functions between the Executive and Congress, by holding that the President could not exercise the seizure power without legislative authority. At the same time, by invalidating an executive order of the President, *Youngstown* dealt a telling blow to the interpretation of the separation-of-powers doctrine which held that each branch of the government was the arbiter of its own powers and responsibilities. When the *Youngstown* decision was made, it seemed dramatic, but more an aberration than the culmination or beginning of a legal trend. It has proved, however, to be an important foundation for the reaffirmation of the proposition that the President is not above the law.

Youngstown *as Symbol and Tool in the Supreme Court,* 1952–1990

Political scientists, historians, and legal commentators were in 1952–53 and have remained since then virtually unanimous in drawing several conclusions about the *Steel Seizure* case as a piece of statesmanship and craftsmanship by the Supreme Court:

- As the selection from Marcus just reprinted indicates, the *Youngstown* holding has been cited and relied upon by the Supreme Court for three major propositions: (1) that there are issues of such national importance that the Court may properly give them accelerated decision, by-passing, if necessary, the normal procedure of full argument and decision in the Courts of Appeals; (2) that policing the boundaries of separation of powers is a necessary and "unavoidable" function of judicial review under the American constitutional system; and (3) that even presidents alleging national emergency conditions must follow what the Justices declare to be the interplay of constitutional executive authority and legislative action (or supposedly deliberate inaction) governing the particular situation.
- The formalistic and leaden quality of the Black majority opinion did not then, nor has the Black opinion since, earned much respect as a written piece of judicial conceptualization of the Presidential-Congressional tension over separation of powers. It has generally been apt quotations from Justices Jackson's or Frankfurter's individual opinions that have been quoted by

subsequent Supreme Courts. (See the Case List for examples of such use in the 1979–1989 period.)

- The fact that every Justice in the majority felt obliged to write a separate concurring opinion, and that most of these are not consistent with each other conceptually, has meant that the *Youngstown* case neither presented the nation with a persuasively unified statement for a majority nor provided a master formula by which future courts could apply the *Youngstown* "rationale" to new circumstances. Chief Justice Rehnquist, who was a law clerk to Justice Jackson during the 1952 Term, has said that he believes the haste with which the case was decided within the Court and the opinions were announced prevented the Justices from working out their individual differences and crafting a doctrinally-consistent single opinion. (Rehnquist, 1987, 92)
- Inside the Supreme Court, from the 1950's to the present, an awareness of expert criticism of this multiple-voice communication of principles has led the Justices to focus openly in Conferences and in between-chambers negotiations on the need to speak with only one voice and with one opinion for the Court in cases of the highest political sensitivity, such as the school segregation cases of 1954–55 and the Nixon tapes case of 1974. For details about how having more time and agreeing on the need for a unanimous judicial communique led to that result in the Nixon tapes case, see the detailed account of how that unfolded in *The Brethren*. (Woodward and Armstrong, 1979, "1973 Term.")
- A highly important legal issue in *Youngstown* was how the Supreme Court should treat the absence of Congressional action in weighing the claim of a president to have emergency-based "inherent" power to act in such a situation—the so-called "silence of Congress" issue. Leading commentators have found it difficult to "divine the precise doctrine" of the Steel Seizure case. More sharply, as Lawrence Tribe has put it, "[j]udicial reasoning that allows Congress to legislate by silence

is constitutionally dubious: the internal system of checks and balances is thwarted because legislative silences are not subject to presidential veto, and external political accountability is diminished since Congress cannot realistically be held accountable by the electorate for laws it 'enacts' by silence" (Lawrence Tribe, 1988, 239–240).

As a final note, it is useful to summarize how *Youngstown* opinions have been used in the Supreme Court during the past decade. Judicial opinions in fourteen Supreme Court cases decided between 1979 and 1989 either cited the holding of the Steel Seizure case or quoted with approval from the opinions of concurring Justices in *Youngstown*. (See the Case List for citations.)

The political issues involved in these cases were predictably diverse rather than involving only one or a few substantive areas. The issues ranged from the legality of the Independent Counsel, the Gramm-Rudman Act, and a $10 maximum-fee for lawyers in veteran's cases to the financial arrangements for securing release of the Iranian hostages, the system of soliciting advice on federal judicial appointments from the American Bar Association, presidential termination of the U.S. treaty with Taiwan, and the personal liability of former President Richard Nixon to private lawsuits.

Statistically viewed, there were sixteen opinions by Justices referring to *Youngstown* (two Justices used *Youngstown* references in two of the cases). In ten of these cases, *Youngstown* was used in majority opinions, in two cases in concurring opinions, and in two cases the reference was in dissenting opinions. Liberals, moderates, and conservatives on the Court all found comfort in citing *Youngstown* opinions, as the following list of citations by Justice and frequency indicates:

Rehnquist	4
Brennan	4
Blackmun	2

Powell	2
Burger	1
White	1
Stevens	1
O'Connor	1
Kennedy	1

The fact that activist liberal William Brennan and activist conservative William Rehnquist each invoked *Youngstown* four times in this period in support of their positions confirms that apt quotations from the opinions in *Youngstown*, particularly from the Jackson and Frankfurter concurrences, supply useful ammunition to ɔoth ends of the Court's current ideological spectrum.

References and Selected Bibliography (1958–1990)

Barron, Jerome A. and Dienes, Thomas C. *Constitutional Law In A Nutshell*. St. Paul, Minnesota. West Publishing Co., 1986.

Berry, Mary Frances. *Stability, Security, and Continuity*. Westport, Connecticut: Greenwood Press, 1978.

Binkley, Wilfred E. *The Man In The White House: His Powers And Duties*. Baltimore, Maryland: The Johns Hopkins Press, 1958.

Blackman, John L., Jr. *Presidential Seizure in Labor Disputes*. Cambridge, Massachusetts: Harvard University Press, 1967.

Cochran, Bert. *Harry Truman and the Crisis Presidency*. New York: Funk & Wagnalls, 1973.

Cornwell, Elmer E., Jr. *Presidential Leadership of Public Opinion*. Bloomington, Indiana University Press, 1965.

Crovitz, L. Gordon and Rabkin, Jeremy A. (editors). *The Fettered Presidency: Legal Constraints on the Executive Branch*. Lanham, Maryland: American Enterprise Institute for Public Policy Research/University Press of America, 1989.

Daniels, Jonathan. *The Man of Independence*. Port Washington, N.Y.: Kennikat, 1971.

Desmond, Charles S., Freund, Paul A., Stewart, Potter and Lord Shawcross. *Mr. Justice Jackson: Four Lectures in his Honor*. New York and London: Columbia University Press, 1969.

Donovan, Robert J. *Tumultuous Years: The Presidency of Harry S. Truman 1949–1953*. New York: W.W. Norton & Company, 1982.

Dorin, Dennis D. "Truman's 'Biggest Mistake': Tom Clark's Appointment

To The Supreme Court," in Levantrosser, William F. *Harry S. Truman: The Man from Independence*. Westport, Connecticut: Greenwood Press, 1986.

Fisher, Louis. *President And Congress: Power and Policy*. New York: The Free Press (A Division of Macmillan Publishing Co., Inc.), 1972.

Goldsmith, William M. *The Growth of Presidential Power: A Documented History*. New York: Chelsea House Publishers, 1974.

Goldwin, Robert A. and Kaufman, Art (editors). *Separation of Powers: Does It Still Work?* Washington, D.C., American Enterprise Institute for Public Policy Research, 1986.

Gwyn, W.B. *The Meaning of the Separation of Powers: An Analysis of the Doctrine from its Origin to the Adoption of the United States Constitution*. New Orleans: Tulane University Press, 1965.

Hah, Chong-do and Lindquist, Robert M. "The 1952 Steel Seizure Revisited: A Systematic Study in Presidential Decision-Making." *Administrative Science Quarterly*. Vol. 20 (December, 1975) 587.

Hamby, Alonzo L. *Beyond the New Deal: Harry S. Truman and American Liberalism*. New York: Columbia University Press, 1973.

Harbaugh, William H. *Lawyer's Lawyer: The Life of John W. Davis*. New York: Oxford Univrsity Press, 1973.

Hart, John; Hodder-Williams, Richard; Lees, John D.; Mervin, David; Shaw, Malcolm (editor); Williams, Phil and Williams, Robert. *Roosevelt to Reagan: The Development of the Modern Presidency*. London: C. Hurst & Company, 1987.

Hartman, Susan M. *Truman and the 80th Congress*. Columbia: University of Missouri Press, 1971.

Higgs, Robert. *Crisis And Leviathan: Critical Episodes in the Growth of American Government*. New York: Oxford University Press, 1987.

Lee, R. Alton. *Truman and Taft-Hartley: A Question of Mandate*. Lexington: University of Kentucky Press, 1966.

Lowi, Theodore J. *The Personal President: Power Invested, Promise Unfulfilled*. Ithaca, New York: Cornell University Press, 1985.

McClure, Arthur F. *The Truman Administration and the Problems of Post-War Labor, 1945–1948*. Rutherford, Madison, Teaneck, N.J.: Fairleigh Dickinson University Press, 1969.

McConnell, Grant. *The Steel Seizure of 1952*. Inter-University Case Program, Case Series No. 52. University: University of Alabama Press, 1960.

McCoy, Donald R. *The Presidency of Harry S. Truman*. Lawrence: University Press of Kansas, 1984.

Marcus, Maeva. *Truman and the Steel Seizure Case: The Limits of Presidential Power*. New York: Columbia University Press, 1977.

Mondale, Walter F. *The Accountability of Power: Toward a Responsible Presidency*. New York: David McKay Company, Inc., 1975.

Murphy, Paul L. *The Constitution in Crisis Times 1918–1969*. New York: Harper & Row, 1972.

Neustadt, Richard E. *Presidential Power: The Politics of Leadership from FDR to Carter*. New York: Macmillan Publishing Company, Revised Edition, 1986.

Nowak, John E., Rotunda, Ronald D. and Young, J. Nelson. *Constitutional Law*. Third Edition, Hornbook Series. St. Paul, Minnesota, 1986.

O'Brien, David M. *Storm Center: The Supreme Court in Ameican Politics*. Second Edition. New York: W.W. Norton & Company, 1990.

Phillips, Cabell. *The Truman Presidency: The History of a Triumphant Succession*. New York: Macmillan, 1966.

Phillips, Harlan B., (editor) *Felix Frankfurter Reminisces*. New York: Reynal, 1960.

Pious, Richard M. *The American Presidency*. New York: Basic Books, Inc., 1979.

Post, Charles G., Jr. *The Supreme Court and Political Questions*. New York: Da Capo Press, 1969.

Rankin, Robert S. and Dallmayr, Winifried R. *Freedom and Emergency Powers in the Cold War*. New York: Appleton, Century, Crofts, 1964.

Rehnquist, Wiliam H. "Constitutional Law and Public Opinion," *Suffolk University Law Review*, Vol. XX (Winter 1986), No. 4, 751.

———. *The Supreme Court: How It Was, How It Is*. New York: William Morrow and Company, Inc., 1987.

Roberts, Charles. *Has the President Too Much Power? The Proceedings of a Conference for Journalists Sponsored by the Washington Journalism Center*. New York: Harper's Magazine Press, 1973.

Rossiter, Clinton. *The American Presidency*. Baltimore, Maryland: The Johns Hopkins University Press, 1987.

Rutledge, Ivan C. "Justice Black and Labor Law," *UCLA Law Review* 14 (January 1967), 501–23.

Sawyer, Charles. *Concerns Of A Conservative Democrat.* Carbondale and Edwardsville: Southern Illinois University Press, 1968.

Scigliano, Robert. *The Supreme Court and the Presidency.* New York: Free Press, 1975.

Schlesinger, Arthur M. Jr. *The Imperial Presidency.* Boston, Massachusetts: Houghton Mifflin Company, 1973.

Schubert, Glendon. *The Judicial Mind: The Attitudes and Ideologies of Supreme Court Justices 1946–1965.* Evanston: Northwestern University Press, 1965.

Schwartz, Bernard. *The Ascent of Pragmatism: The Burger Court in Action.* Reading, Massachusetts: Addison-Wesley Publishing Company, Inc., 1990.

Schwartz, Frank. "Truman's Seizure of the Steel Mills as an Exercise of Active-Positive Combat," in Levantrosser, William F. *Harry S. Truman: The Man from Independence.* Westport, Connecticut: Greenwood Press, 1986.

Sorensen, Theodore C. *Watchmen in the Night: Presidential Accountability after Watergate.* Cambridge, Massachusetts: The MIT Press, 1975.

Steinberg, Alfred. *The Man from Missouri: The Life and Times of Harry S. Truman.* New York: Putnam, 1962.

Swindler, William F. *Court and Constitution in the Twentieth Century: The New Legality 1932–1968.* Indianapolis and New York: Bobbs-Merrill, 1970.

Tribe, Laurence H. *American Constitutional Law.* Second Edition. Mineola, New York: The Foundation Press, Inc., 1988.

Westin, Alan F. "The Case for America," Introduction to Friedman, Leon (editor). *United States vs. Nixon.* New York: Chelsea House Publishers, 1974.

Wilmerding, Jr., Lucius. "Seizure of Industry under War Powers: Truman and the Steel Mills," in Caraley, Demetrios (editor). *The President's War Powers: From the Federalists to Reagan.* New York: The Academy of Political Science, 1984.

Woodward, Bob and Armstrong, Scott. *The Brethren: Inside the Supreme Court.* New York: Avon Books, 1979.

Yarbrough, Tinsley E. *Mr. Justice Black and His Critics.* Durham and London: Duke University Press, 1988.

Case List of Opinions in the Supreme Court citing Youngstown, 1979–1989

Chrysler Corporation v. Brown	441 U.S. 281 (1979)
United Steelworkers v. Weber	443 U.S. 193 (1979)
Goldwater v. Carter	444 U.S. 996 (1979)
Dames & Moore v. Regan	453 U.S. 654 (1981)
Weinberger v. Romero-Barcelo	456 U.S. 305 (1982)
Nixon v. Fitzgerald	457 U.S. 731 (1982)
Northern Pipeline Construction Co. v. Marathon Pipe Line Co.	458 U.S. 50 (1982)
Walters v. National Association of Radiation Survivors	473 U.S. 305 (1985)
Thornburgh v. American College of Obstetricians and Gynecologists	476 U.S. 747 (1986)
Bowsher v. Synar	478 U.S. 714 (1986)
Commodity Futures Trading Commission v. Schor	478 U.S. 833 (1986)
Morrison v. Olson	56 LW 4835 (1988)
Mistretta v. U.S.	57 LW 4102 (1989)
Public Citizen v. U.S. Department of Justice	57 LW 4793 (1989)